Start of Play

DAVID UNDERDOWN

Start of Play

CRICKET AND CULTURE IN
EIGHTEENTH-CENTURY ENGLAND

ALLEN LANE
THE PENGUIN PRESS

ALLEN LANE
THE PENGUIN PRESS

Published by the Penguin Group
Penguin Books Ltd, 27 Wrights Lane, London w8 5TZ, England
Penguin Putnam Inc., 375 Hudson Street, New York, New York 10014, USA
Penguin Books Australia Ltd, Ringwood, Victoria, Australia
Penguin Books Canada Ltd, 10 Alcorn Avenue, Toronto, Ontario, Canada M4V 3B2
Penguin Books India (P) Ltd, 11, Community Centre, Panchsheel Park, New Delhi – 110 017, India
Penguin Books (NZ) Ltd, Private Bag 102902, NSMC, Auckland, New Zealand
Penguin Books (South Africa) (Pty) Ltd, 5 Watkins Street, Denver Ext 4, Johannesburg 2094, South Africa

Penguin Books Ltd, Registered Offices: Harmondsworth, Middlesex, England

First published 2000
2

Set in 10.25/13.5 pt Linotype Sabon
Typeset by Rowland Phototypesetting Ltd, Bury St Edmunds, Suffolk
Printed in England by The Bath Press, Bath

A CIP catalogue record for this book is available from the British Library

ISBN 0–713–99330–8

To all those who taught me
that cricket should be fun

'Cricket's the game for the low and the great.'
'The Jovial Cricketers', 1776

'What do they know of cricket who only cricket know?'
C.L.R. James, *Beyond a Boundary*

Contents

Acknowledgements

Where to begin when so many people have contributed – often unknowingly – to the writing of this book? I could start with Acland Ellis, and John Sealy and Reg Tincknell and all the rest of my old friends in the Wells Wednesday XI of fifty years ago – but they are already included in my dedication. In a more immediate sense, the book began as a vaguely formulated idea which I am grateful to Caradoc King for encouraging me to pursue, rather than dismissing it out of hand. It began to take shape in visits to the record offices of the original cricketing counties: the Centre for Kentish Studies at Maidstone, the Hampshire Record Office at Winchester, the East and West Sussex Record Offices at Lewes and Chichester, respectively. To the staffs of all these I am deeply grateful for the way in which they met, and often anticipated, my needs. At Lewes Christopher Whittick was wonderfully hospitable and gave generously of his time as he helped me to find my way through the East Sussex records. At Chichester I was fortunate enough to find in Tim McCann both a marvellously helpful expert on the Goodwood archives and on the early history of Sussex cricket, and also a fellow Somerset enthusiast. Research trips into Sussex were always made enjoyable and enlightening by his shrewd opinions about cricket past and present.

No historian of eighteenth-century England can fail to acknowledge the courteous reliability of the staffs of the Public Record Office and the British Library; in the case of this book those of the Newspaper Library at Colindale deserve special mention. I am also grateful to Sally Hofmann for her help with the archives of the Honourable Artillery Company. In the United States I have benefited from the splendid professionalism of the staffs of the Sterling Memorial and Beinecke Libraries at Yale University, and the C. C. Morris Cricket Library at Haverford College in Pennsylvania. I particularly wish to thank Carol Babb at Haverford for her patience with my requests for photocopies, and her frequent suggestions of other relevant sources. I am also grateful to Christine Ferdinand, Howard Milton, Ashley Mote and David Vaisey for answering various queries, and to Malcolm Warner at the Yale Center for British Art for his valuable advice about possible illustrations.

Having spent most of my career as an historian immersed in an earlier period, I owe much to the tolerance of friends and colleagues who have guided me through the intricacies of the eighteenth century. Parts of chapter 1 of the book are adapted from my 'Regional Cultures? Local Variations in Popular Culture during the Early Modern Period', in Tim Harris (ed.), *Popular Culture in England, c.1500–1850* (1995), and published here with the permission of Macmillan Press Ltd. The book also contains ideas that were aired in papers given before audiences in the United States: at meetings of the Northeastern Conference on British Studies, the Pacific Coast Conference on British Studies and the American Society for Eighteenth-Century Studies. I am grateful to all those who took part in the subsequent discussions. More recently I have benefited from the generous help of Jim Rosenheim and Tim McCann, each of whom read several chapters of the book in manuscript, and Paul Monod, who cheerfully took on the task of reading the entire text during a busy summer. He coped brilliantly with the peculiarities of a (to him) strange and unfamiliar sport, and made many astute and helpful comments. Stuart Proffitt has been a model editor, providing much friendly criticism, including numerous organizational suggestions, all of which have made this a better book. For any historical howlers or heresies which have escaped the notice of these readers I take full responsibility.

Anyone reading this or any other book on early cricket will appreciate the extraordinary contributions of Stephen Green, Curator of the MCC Library at Lord's. I have regularly benefited from his expertise during visits to Lord's, from his ability to produce photocopies even of works whose exact titles I was unable to provide, and from his reading of the entire text. I thank him profoundly for his help. Finally, as always, I gratefully acknowledge Susan Amussen's patient willingness to listen to so much about eighteenth-century cricket and culture, and yet still be able to respond to it with wonderful historical insight. Her companionship and imaginative inspiration have made this book a constant pleasure to write.

Abbreviations

Arch. Cant.	*Archaeologia Cantiana*
BL	British Library
CKS	Centre for Kentish Studies
DA	*Daily Advertiser*
DNB	*Dictionary of National Biography* (Oxford: Oxford University Press, 1921–2)
ESRO	East Sussex Record Office
HAC	Honourable Artillery Company
HC	*Hampshire Chronicle*
HRO	Hampshire Record Office
JCS	*Journal of the Cricket Society*
N&Q	*Notes and Queries*
PRO	Public Record Office
SAC	*Sussex Archaeological Collections*
S&B	*Scores and Biographies*
SJ	*Salisbury Journal*
VCH	*Victoria County History*
WSRO	West Sussex Record Office

List of Illustrations

Preface

I first walked over Broadhalfpenny Down on a still, grey September morning. There was rain threatening, and the Hampshire countryside was almost uncannily silent. I had driven from Chichester through the featureless suburban sprawl north of Portsmouth. Then I was out of it, a left turn in Clanfield, and suddenly, long before I expected it, there was the famous Bat and Ball pub, and across the road a clunky monument and a green field with a cricket pavilion, sightscreens, and a square that bore the scars of recent matches. A noticeboard by the pavilion told me that this was the ground of the Broadhalfpenny Buccaneers, and that they still had a few home fixtures left in the season. But it was also the ground of Richard Nyren, John Small, Tom Sueter, and all the rest of the ancient Hambledon heroes. I already knew that I had to write a book about it.

Like anyone with an interest in cricket's past, I had absorbed a good deal about Hambledon, both as historical fact and as imagined, romantic symbol. Anyone with the slightest knowledge of cricket history remembers John Nyren's wonderfully evocative, nostalgic account of the Club's great days in the 1770s and 1780s.[1] The 'high feasting' on Broadhalfpenny Down, the team's windswept home ground on the hill above the village; the prodigious eating and drinking; the 'fine brawn-faced fellows of farmers' who congregated there on match days; the rich and memorable characters who made the club famous for both cricket and singing throughout the southeastern counties; the unforgettable victories over teams labelled 'All England'; the cheering throngs 'baying away in pure Hampshire' whenever a Hambledon man made a good hit; the marvellous vividness of an old man's recollections of his boyhood: all the remembered ingredients of cricket's first age of innocence.

Much has been written about Hambledon, in books by celebrated authors – E. V. Lucas, Neville Cardus, H. S. Altham, a score of others. It has inspired songsters and poets, from the Revd Reynell Cotton in the eighteenth century to Francis Brett Young in the twentieth. The Club's records have been exhaustively mined and edited by F. S. Ashley-Cooper and Ronald Knight, by the latter in the context of a huge collection of other historical materials pertaining to the Club. Hambledon village has its own historian in the person of John Goldsmith. Broadhalfpenny Down has been the subject of a recent book by Ashley Mote. In 1976 John Arlott thought it unlikely that enough new material on Hambledon cricket could be found to justify Knight's projected series. Fortunately he was wrong.

Yet in spite of this vast outpouring of print, Hambledon has never really been put into historical context, and that is what this book sets out to do. At first sight the Club seems a perfect symbol of the unspoilt harmony of the traditional village community, with lords and labourers sharing their rustic pleasures in the green fields of preindustrial England. Who can forget Nyren's wonderful stories – of the 'little farmer', Lamborn, baffling the Duke of Dorset with his off-breaks, the new spin that this humble shepherd had perfected while looking after his father's sheep on the downs; or of Nyren's father, Richard, that 'thoroughbred old English yeoman', firmly yet courteously standing his ground in an argument with the Duke, and being congratulated by Sir Horace Mann when he proved to be in the right? Yet this was in fact a divided, contentious village, and Hambledon's years of greatness were precisely those in which the old ideals of generous paternalism and grateful deference (never fully realized, of course) were being undermined by commercial agriculture and growing rural poverty: the years of Goldsmith's lament for a vanishing past in 'The Deserted Village'. Was there any connection, I wondered, between Hambledon's later decline and the process which Goldsmith had depicted? For there appeared to be no doubt that the cricket club's collapse occurred during the period of misery and demoralization that afflicted agrarian England during the last decade of the eighteenth century.

At this time I had supposed – like most other cricket historians – that the Hambledon Club did indeed disappear in the 1790s, when the combined effects of war and the migration of the game's noble patrons to London brought an end to those heroic contests in rural Hampshire. But then I discovered that the club did *not* die in the 1790s: it survived until 1825; and while its later years lack the high drama of the great days that Nyren records, they nevertheless have much historical interest. They also raise the same questions as the first phase of decline thirty years earlier, for by the 1820s conditions in the English countryside were even more desperate than at the end of the previous century. William Cobbett, who chronicled the grim tale of rural misery in his splendidly opinionated *Rural Rides*, twice visited Hambledon in the mid-1820s, observing there the same symptoms of decay that he found all across arable England. Eventually, in 1830, the storm broke, and Hampshire, like the rest of the southern and southeastern counties, was convulsed by the violent agrarian riots known to posterity by the name of their mythic leader, the imaginary Captain Swing. Hambledon had its own Swing rioters, and once again I find myself asking whether there was a connection between the death of a cricket club and the malaise that afflicted the community of which it was a part.

This book will trace the rise and decline of cricket at Hambledon, relating that great team to the wider culture of its period. In a way the cricket club serves as a metaphor for two connected developments: the rise and decline of rural cricket in southern England in the century before the Napoleonic wars, and the survival and subsequent decay of the vitality of rural life in the same period. Why, in the end, should it matter to us that a Hampshire village should have had a brilliant cricket team more than two hundred years ago, and then have dwindled into obscurity? It matters, surely, because it puts us in touch with important elements in our past – not just with the place of cricket (or any other sport) in that past, but also with the history of the communities in which cricket was played, some of whose traditions we have inherited. It may also matter, perhaps, because it reminds us that when we alter the context in which a game is situated it may have consequences which we might never anticipate. The subordination of the Hambledon Cricket Club to the needs of its aristocratic patrons, for example, both reflected and contributed to the decay of one part of rural England. Is it totally fanciful to suggest that the subordination of modern cricket to the interests of its corporate sponsors may have an equally profound impact on our culture?

So it may be worth taking the time to step back and investigate the life of the rural England in which cricket developed all those years ago. There is no shortage of writing on the game, even in the pre-Hambledon years. Much of it has focussed on cricket as played by the elite, by dukes and earls and the teams they patronized, and on the cricket sponsored by London promoters at places such as the Artillery Ground. But, as I shall show in this book, cricket was 'a game for the low and the great'.

Aristocratic cricket was merely the tip of an iceberg, and if we are to understand the game we need to swim deeper and discover what was going on in Sussex villages such as Hurstpierpoint and East Hoathly in the fifty years or so before Hambledon reached its pinnacle of glory. We also need to confront the sort of questions which historians of sport, and indeed serious historians of any kind, inevitably pose about this or any other subject: Why then? Why there? Why these people and not others? What do these peculiar rituals (for cricket is nothing if not ritual) really mean? Above all, in this case, what can we learn about a society and its culture from a popular sport as it grows and develops, with its striking social mixing and its apparent blurring on the field of class lines which remain intact off it?

The decline of Hambledon obviously did not mean the end of serious cricket in England. What it meant was the transfer of the game's centre of gravity from rural England to London. When in September 1786 the members of the Hambledon Club elected the Earl of Winchilsea as their new president, they were unwittingly driving the first nail into the Club's coffin. Winchilsea was one of the most eminent of the cricketing noblemen who poured money and patronage into the game, and, as we shall see, there was much that was admirable about him. Yet in the end it was he and his like who betrayed Hambledon, preferring the interests of their aristocratic friends in London's White Conduit Club to those of the less exalted Hampshire gentry and their rustic neighbours. Winchilsea was one of the backers of the new London ground which the professional, Thomas Lord, opened in 1787, and was among the great and the good who at about the same time transformed the White Conduit Club into the Marylebone Cricket Club – the MCC. Some of the leading players had for years been employed by noblemen such as the Duke of Dorset and the Earl of Tankerville, but until the later 1780s they were still essentially part of the rural scene. Now they were bought up by the MCC and its aristocratic backers, and were no longer symbols of the kind of local patriotism that John Nyren so unforgettably depicts at Hambledon. They were simply the hired hands of what we now call the 'leisure industry'.

Nyren hated London, even though he eventually lived there. The tension between the capital and the provinces has of course long been a feature of English cultural life, affecting literature and the other arts as well as sport. Rural folk have always tended to see London as at best the site of pompous wealth and conspicuous consumption, at worst as the national sink of vice, corruption and iniquity; the country, on the other hand, has always been equated with virtue, hard work, and honesty. This is, of course, a caricature, yet it is hard to escape the fact that from very early in cricket's history London's dominance has ensured that money will take precedence over the healthy local patriotism that inspired Hambledon and the other great teams of the period before Winchilsea's foundation of the MCC.*

The relationship between cricket and the society in which it is played, and the tension between London and the provinces, will be among the central themes of this book. What I hope to show is that Hambledon was only one part, albeit an important one, of eighteenth-century cricket, and that the game was embedded in a vigorous and vibrant rural culture that would have flourished even if milords such as the Duke of Dorset had never ever existed, or had taken the advice of their critics and gone off to the colonies to defend the British Empire.

In the first four chapters I survey cricket's place in the culture, both popular and elite, and we encounter the principal social forces that shaped it and other recreations: the plebeian, the patrician, and the commercial. In the next two I explore the heyday of the Hambledon Club in the 1770s and 1780s, again looking at both the club and the sport in the context of the society and culture of those decades. Two further chapters and an epilogue will trace the decline of Hambledon from the 1790s to the period of Captain Swing and the New Poor Law, and the corresponding take-over of English cricket by the MCC establishment.

It will not have escaped the reader that there are some political

---

* Here I should declare a personal interest. I am a country boy, Somerset born and bred. So I cannot help observing that for as long as I can remember English cricket has been dominated by London, the selection of the national team affected by a marked metropolitan bias, chosen by selectors who always seem to be heavily influenced by the public discourse of a London-based media. Throughout my lifetime, Surrey and Middlesex players of no particular distinction have regularly appeared in England sides, selected again and again in spite of repeated failures. Sometimes, at last – at last! – they have succeeded, as what county player of decent quality would not after so many chances? Meanwhile, even the most brilliant players from unfashionable provincial sides – from Harold Gimblett in my boyhood to Matthew Maynard in recent times – have been given only the most limited opportunities, and almost instantly discarded if they did not come off on their first appearance.

assumptions underlying this book, as there are in most other historical works that are worth reading (even if their authors do not always acknowledge them). But I hope that my assumptions will not obscure something more crucial than any of them: that cricket ought always to be played for fun, not just for money or power. It may be played for those things too, but if the pleasure, the enjoyment, is missing it is scarcely worth spending our time on it. At its best this marvellous game inspires a joy that transcends its inevitable immersion in the issues of 'class', commerce and nationalism which always turn up in cricket – as in everything else – in the English past. A letter from a Sussex woman, Mary Turner of East Hoathly, to her son Philip in 1779, vividly captures what ought to be the true spirit of the game. 'Last Monday,' she told the boy, away at school in Brighton, 'your father was at Mr Payne's and played at cricket, and came home pleased enough, for he struck the best ball in the game, and wished he had not anything else to do, he would play at cricket all his life.' There is nothing here about money or gambling or class interest – just the sheer joy of hitting the ball out of sight, and Mr Turner's pleasure in doing so rings down the ages, for all of us.[2]

Like young Philip Turner, I too was lucky in having a father who wished that he could have played at cricket all his life. Once in his youth he played in a club match with W. G. Grace: I cannot expect everyone to believe this, but I solemnly swear that it is true. The pleasure he took in coaching his sons in the garden, in watching us in school and club matches as we grew older, and in taking us to see his beloved Gloucestershire, and even my own beloved Somerset, must have had a meaning for him that I could only understand when, years later, I in my turn shared with my own sons the pleasures of watching county cricket at those cheerful, unpretentious, west-country grounds. Cricket, more than most games, creates deep links across the generations, which is why for the imaginative observer the match being watched exists on several different levels; not only in the present, but constantly reminding us of other matches, other players; taking us back past Richards and Botham, Procter and Graveney, past Hammond and Jack White, past Sammy Woods and Jessop and W. G., all the way back to Hambledon and even beyond. This surely is the main reason why cricket has such a rich and varied historical literature.

With all its imperfections, this book now becomes part of that literature. I hope it will be read and enjoyed by those who share my passion for cricket. But I hope it will also be read and enjoyed by those who do not, yet are seriously interested in the English past, and particularly in the society and culture of the eighteenth century. C. L. R. James's adaptation of Kipling's question – 'what do they know of England, who only England know?' – which is an epigraph to this work, occurs in the best book ever written on the game. *Beyond a Boundary* is indeed about cricket, but it is also about something more important, West Indian identity, and it can be read and appreciated even by those unable to follow every detail of James's analysis of George Headley's batting. It would be arrogant and misleading of me to compare this book with *Beyond a Boundary*, but if it provides some of its readers with even a small part of the insight and pleasure that they can obtain from James's masterpiece, the effort that has gone into it will have been worthwhile.

I

Cricket and Culture: the Prehistory

There was high feasting held on Broadhalfpenny during the solemnity of one
of our grand matches. Oh! it was a heart-stirring sight to witness the multitude
forming a complete and dense circle round that noble green. Half the county
would be present, and all their hearts with us – Little Hambledon, pitted
against all England was a proud thought for the Hampshire men. Defeat was
glory in such a struggle – victory, indeed, made us only 'a little lower than
angels'. How those fine brawn-faced fellows of farmers would drink to our
success! And then, what stuff they had to drink! – Punch! – not your new
Ponche à la Romaine, or *Ponche à la Groseille*, or your modern cat-lap milk
punch – punch be-devilled; but good, unsophisticated John Bull stuff, – stark!
– that would stand on end – punch that would make a cat speak! Sixpence a
bottle! We had not sixty millions of interest to pay in those days. The ale, too!
– not the modern horror under the same name that drives as many men
melancholy-mad as the hypocrites do; – not the beastliness of these days, that
will make a fellow's inside like a shaking bog – and as rotten; but barley-corn,
such as would put the souls of three butchers into one weaver. Ale that would
flare like turpentine – genuine Boniface! – This immortal viand (for it was
more than liquor) was vended at twopence per pint . . . Then the quantity the
fellows would eat! Two or three of them would strike dismay into a round of
beef. They could no more have pecked in that style than they could have
flown, had the infernal black stream (that type of Acheron!) which soddens
the carcass of a Londoner, been the fertilizer of their clay. There would this
company, consisting most likely of some thousands, remain patiently and
anxiously watching every turn of fate in the game, as if the event had been the
meeting of two armies to decide their liberty. And whenever a Hambledon
man made a good hit, worth four or five runs, you would hear the deep
mouths of the whole multitude baying away in pure Hampshire – 'Go hard!
– go hard! – *Tich* and turn! – *tich* and turn!'[1]

John Nyren's Hambledon. The 'cradle of cricket'. Those glorious days of high drama (and high feasting) on Broadhalfpenny Down: we may suspect that these are the nostalgic recollections of an ageing romantic, yet anyone writing about the eighteenth-century game cannot escape them, and probably should not want to. Nyren's book is a classic, and whether he wrote it himself, or whether the version we have is an 'as-told-to' one recorded by his friend Charles Cowden Clarke in 1832 is not important: in either case it originated with Nyren. Blessed with a good memory and a fine way with words, Nyren had excellent credentials for writing about the cricket of his boyhood more than fifty years earlier. 'I was born at Hambledon in Hampshire,' he proudly proclaims, 'the *Attica* of the scientific art I am celebrating.' He was the son of a famous player, Richard Nyren, who captained the team in its great days, and also kept first the Bat and Ball and then the George Inn in Hambledon. The younger Nyren was born in 1764, so his boyhood coincided with the Club's years of fame, giving him those vivid memories of the Hampshire countryside and its inhabitants which he eventually recorded as an exile in London. They were first published in 1832 in a magazine called *The Town*, and were made into a book, with Cowden Clarke's assistance, in the following year.[2]

Nyren describes a sport that by the 1770s had reached a high level of development. It had recognized, accepted rules – or laws, this being the eighteenth century – the first printed version of which dates from 1744. It was played by teams sufficiently well known to attract large and enthusiastic crowds, and, at least at Hambledon, to arouse passionate local loyalties. The game was of course very different from the one we know by the same name in our own day. The number of players was usually the same – eleven a side – though matches were sometimes played which involved fewer or more than that number. Bowling was underarm, and before the 1760s the ball came skimming at the batsman with only minimal bounce. The bat, consequently, was curved like a hockey stick, and it was only during the Hambledon era that bowlers developed the knack of making the ball kick up at the batsman. This, as well as the addition of the third stump to the two widely spaced ones previously used, made it necessary to switch to the 'straight' bat, which was later to become something like a metaphor for cricketing virtue. But the methods of dismissal were similar to those of today: bowled, caught, stumped, run out, though the lbw rule came in only in 1774. Pads, gloves, and other kinds of protection were absent, which meant that lbw dismissals were uncommon, for no one was likely to risk injury by deliberately putting their legs in the way. Batting was no easy matter on the primitive, rough pitches that were the norm, so scores (recorded by cutting notches in sticks – a sign that early scorers were often illiterate) tended to be low. In the early eighteenth century even two-innings matches usually ended in a day. This did not, of course, make them any less exciting.[3]

A version of the game that Nyren describes with such enthusiasm had originated centuries earlier among the peasantry of southeastern England, in the 'forest' counties of Surrey, Sussex, and Kent. This bald statement side-steps many heated debates about cricket's early history. Was it, to choose only a few of the theories that have been advanced, a Celtic game, a French game, a shepherds' game, an aristocratic game which the young Prince Edward, afterwards the unfortunate Edward II, is said to have been learning early in the fourteenth century? And what are we to make of those pictures of people with bats and balls that we sometimes find in medieval illuminated manuscripts or stained-glass windows? For our purposes, fortunately, none of them matters, for the almost total absence of written sources regarding cricket before about 1600 ensures that there is nothing that the historian can usefully say about it. We can imagine that all over England young people probably played whatever forms of the numerous bat-and-ball games – stoolball, trap-ball, tip-cat, cricket – were popular in their localities. But as to whether those games were organized, ritualized and codified, we can only speculate.

We can speculate, but what do we *know*? One thing we do know is that the first absolutely certain reference to cricket locates it at Guildford, Surrey, around the middle of the sixteenth century. In 1598 John Derrick, aged fifty-nine, testified in a lawsuit over whether a piece of land had been held in common. When he was a boy at the Free School he and his schoolfellows used to play cricket in the field in question (which was also used for bear-baiting); so young Derrick and his friends were playing something they called cricket by 1550 or so.[4] The game must have spread widely in the southern counties during the latter part of the sixteenth century, for after 1600 written records of it begin to multiply. By the time we reach the eighteenth century there is no shortage of information to help us to determine both its place in English culture, and its regional origins.

*

3

The area in which cricket first developed, to the south and southeast of London, has a distinctive geographical unity. At its heart lay the ancient forest of the Weald, stretching across Kent and Sussex from its easternmost limit a few miles inland from Folkestone, and at its western end linking up with the forests of Bere and Waltham in southern Hampshire. On either side of the Weald were the chalk hills, the North and South Downs, which presented – and still present – the dramatic visual contrasts which make the scenery of the region so unforgettable. Daniel Defoe noted the contrast between the Weald and the lower slopes of the Downs, as he noted almost everything else worth seeing, during his wanderings through England in the early eighteenth century. Travelling between Guildford and Westerham on the Kent–Surrey border he admired the 'gentlemen's houses, populous villages, abundance of fruit, with hop-grounds and cherry orchards' at the foot of the North Downs to his left. On the other side, to his right, lay the Weald, all 'waste and wild grounds, and forests, and woods', notable only in being still the centre of an important, though now declining, iron industry. Defoe was not greatly impressed with the Downs themselves, adversely comparing their poor chalky soil with the richness of the vales that surrounded them.[5]

The Weald and the Downs: the interaction between them was to shape the entire development of the region, and much of the early history of cricket. The southeast of course contains other, smaller geographical zones: barren Bagshot Heath; the coastal wetlands along the Thames estuary and in Romney Marsh; the narrow, fertile plain between the English Channel and the western part of the South Downs. But most people in the three counties lived in either the Weald or the 'upland'. When they looked around them, at the wooded, shadowed Weald, or at the great bare sweep of the Downs, how could they not be aware of where their roots were? As early as 1610, near Chevening in Kent, there was a cricket match between teams from the Weald and the Downs.[6]

As we travel by motorway or commuter train through what is now London's suburban stockbroker country, or glide through it on Eurostar, it is hard to imagine how remote and primitive much of this land was until the new turnpikes were built in the eighteenth century. People visited London, of course, and the civilizing impact of the coffee-house, the newspaper and the assembly rooms was beginning to be felt in many a small town. But apart from the gentry, the clergy and the middle-class professionals, country folk were just that: country folk. London was slowly spreading into the adjacent parts of Surrey and Kent, but the more remote parts of all three counties were still largely cut off from the capital. When Horace Walpole went down into Kent in 1780 he likened it to Africa, and complained bitterly of the 'jolting over stony roads' to which he was subjected. Roads in the muddy Weald were particularly bad and often impassable, and Defoe thought that this seriously hampered economic development, making it difficult and expensive for the farmers to get their corn to market. Oxen, used in most other places only for ploughing, here had to pull carts and even carriages. Sussex was particularly isolated, and its inhabitants were often dismissed by superior Londoners as uncivilized barbarians. Not that all of them resented being off the map: there were those who criticized the new turnpikes for having exposed the honest country people to the corrupting influences of the metropolis.[7]

The Weald and the Downs: let us begin with the Downs. The typical downland landscape is the sweeping, unfenced hillside, strewn with the ancient burial mounds which tell of prehistoric settlement. The North Downs contained more woodland, as did the western ridges of the South Downs towards the Hampshire border. But the common impression of the Downs as one huge, close-cropped sheep pasture is not entirely misplaced. Many villages still grazed their sheep in common, though by 1700 individually owned flocks were growing in size. The great sheep fair at Findon, on the Downs above Worthing, was always one of the high points of the agricultural year. The Downs also supported much arable farmland on the lower slopes. One wealthy Steyning farmer sent out nearly 1,000 sheep to graze on the downland pastures, but he also had over 200 acres sown with wheat and barley.

Downland villages, strung along the nearby valleys, tended to be compactly built with clearly defined central cores – 'nucleated villages', to use a term popular with historians. Compared with the Weald, they were also more likely to have remnants of the old common fields, in which the traditional system of semi-collective agriculture still prevailed, with the inhabitants sowing the same crops and harvesting them at the same time. Strong habits of cooperation were ingrained in such places, and the annual village festivals which proclaimed their identity always stressed the values of neighbourliness and unity. Downland villages sometimes had places – often ancient trees – around which the inhabitants liked to congregate. At Selborne in Hampshire there was an old oak with seats around it. It was 'the delight of old and young', the naturalist Gilbert White tells us, 'and a place of much resort in summer evenings, where the former sat in grave debate, while the latter frolicked and danced before them'.[8] Open fields survived in places near the South Downs and in the Kent chalk country, but as time went on there were more individually owned farms everywhere, and they became larger in size. This in turn led to the appearance of a few major farmers producing for the market, and fewer small freeholders and copyholders engaged in subsistence agriculture. There were important cultural consequences of this growing gap between rich and poor, as well as of the contrasts in economic activity and settlement patterns between the chalk country and the Weald.

The Weald was both agricultural and industrial. There were still large tracts of woodland, but much of the huge oak forest had long since been cleared and turned into farmland, primarily for the rearing of cattle. But such farms were relatively small, and in Kent they were becoming smaller, for here 'gavelkind' – the equal division of an inheritance among heirs – was the local custom. The decline of the Weald's two principal industries – iron-working and cloth-making – meant that many of the small towns and villages were beset by poverty and unemployment. There had been over fifty furnaces in the Sussex iron country during the industry's heyday in Tudor times, but by 1714 the number was down to fourteen. The last one in the county, at Ashburnham, closed in 1796, and in Kent production had ended a few years earlier. The industry's voracious demand for timber has usually been blamed for its decline, though it appears that market forces also contributed to it. The Wealden cloth industry, formerly the main source of employment at such places as Cranbrook and Tenterden, was also in serious trouble, and only survived rather pathetically at Cranbrook because of a local demand for cheap cloth to make sacks for hops.

Many Wealden parishes were areas of scattered settlement, containing hamlets and isolated farms that were at some distance from each other and from their defining centre, the parish church. In this they resembled the villages of the dairy-farming north Wiltshire 'cheese country'. Places such as this tended to be more individualistic, less unified, than the arable villages of the downlands, and this had important cultural consequences. The relative strength of religious denominations is a good example, the Anglican parish being a far more inclusive entity than the nonconformist congregation, which was more likely to emphasize individual interpret- ation of scripture. 'Chalk is church and cheese is chapel' as the Wiltshire

6

saying put it. There were, of course, parishes which spanned the two types: large in area, with dispersed settlements surrounding a nucleated core. The cultural identity of such places tended to be equally mixed: more individualistic than the arable downlands, more collectivist than the pastoral former woodlands. Hambledon is a good example.[9]

The southeastern counties contained other people besides farmers, however. All across the lowlands, whether in the Weald or along the Downs, stood the stately homes that impressively asserted that this was still a country dominated by the aristocracy. Indeed, in some ways, it was becoming more dominated by them than ever, for during the century after 1660 efficient management, successful investment in urban property and creative inheritance devices to prevent estates being broken up vastly increased the nobility's already massive landholdings. Near Sevenoaks stood the Sackvilles' great mansion at Knole. In its immense park great herds of deer grazed amid the oaks, beeches and chestnut avenues. Not far away was the ancestral house of the Sidneys at Penshurst, another monument to the success of the Tudor nobility, with not just one deer park but two. In Sussex the Percys had their south-country residence at Petworth, equally impressive for both its Tudor house and its surrounding parkland; in the early eighteenth century it was occupied by a son-in-law, the Duke of Somerset. A few miles away on the other side of the South Downs was the Duke of Richmond's Goodwood, a house that, like Knole, was to play a major part in the story of eighteenth-century cricket. A score of houses of lesser, but still prosperous, gentry families adorned the lower slopes of the Downs in all three counties: Danny, Glynde, Firle in Sussex, and a whole line of them between Guildford and Leatherhead in Surrey, for example.

The character of the countryside was also shaped by the many small towns, of varying degrees of prosperity, which lay scattered across it. There were the old market towns, ranging from small places such as Petersfield to larger ones such as Farnham, which Defoe describes as 'the greatest corn-market in England'; it was also a great market for hops. Many places had grown up around the castles which defended them: the Sussex towns of Arundel and Lewes, both originally built to guard gaps in the Downs, are obvious examples. In nearly all of them, as we shall see, the growth of a genteel culture based on coffee-houses, assemblies, music societies and the like enabled them to share in what has recently been called an 'urban renaissance'.[10] In the vanguard were the spa towns where ladies and gentlemen came to take the allegedly medicinal waters as pretexts for enjoying the leisured social round – and the brisk marriage market – rapidly developing in them. The most successful such towns in the southeastern counties were Tunbridge Wells in Kent and Epsom in Surrey. At Tunbridge Wells Defoe found good company, but along with the usual music and dancing he also found plenty of 'gaming, sharping, [and] intriguing'. More to his taste was Maidstone, not a spa town, but one which combined business with 'mirth and good company'. Epsom was another spa 'adapted wholly to pleasure', near enough to London to encourage something like the modern habit of commuting. The nearby Downs were already famous for horse-racing, always crowded with visitors on race days.

Other towns remind us that the region was also inescapably bound up with the sea. Along the Thames were the naval dockyard towns of Woolwich, Rochester and Chatham, with Greenwich serving as a refuge, Defoe tells us, for 'persons of quality and fashion' – the families of officers, active or retired, in other words. On the south coast, Portsmouth dwarfed every other navy town, providing enough civilian employment for Defoe to reflect that the dockyards were 'like a town of themselves'. Smaller ports such as Shoreham had a thriving coastwise trade, as well as skilled workmen getting their livings by the building and repairing of ships. Southampton was in a state of some decay. Until the early sixteenth century fleets of Venetian galleys used to call there, but since then, like other provincial ports, it had seen much of its trade gobbled up by London. Later in the century it was to make something of a recovery as a resort town. The sea was an ever-present reality; labourers in the villages near the coast often supported themselves by part-time fishing, and the whole coastline was famous for the determination and violence of its smugglers.

The region was also closely linked with the country's great metropolis. By 1700 London was a sprawling giant of some half a million people, its population constantly swollen by the arrival of hopeful migrants from the countryside, looking for work or excitement or an escape from rural poverty. The wilds of Kent and Sussex might be remote and isolated, but they could not escape London's massive shadow. There can have been few people in the region who did not have relatives there – starting out as servants or apprentices and going on to lives of success, crime or uneventful marriage, as the case might be. All roads led to London. The surplus grain production of the region was naturally marketed in the capital, and a ring of orchards and market gardens was constantly expanding, stimulated by Londoners' insatiable demand for fruit. Visitors from the city always spoke admiringly of the Kent countryside, the 'garden of England', especially of the cherry orchards. 'We rode,' a traveller wrote in 1735, 'between hop grounds and cherry orchards most part of the way from Tunbridge to Rochester.' Almost a century earlier, the exiled royalist Sir Edward Hyde had bitter-sweet memories of 'eating cherries at Deptford'. At the upper levels of society the relationship between London and its hinterland was a two-way one: rural squires and noblemen made the journey to London for business or social reasons, while the metropolitan upper class regularly found their way to Epsom or Tunbridge Wells or other centres of fashionable civility.[11]

In the course of these migrations members of the London elite must certainly have encountered a peasant game called cricket; some of them found it sufficiently interesting to learn to play themselves. But cricket was only one of the popular sports that would have been familiar to them, and before we engage with cricket we need to look briefly at some of them if we wish to understand the English cultural landscape. It is striking how often they were regional in nature, played in one area but not in another, or with clearly marked regional variations. About many of them, alas, we know too little to be able to decide how far they expressed important aspects of the local culture, though we may suspect that many did.[12]

For the English countryside was alive with a rich variety of these local sports. Some, like the famous bull-runnings at Stamford and Tutbury, are fairly well known; of others we have only tantalizing glimpses. What, we may wonder, was the meaning of the game traditionally played on Palm Sunday with a ball and sticks at Cley Hill in Wiltshire? It was accompanied by various kinds of childish fun (according to a local antiquary, the villagers of Corsley used to climb the hill and 'divert themselves with tumbling and rolling from top to bottom'). Another widely played but still rather obscure sport, popular in the northwest midlands, was 'Prison Bars', in which teams of players tried to drag opponents from one 'camp' or base into another. Like other local contests, it occasionally had aristocratic sponsorship. Earl Gower put on a match between teams from Cheshire and Staffordshire at his seat at Trentham in 1764 which attracted 'a prodigious concourse of people', including the Duke and Duchess of Bedford. Yet another sport with a distinctly regional flavour was fives – a primitive version of squash – which was especially strong in east and southeast Somerset. The central feature of the game was the bouncing of a ball off a large stone wall, and since in this period the most suitable walls were usually those of churches, fives-playing in churchyards was common: players often got into trouble for desecrating the sabbath or breaking windows in the church.[13]

By far the most widely played English plebeian sport in earlier days had been football. It was a communal, collectivist game, far more violent than modern soccer or rugby even at their most aggressive. Any number could play, there were no identifiable positions, and the playing area was the entire open space between the two competing villages. It was an effective bonding mechanism for young males, a shared experience of violence, in which injuries were marks of honour, and either victory or defeat could leave the participants with inspiring memories of collective action. The Cornish writer Richard Carew describes the players returning from a game (known in the Duchy as 'hurling'), 'as from a pitched battle, with bloody pates, bones broken and out of joint, and such bruises as serve to shorten their days'. Yet, he continues, 'all is good play, and never attorney nor coroner troubled for the matter': the bonding mechanism worked, in other words. Football's structure well reflected the social organization of the ancient open-field village. Where cooperative agriculture was the norm people were not very inclined to play sharply distinguished individual roles or pursue their own economic self-interest at the expense of their neighbours. The game was played in town as well as in country – Shrove Tuesday was a popular date for urban contests. Most typically, though, it expressed the culture of the preindustrial community, affirming local identity through legitimized violence. Its virtual disappearance in the rural areas of southern England in the eighteenth century may be connected with the replacement of the old, cooperative agriculture by the more individualistic and market-oriented farming that became widespread during the century.

There were, to be sure, other, more structured kinds of football, of which camp-ball, played throughout East Anglia, is the best known. Camp-ball was played by limited (and equal) numbers of players on each side, and it had recognizable rules. It may well be that its formal character reflects the more developed economy and more structured society of the eastern counties, compared with the open-field midland

and western regions in which ordinary football was played. But camp-ball could be just as violent as the other kinds. One variant was called 'savage camp', and permitted kicking opponents and virtually any other kind of brutality. In the Lancashire hills, we are told, 'township plays against township, with irons fixed in front of their heavy clogs'. It is not surprising that fatalities in both kinds of football were frequent.

One popular west-country sport in the seventeenth century was stool-ball, a game resembling modern baseball. Here we are at last getting close to cricket, for the core of both games is the individual confrontation between batsman and bowler, or pitcher. But both also required the combined action of the individual and the team. There were two kinds of stoolball, and most of the literary references are to the simpler form, in which the hand or a small paddle was used to hit the ball. This was to be found all over England, but it was little more than a children's game, played by boys and girls at village revels – the Jacobean writer Nicholas Breton describes the young people 'playing at stoolball for a tansy and a banquet of curds and cream'. The more serious form, played by adults with a hard ball and a wooden bat and known locally as 'stobball' or 'stopball', was confined to north Wiltshire and the adjoining counties. This kind of stoolball was an appropriate expression of the culture of the pastoral 'cheese country', reflecting the individualism promoted by the relatively scattered rather than nucleated settlement pattern, the structure of agriculture – carried on in enclosed family farms rather than more collectively in the open fields – and the lack of strong manor courts, whose absence accustomed the inhabitants to a somewhat greater degree of self-government than was the rule in the more firmly controlled arable parishes. Yet we should not exaggerate the individual-ism. Stoolball players were still members of teams; their parishes were still communities.[14]

So of course were the parishes in which cricket was first played. The 1598 Guildford record notwithstanding, Kent and Sussex can, like Surrey, also claim to be among the cradles of the sport. Let us begin with Kent. We have already encountered cricket near Chevening in 1610. A later lawsuit describes the match as 'a cricketing between the Weald and Upland'; evidently cricket was already sufficiently widely played for regional teams to be possible. A few years later, in 1629, the curate at Ruckinge, in the same county, was charged with playing on a Sunday after evening prayer. Cricket was being played at Harbledown, near Canterbury, in the next decade; a puritan minister made himself disliked by his denunciations of drunkenness and of 'profaning the Sabbath by cricket-playing'. Another puritan cleric, at Maidstone in 1640, also denounced the game, along with stoolball, morris-dancing and cudgel-playing, all of them 'profane' amusements that his parishioners preferred to his edifying Sunday sermons. By 1668 cricket at Maidstone was sufficiently well attended for the promoter to need a licence to sell ale. Nearby Coxheath long remained a venue for big games, and in 1646 a local man wagered six candles on the result of a match there.[15]

The game was equally popular in early seventeenth-century Sussex. It was being played at Sidlesham in 1611, and at Boxgrove, a few miles from Chichester, several young men were prosecuted in 1622 for playing on Sunday evenings. Cricket was evidently a regular Sunday recreation in the village; church windows had been broken, and a child, it was alleged, was 'like to have her brains beaten out with a cricket bat'. The ungodly miscreants responsible included one of the minister's servants; two others appear to have been sons of the churchwardens, who were accused of 'defending and maintaining them in it'. Not far away, at East Lavant, there were other prosecutions for playing Sunday cricket, and there is also evidence of the game at both Midhurst and Arundel by 1648. It could be a dangerous activity. In 1624 a West Hoathly man was killed during a match on Horsted Green, and there was a similar tragedy in 1647 at Selsey, a few miles south of Boxgrove.[16]

Almost all of this early cricket took place on the boundary between the chalk downs and the Weald. Guildford, Chevening (just outside Sevenoaks, which in the eighteenth century was to be another famous stronghold of cricket), and Maidstone are scattered along the North Downs. Lavant and Boxgrove are on the edge of the South Downs. The next parish to the east is Eartham, where Richard Nyren was born in 1735. Immediately east of Eartham is Slindon, which had a famous team in the generation before Hambledon's ascendancy. Sussex historians who proudly locate the cradle of cricket in the triangle of West Sussex bounded by Arundel, Chichester and Midhurst, are ignoring evidence for the equally early development of the game in Kent, but they are certainly right in claiming it as *one* of the cradles. By the end of the seventeenth century cricket was a familiar part of the Sussex scene. It was not always the placid affair that we might expect. When in 1693 a group of Sussex people were convicted of assault they pleaded that they

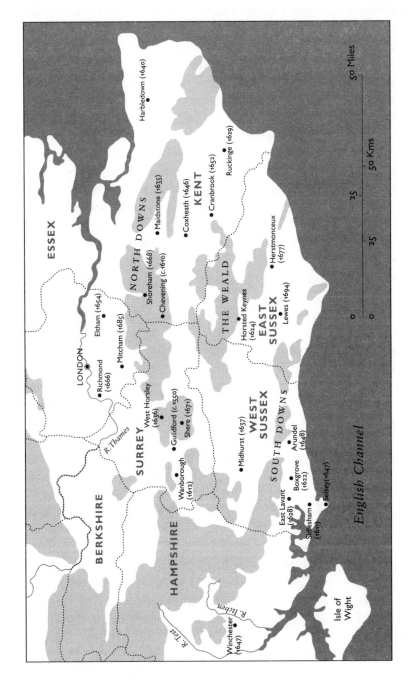

Cricket Sites before 1700

had been 'only spectators at a game of cricket', implying that violence at matches was common enough to be excusable. Already the game was beginning to assume its eighteenth-century character. In July 1697 a London newspaper reported that there had recently been 'a great match at cricket' in Sussex, for fifty guineas a side.[17]

Cricket, then, originated in the 'forest counties'. The area between the Downs and the sea running west from Arundel to Chichester and beyond into Hampshire was originally one continuous tract of forest. Much of it, as we have seen, had been cleared by the seventeenth century, but Bere Forest in Hampshire survived, and Boxgrove was in the old forest of Arundel, of which traces still remained. Herstmonceux, where cricket was played at least by the 1670s, is further east, in the valley between the hills of the Sussex Weald and the eastern end of the South Downs. 'The Dicker', an early cricketing site near Herstmonceux, was surrounded by a tract of woodland, part of Waldron Forest; it was described in 1600 as a 'great waste ground or common'. Other early traces of cricket take us further into the Weald: to Horsted Keynes (1624), Cranbrook (1652) and Ruckinge at its eastern end. Harbledown is on the edge of Blean Forest, but also close to the Downs. This was countryside with plentiful supplies of wood and skilled craftsmen to make the necessary implements of the game. But although cricket developed in the woodlands of the Weald, it was played on the open chalk downlands, the most suitable terrain for a game that needed plenty of space, and for which the springy turf, closely cropped by huge flocks of sheep, provided ideal playing conditions. The 'hard-ball' form of stoolball evidently required as much space as cricket, and equally well-cropped turf. John Aubrey tells us that on Colerne Down in Wiltshire, a great site for stoolball matches, the turf was 'very fine, and the rock ... within an inch and a half of the surface which gives the ball so quick a rebound'.[18]

Bat and ball games such as stoolball and cricket thus seem to express some of the individualism characteristic of the woodland or pasture villages, even if cricketers had to move to the open downlands to find the best playing conditions. But why cricket in the southeast and stoolball in Wiltshire? Until the eighteenth century there may not in fact have been much difference between the two sports. It has been argued that cricket was originally a Celtic game, and that its early strength in Hampshire, Sussex and elsewhere can be attributed to some supposed Celtic survival in those counties.[19] But this does not seem very plausible: if cricket was a Celtic sport, why is it totally invisible in Wales in the early modern period? In the end cricket swamped all the other local variants, partly because the aristocracy took it up, thus giving it resources and national notoriety, but also because it was intrinsically a better game.

Let us turn to the class origins of cricket. It is no secret that some sports have always been related to particular social classes. The nobles of medieval and early modern times proclaimed their conceptions of honour and self-worth in the tournament and on the hunting field; but jousting and hunting were not appropriate pursuits for the common people. 'It is not fit that clowns [i.e., rustics] should have these sports,' King James I once declared. The society in which early cricket was embedded was of course an intensely hierarchical one. Yet all the evidence suggests that cricket was originally primarily a peasant game. In the Boxgrove incident the two churchwardens, both of whom had sons among the players, were reasonably prosperous husbandmen, each living in a six-roomed house. But the absence of information about the others suggests that they must have come from further down the social scale. This does not mean that the gentry had completely abandoned their neighbours' recreations. Among several local men charged with playing 'a certain unlawful game called cricket' at Cranbrook in 1652 was John Rabson, Esq. But the other players were less genteel: they included two clothiers, a barber, a husbandman, and a labourer. The Ruckinge curate claimed that his fellow-players in 1629 included 'persons of repute and fashion', while among the participants in the Coxheath match in 1646 were six gentlemen, several of them of royalist persuasion, including a son of Sir Robert Filmer, author of the famous *Patriarcha*. But these were the local gentry who, like John Derrick at Guildford, may well have played cricket in their schooldays. They were men rooted in their neighbourhoods, not the more remote noblemen who were to be so important in the following century.[20]

Later in the seventeenth century cricket was taken up by members of the aristocracy, and once this happened the game's geographical distribution became blurred, as the nobility participated in a national culture, not one that was primarily local in scope. The Earl of Sussex attended a match near Herstmonceux in 1677, the aristocratic Pelhams were betting on cricket in Sussex at least by 1694, and the Duke of Richmond – the first of a dynasty of enthusiastic cricketers – was sponsoring a team by 1702.[21] In 1728 a French traveller in England, Cesar de Saussure, came across a mysterious bat-and-ball game that he had never seen before. He tried to explain it to his fellow-countrymen, in the process betraying the foreigner's typical bewilderment at its complexities. 'The English', he said, 'are very fond of a game they call cricket ... They go into a large open field, and knock a small ball about with a piece of wood. I will not attempt to describe this game to you, it is too complicated, but it requires agility and skill, and everyone plays it, the common people and also men of rank.'[22]

This aristocratic involvement notwithstanding, even in the eighteenth century the game's heartland was where it had always been: in the southeastern corner of England, in the 'forest counties' of Kent, Surrey and Sussex – an area which needs to be expanded by only a few miles to include the eastern part of Hampshire in which Hambledon is situated. Cricket, the game's early historian, James Pycroft, insisted, was originally played mainly by 'the lower orders', and for this reason, he said, 'we find the yeomen infinitely superior to the gentlemen'. Well into the eighteenth century cricket was still primarily a rustic, village game.[23]

To understand it, however, we still need to look more closely at the aristocracy and gentry, who after all owned most of the land and had most of the political authority. Without some understanding of their politics and of the sources of their wealth, their role in eighteenth-century cricket will be incomprehensible. So let us go back a bit. The gentry had split into two armed camps in the civil wars of the 1640s, but then achieved a partial reconciliation in 1660 and recovered their power. But throughout the Restoration era they were never in full agreement over religion and politics, and by Queen Anne's reign in the early eighteenth century the 'rage of party', as contemporaries regretfully described it, divided them into Whigs and Tories. Broadly speaking, Whigs stood for the principles which had triumphed in the Revolution of 1688: limited monarchy, parliamentary government, a degree of religious toleration (for Protestant nonconformists, at any rate). They were more inclined to welcome the new world of money and banking which many of the rural gentry affected to fear and despise. The country squires were more likely to be Tories: passionately Anglican and monarchist, but often covertly Jacobite, toasting the 'King over the water', the exiled James II and his descendants, the Old and Young Pretenders. Their failure to prevent the Hanoverian succession in 1714 condemned them to the political wilderness, at least as far as power at Westminster was concerned. But they remained strong in the counties, standing for the independent 'Country interest' against the corruption of the 'Robino-cracy', Sir Robert Walpole's entrenched regime. In the person of Squire Western, Fielding's *Tom Jones* provides a memorable caricature of the hard-drinking, hard-riding, Tory hunting squire. In the decades after 1720 Western and his like were able to confirm their prejudices by subscribing to Bolingbroke's *Craftsman*, significantly subtitled *The Country Journal*.

Some of the squirarchy's bitterness was caused by a strong sense that the economic tides were flowing against them. The population growth of the sixteenth century, which by driving up food prices had benefited agricultural producers, continued, though at a slower rate, until the civil wars. But the population stabilized during the second half of the seventeenth century, and this, coupled with the continuing advance of agricultural productivity, meant falling food prices. This was good news for the working population, and may have enabled them to enjoy more leisure. Some of them certainly now had enough spare time to play cricket and other sports, which they had not been able to enjoy in harsher times when subsistence was the first priority. But there was another side to the situation. Tenant farmers now found it increasingly difficult to pay their rents, and their landlords, the gentry, suffered accordingly. The great nobles, on the other hand, found ways to prosper even in this harsh climate. The sheer scale of their operations made it easier for them to borrow large sums; newly invented inheritance devices helped to keep their estates intact; and a lucky few, the Earls of South-ampton and Bedford among them, made huge profits from urban devel-opment. During the French wars that followed the 1688 revolution a new Whig aristocracy began to emerge, its coffers swollen by war contracts, the profits of government office, and in a few cases by success-ful investment in the stock market – though that was always a risky business, as the great crash of 1720, the 'South Sea Bubble', attested.

The Tory gentry of the shires hated all this, and everything else about the 'moneyed interest', even if (or perhaps because) some of them occasionally had disastrous flutters in the market. Their taxes, they firmly believed, supported the waste and corruption of the Court, while the spread of a market economy was destroying the stability and har-mony of rural life. Their attachment to Jacobitism – the cause of the exiled Stuarts – was part of that 'politics of nostalgia' that animated so much of the Tory mind-set.[24] It was a nostalgia for an imagined past whose components were a paternalist gentry extending charity and protection to inferiors when they needed (and deserved) it; a contented peasantry whose members worked hard, lived virtuously and showed appropriate gratitude for the benefits provided by those in authority over them; and subscription to the values of deference and obedience taught them by the Church of England – with none of the troublesome independence and self-assertiveness that were all too often the lessons learned from nonconformist preaching. This whole system, the gentry fondly believed, was bound together both by religion and by the periodic festivals – the rural sports and village feasts – in which the identity of their communities was reinforced and expressed, and over which they benignly presided. It is easy to see how support for village cricket might be one outcome of these attitudes.

Like most invocations of a vanished past, the gentry's conception of the 'good old days' contained a large element of illusion and self-deception. The traditional arable parish, with its basis in unwritten custom rather than written law, its fairly wide distribution of property through the villagers' possession of strips in the common fields, and its semi-communal method of production, had always put subsistence for the many ahead of profit for the few. But that idealized cooperative community was beginning to erode even in the sixteenth century, when the lure of rising prices for their commodities had persuaded many a farmer to switch to production for the market. This could only be done by the enclosure of the open fields and of common land, so that individually owned farms could produce their crops more efficiently and economically. Those who could afford the capital outlay did well out of the transformation. But in the villages affected by enclosure many others did not, losing their small holdings and either leaving the village or remaining as labourers working the fields for others. In the early years of the seventeenth century people such as the Yorkshireman William Fennor were already lamenting the passing of the old days of 'honest neighbourhood, where all the parish did in one combine'.[25]

We should not exaggerate either the speed or the universality of the process. Many parts of England, especially in the pasture areas, had never had open fields, and had always practised some form of individualist agriculture. And even in the arable-farming counties of southern England much land was still unenclosed long after the middle of the eighteenth century. If this had not been the case, the growth of cricket would have been immensely more difficult, for the game obviously required access to large open spaces. Which, of course, is why so much cricket was played on stretches of common land, such as Hambledon's sheep pasture, Broadhalfpenny Down. It was, indeed, only in the 1750s and 60s that the great age of enclosure by parliamentary enactment really began. Yet even in the early years of the century people were aware that they lived in days of great change. That awareness is neatly captured by the unknown artist who in the 1720s painted the two Gloucestershire landscapes now in the Cheltenham Art Gallery. At Alderton, villagers sing and dance as they cut the hay in the great common field; it is a team effort, and there are musicians and morris dancers. Around nearby Dixton there is also a green countryside, but the fields are enclosed and the landscape is almost empty of human beings, except in the neighbourhood of the manor house, where the returning squire is being greeted by a handful of family members and servants. No doubt the joy and harmony at Alderton is exaggerated and idealized, but the two paintings nevertheless make a powerful statement. Almost fifty years before Oliver Goldsmith, the 'Deserted Village' is being visually portrayed.

This brief survey of agricultural England is of course vastly oversimplified and misleading, omitting as it does both the towns and the growing number of industrial regions. Many small towns were not very different from the villages that surrounded them in that they too were to a greater or lesser extent controlled by the great landowners. However, some places were left to go their own way, as happened at Farnham in Surrey, where, as we shall see, the inhabitants converted part of the Bishop of Winchester's park into a cricket ground, without bothering to ask anyone for permission. But other towns were more volatile than the agricultural villages, more likely to burst into riot during times of high prices or low wages. The fall in grain prices during the century after the Restoration may have been bad for the gentry and the major farmers, but it was good for the urban consumers who had to buy their own food. Yet there were numerous bad years during the eighteenth century when harvest failures interrupted the generally low level of food prices and led to hardship and discontent among the poor: 1740, 1756–7, 1766, for example. As we shall see later in this book, by 1770 or so the upward movement of population brought a more consistent increase in prices and corresponding distress. But even before that, this was far from being a placid or quiescent society.

Riots could be sparked by other things besides high food prices. In

1738 both the Kingswood colliers near Bristol and the Wiltshire and Devon weavers rioted in protest against wage cuts; four of the ringleaders in Wiltshire were executed. In 1767 the introduction of machinery led to more disturbances in the clothing districts: rioters near Warminster destroyed a new 'gig mill'. But food prices were the usual culprits. The riots in 1756 were particularly widespread in the midland counties. But discontent also surfaced in Berkshire: a Newbury mealman received a threatening letter warning him that his mill would be demolished if he did not 'stop carrying the flour to Bristol' (thus driving up prices in the local market). In the following year the disorders in the southern counties became more widespread. At Fordingbridge in Hampshire a group of men armed with axes and clubs extorted money from local millers, saying 'they would not eat barley-bread any longer'; they then went on to Ringwood on the same errand. There was also trouble in Sussex, where a large party of rioters had to be dispersed by dragoons after they had seized corn at Petworth and Arundel. It is interesting that both were small towns dominated not by resident squires, but by more remote great noblemen: the Duke of Somerset at Petworth, the Duke of Norfolk at Arundel.[26]

These disorders were rarely, if ever, motivated by blind desperation. Underlying virtually all of them was the belief in a traditional social order which protects the interests of the poor consumer. There was often the expectation, not always misplaced, that local authorities would uphold the ancient statutory market regulations, to allow the poor to buy when the price was low, rather than waiting for outsiders buying in bulk to dictate the price. The ever-expanding market economy was all very well in theory, but for the poor it often brought unemployment and starvation. In contrast, against it stood the ancient values of the 'moral economy': the just price, the condemnation of profiteering by greedy dealers and capitalists. Threatening letters sent to exploiters and violators of the old neighbourly norms angrily warned of the likelihood of violence. A miller near Christchurch was told that if he did not reduce the price of his flour, his 'barn, stable, and all that thereunto belongeth shall be laid in ashes'. If the situation was bad enough and nothing had been done to alleviate the distress caused by high prices, rioters would confiscate corn at the markets and either give it away or sell it at what was thought to be the just price.[27]

The targets in these incidents were almost always the dealers and millers who were alleged to be violating the traditional rights of the poor. Attacks on gentlemen's houses were unusual, though there were a few in 1756–7, mostly provoked by rumours of impending conscription for the new Militia. In a later chapter we shall encounter an interesting one at the Sackvilles' great palace of Knole. But for the most part the gentry performed their traditional role of trying to protect the poor of their villages from the predatory outsiders who were reducing them to penury. They were, of course, caught in the middle between their need to maintain law and order and thus placate the farmers who were their neighbours and likely to be personally known to them, and the poor whose discontent in times of distress might lead to a lot of windows being broken. Townspeople whose prosperity depended on unhindered access to their market-places also expected the disorders to be put down. At Stockbridge in 1757 a group of townsmen and grain dealers promised the local farmers that they would no longer be 'insulted in their persons, and plundered of their properties by an outrageous mob' and that they could safely bring their goods to market there.[28]

So this was a society of many contradictions. It was hierarchical and often oppressive, yet the prevailing ideology of the 'freeborn Englishman' accepted by both Whig and Tory gentlemen allowed for a good deal of independence on the part of the lower orders. That independence was reflected in the occasional violent outburst over wages or food prices. It was also expressed more peacefully in the games the ordinary folk played, which sometimes – if only temporarily – breached the cultural gulf between the upper and lower classes. A sport such as cricket might perhaps encourage greater social cohesion by reinforcing a sense of local identity which could cut across class lines. To put it more crudely, it might make the lower classes more content with their lot, more inclined to submit to the authority of their superiors. Before we can decide whether it did this or not we need to explore the game's further development and its place in the culture of eighteenth-century England.

2

'Good Old English Entertainments': Village Games in the Eighteenth Century

One day in May 1774 a Sussex lawyer named John Baker encountered an idyllic scene at Southwater, a few miles from Horsham. Outside the village inn, he noted, was 'a maypole with garlands on it, and several couple of men and women dancing by [the] roadside before the door'. Now there is nothing very remarkable about maypole-dancing in an English village in May, yet Baker was intrigued by it, because the date was the 12th, which would have been the 1st under the old calendar before it was changed by law in 1752. So this was 'Old May Day', and more than twenty years later the Southwater villagers still regarded it as the right one for their May festivities. Rural Sussex was full of this kind of conservatism. Walter Gale, the schoolmaster at Mayfield, believed in astrology and presages such as the double striking of the church clock, which he decided foretold his sister's death. A few days after the merry-making at Southwater Baker's servants all went to be 'churched' – the ecclesiastical ritual normally used when women gave thanks for their safe delivery in childbirth – after they had, in the scientific modern way, been inoculated against smallpox.[1]

Anyone entering the social and mental world of eighteenth-century English men and women is immediately struck by this kind of overlapping between old and new. On the one hand was a very traditional kind of culture, expressed in the village feasts and festivals of the old agricultural and church calendars. That is what Baker encountered at Southwater. But at the same time new kinds of leisure were becoming available as inn- and tavern-keepers responded to the beckoning lure of profit, and began to promote sporting contests at or near their hostelries, attracting, they hoped, throngs of thirsty customers. Some of these pub-sponsored affairs were connected with the traditional festivals – Whitsun week, for example – but others were straightforwardly commercial. Sometimes they were encouraged by members of the elite, sometimes not. At Epsom races in 1748, a newspaper reported, 'the Bull-baiting and Cocking was honoured with persons of the highest distinction, who expressed the greatest approbation of such good old English entertainments'. Yet in other places the local magistrates disliked them because of the drunken disorders that accompanied them. In 1767 the Hampshire JPs complained of the 'pernicious practice' which permitted publicans 'to advertise and encourage revels and such like unlawful meetings of idle and disorderly persons . . . for their private gain and advantage'. Such disgraceful assemblies led 'the lower sort of people' to be 'seduced from their respective labours and employments'; the JPs would in future grant no licences to hostelries which allowed them.[2]

Cricket was a major part of this fabric of popular festive practices. It may surprise the modern reader, taught that the Protestant Reformation drastically curtailed the number of holidays by abolishing the 'popish' saints' days, to discover how many were still left. Thomas Marchant, a wealthy yeoman at Hurstpierpoint in Sussex, kept a diary of his farming activities in the early eighteenth century in which he regularly recorded the days on which his labourers 'kept holiday'. Besides the obvious dates at Easter, Whitsuntide and Christmas, they normally took off 'Holy Thursday' (Ascension Day) and Midsummer Day (24 June), and they were sometimes let off work for Candlemas in early February, Lady Day (25 March), Michaelmas, All Saints' Day (1 November), and St Andrew's Day (30 November). Often these days coincided with nearby fairs; in 1719, for example, there were St George's Day fairs at Nutley and Henfield, and Marchant's servants duly 'kept holiday'. Among other holidays less regularly noted in Marchant's diary are the anniversary of Charles II's Restoration on 29 May (1727), and 5 November, Gunpowder Treason Day (1716 and 1718). Add to these the annual harvest suppers, and such feasts as the one given by March- ant's uncle for his 'hop-pole carriers', and one almost begins to wonder how anyone got any work done. On a Monday in July 1718 Marchant records that his reapers went to Henfield Fair; on an August evening a year later they simply 'played the fool' after work.[3]

Among the most important dates in the leisure calendar were the annual parish festivals, usually called wakes in the north of England, revels in the south. In some places they were still known as 'Whitsun ales', though most of them had lost their connection with their parishes, which no longer sponsored 'churchales' to raise money for keeping the church fabric in good repair.[4] But ritual merrymakings of a more secular kind made a rapid comeback from the Puritan campaign against them which had reached its climax in Oliver Cromwell's time. Virtually every rural parish had them; they were particularly common around Whitsuntide in the early summer and in late August or September after the harvest was in. A contributor to the *Gentleman's Magazine* in September 1738 remarked that on nearly every Sunday at that time of year there was a revel in one of the neighbouring parishes; they attracted 'great numbers of both sexes, in their holiday clothes . . . to partake of the entertainment of their friends and relations'. Some village feasts had a long history: the one at Wanborough in Wiltshire, noted as 'a great revel' in a 1757 newspaper, had been similarly described by the antiquary John Aubrey in the previous century; it was kept up, Aubrey noted, with 'great merriment every year'.[5]

The parish festivals had the important function of asserting the identity and solidarity of the local community, binding it together against outsiders. There was always plenty of eating and drinking, as well as dancing, courtship, and sexual dalliance. At Bletchley in 1766 there were morris dancers, and at many other places there were ploughing contests, smock races and suchlike 'merry doings', as the Revd James Woodforde described the celebrations in his village. Some of them were attended by huge crowds, as at the annual Cotswold Games near Chipping Campden and the 'Scouring of the White Horse' on the chalk down near Uffington, which was said to have attracted 30,000 people at Whitsun 1780. The programme included a 'jingling match', in which eleven blindfolded contestants had to chase a man hung with bells. There was wrestling and cudgel play, and an advertisement for the 1776 Scouring promised other rustic diversions, including horse-racing (one of the races was for carthorses), sack races and cheese-rolling down the hillside. Often the drinking got out of hand. During their merrymaking in the Whitsun holidays in 1770, some weavers at Aldbourne fired off a cannon, causing extensive damage to a nearby house. There was 'great rioting, fighting and quarreling' during a parish feast at Shenley, Buckinghamshire, a visitor reported in August 1767 – scarcely the neighbourly harmony that the festivals were supposed to promote. But who did not know the old saying, that it was 'no festival unless there be some fightings'?[6]

Many popular features of the wakes and revels were indeed institutionalized forms of violence: the wrestling and cudgel-playing contests in which the young men of the village demonstrated their masculinity, for example. Some were bonding rituals against outsiders, as in many a football or hurling match, or the 'skimmington' riots in pre-civil war Wiltshire, and the battles over maypoles or 'summer birches' in eighteenth-century Wales.[7] Much of the violence was jocular or semi-jocular, tongue in cheek, so to speak. This was certainly the case with the old custom of the skimmington and the performance of 'rough music'. These ancient rituals – in which crowds of villagers would march in disorderly processions to surround the houses of violators of sexual norms, raucously ridiculing their misdeeds – were still widely practised in both town and country. A correspondent of the *Salisbury Journal* in 1755 provided a description of the rough music for which his parish, apparently, was famous. It consisted, he said, of 'performances on cow-horns, salt-boxes, warming-pans, sheep bells, &c, intermixed with hooting, hallowing, and all sorts of hideous noises, with which the young wags of the village serenade their neighbours ... particularly those families in which (as the phrase is) the grey mare is the better horse'.[8]

This noisy ritual was, however, no longer exclusively used against women who dominated or beat their husbands, as it had been in previous centuries. At Billingshurst in Sussex in 1748 it was directed at a man who had been mistreating his wife. The village women performed rough music in front of the offender's house, then put him in a blanket and ducked him several times in a nearby pond, to the delight of upwards of 200 spectators. But although the offence that triggered a skimmington usually had something to do with relations between the sexes, it could also be used (as it had been in the seventeenth century) against other violators of community norms. At Birmingham in 1750 a woman who had informed against people selling liquor without licences was 'ducked, daubed, [and] washed' by a mob, who then conveyed her to the prison. The ritual could also be appropriated by people with very different agendas. Needing recruits for the navy in 1742, members of a press-gang disguised themselves as a skimmington procession, marching behind fiddlers from Greenwich to Deptford with horns on their heads. They attracted a large crowd, including numerous former sailors, who were promptly conscripted and sent to sea again.[9]

The old festive rituals through which the local community expressed and policed its cultural norms – over personal morality, over gender relations, over acceptable levels of violence – were still alive and well in eighteenth-century England, even if they were no longer sanctioned by the church or the state. The famous 'Court of Cuckolds' at the Horn Fair at Charlton near Blackheath, for example, was still being kept up in 1748; earlier in the century Daniel Defoe had dismissed it as a licentious 'rabble of mad people' and called for it to be suppressed. Itinerant musicians still toured the villages; three turned up at Hurstpierpoint in August 1721. Popular songs and stories had been hawked in print for more than a century, yet there were still ballad-singers travelling through the countryside, entertaining crowds at fairs and revels; one was arrested for begging in Hampshire in 1741, while two others abandoned their horse, a pathetic windbroken grey mare, at a pub in Devizes in 1748. Ancient rituals associated with particular trades and crafts, such as the weavers' processions in February in honour of their patron saint, Bishop Blaize, continued throughout the century, and made 'a pleasing appearance' at Alton in 1774. At Southampton twenty years later the procession attracted large crowds, many of them from the surrounding countryside.[10]

Public feasting was closely associated with national holidays such as Gunpowder Treason Day on 5 November, commemorating the miraculous preservation of James I and his Parliament when Catholic conspirators had plotted to blow them up in 1605. Many places had their bonfires and fireworks, and as always there was a good deal of drinking. The political content – anti-Catholic, anti-Tory – may have been less explicit than it had been in the later seventeenth century, and in some places (as at Castle Cary in 1769) an unpopular local dignitary might be burnt in effigy alongside the usual suspects: the Pope and the Devil. The 5 November celebrations at Lewes were famous for their boisterousness (it was the custom to roll blazing tar-barrels through the streets), and there was a serious riot there in 1785 when the magistrates tried to suppress them. Something similar happened three years later at Southampton. The *Hampshire Chronicle*, however, thought that by 1773 Guy Fawkes' Day was celebrated with more vigour in the American colonies, where 'they annually burn the Pope, the Devil, and the Pretender; and sometimes . . . a Governor or two'.[11]

In so far as 5 November still retained political meaning, it was a Whig festival. At the other end of the political spectrum, the anniversary of Charles II's Restoration on 29 May appealed most to Tory loyalists and Jacobites. It was still widely celebrated, sometimes under the name of Oak Apple Day, from the King's salvation in the oak tree after the battle of Worcester. Again there were bonfires and the ringing of church bells, and people adorned their houses with oak leaves or wore them as personal decorations. It was yet another excuse for communal feasting and drinking, but could lead to violence if the support for the Pretender became too vocal. There were many similar outbreaks on the Pretender's birthday, 10 June.[12]

These political commemorations were contentious and divisive, but the ordinary village festivals were usually more harmonious. As a *Gentleman's Magazine* contributor observed in 1738, people went to them 'to divert themselves with . . . rural games, and athletic exercises'.[13] Cricket was one among many diversions that competed for popular attention. Cock-fighting, bull-baiting and other brutal spectacles were enjoyed throughout the land, in urban as well as country settings. As we saw in the previous chapter, different regions had their own particular sports: camp-ball in East Anglia; stoolball in the 'cheese' country of north Wiltshire and the adjoining counties; fives in east Somerset and north Dorset; wrestling in Devon and Cornwall; different varieties of hurling in the eastern and western parts of the Duchy.

Other sports had wider geographical appeal. Foot-races for both men and women – in the latter case known as 'smock races' because of the prizes on offer – were regular features of fairs and parish revels. There was a smock race in one of Thomas Marchant's fields at Hurstpierpoint in June 1721. Sometimes the races were highly organized, as were the two-mile races (the same distance for both men and women), held during Marlborough Races in 1739, for which men had to pay an entrance fee of half a crown, women of a shilling. A correspondent of the Duke of Richmond in 1734 noted that smock races were commonly held at 'horse matches', and that one London woman – the servant of a butcher's wife – had recently made quite a name for herself by twice winning smock races in the capital. By this time a few London tracks were already charging for admission. Team races were not unknown: in 1769 a team of men from Sandwich defeated one from Canterbury 'with great ease'. Other foot-races were spontaneous, spur-of-the-moment affairs, though this did not prevent people from betting on them. Thomas Turner, who kept the village shop at East Hoathly, Sussex, won 1s.3d. on a race in the Duke of Newcastle's park at Halland in 1757. Turner himself was the victor in a another race one summer evening in 1762, the prize being a bottle of cider.[14]

One formerly popular sport – football – seems to have been in decline in the southern counties during the eighteenth century. It had been widely played in the Wiltshire and Dorset downlands a hundred years earlier, but after 1700 it is rarely reported, apart from the survival of the traditional Shrove Tuesday matches in a few places. Turner's diary never mentions it in Sussex. It may be that football went unreported because it was a totally plebeian game, of no interest to the gentry or middle class. But so were the cudgel-playing contests, which were frequently advertised because they attracted crowds to whom publicans might expect to sell food and drink. The lack of advertisements for football suggests that it was not a sport that offered much opportunity for profit. Football certainly survived in northern and midland England during the century, as did its local variants – camp-ball in East Anglia, and hurling in Devon and Cornwall. But for reasons that are obscure it had evidently lost its hold in the villages of the southern and southeastern counties.[15]

A far more popular sport at rural festivals in southern England was cudgel-playing, of which there were several varieties, including backsword and singlestick fighting. There were cudgelling contests at the Bell Inn at Great Cheverell, near Market Lavington, on Whit Monday and Tuesday in 1751, for prizes of three guineas each day: 'When a man has broke two heads,' the pub's advertisement announced, 'he must get off the stage, and fresh men must mount.' In another Wiltshire village, Stapleford, the Pelican regularly advertised Whitsun Games in the 1760s, with backsword, wrestling, and foot-racing contests, the victors all being rewarded with silver-laced hats. There were Whitsun Games, too, at Stubbington near Titchfield in Hampshire, featuring singlestick, wrestling and bowling contests, along with 'dancing, singing, and other innocent diversions, too tedious to mention', as the proprietor of the Huntsman and Hounds primly announced in 1767.[16]

Champion cudgel-players developed fearsome skills at breaking heads, and organizers sometimes found it necessary to exclude them from competition so that those less proficient would not be deterred from trying their luck; the Weymouth Arms at Warminster, for example, announced that two men named Neant and Edwards would not be allowed to compete in their next meeting in 1757. Even when the local champions were absent, cudgelling was a bloody and dangerous sport: a Wimborne labourer was so badly beaten in 1738 that he died shortly afterwards. One way of reducing the danger was to have separate contests for those under twenty-one; this was done at Southwick, near

Portsmouth, for example. Complaints by moralists in the 1760s that the nation was getting soft receive some support from the frequent announcements during that decade that competitors might wear protective padding; until then this had almost invariably been forbidden. With or without padding, many a village lad was willing to risk his head either for the prestige or for the money at stake. Two or three guineas was a goodly sum for an agricultural labourer, and sometimes even the losers were rewarded: the Black Dog at Broadmayne, Dorset, for example, announced in 1760 that 'every one who has his head broke' would receive one shilling. The lure of prize money inevitably led to allegations of cheating, as happened to a contestant named Beech, from Winkton near Christchurch, who was charged with being 'apt to take advantages in play'. Beech was sufficiently concerned about his good name to get a certificate testifying to his innocence, signed by 'many respectable gentlemen', and have it posted in a local barber's shop.[17]

Cudgel-playing might be an obscure individual contest promoted by some nameless alehouse-keeper, but it occasionally had more respectable sponsorship. The Earl of Stafford gave prizes for a competition in Northamptonshire in 1721, while the second Duke of Marlborough offered a prize of five guineas for the winners of a match between the 'gamesters' of Berkshire and Buckinghamshire in 1744. Cudgelling as a team sport was also common. There was team backsword at Wotton-under-Edge, Gloucestershire, in Whitsun week, 1774, while teams representing Somerset and Wiltshire several times fought each other at Corsley Hill Fair, and at Marlborough and Wells Races, respectively.[18]

The organizers of horse-racing meetings often used cudgel playing to attract rural spectators. At Bridgwater Races in 1738 they advertised 'cudgel playing each morning, and also a Plate on Thursday to be run for by countrymen's horses'. Cudgel matches were regular features of the smaller meetings at such places as Market Lavington and Lambourn before these were ended by parliamentary action in 1740, but for years after this date it was customary for meetings to offer cudgel playing for the plebs, balls and assemblies for the quality. This was still the case, for example, at both Wells and Marlborough Races during the 1760s. Wells in 1767 advertised 'public breakfasts, ordinaries, balls, backsword playing, &c, as usual' – an indication of the varied tastes of people flocking into the city for the races.[19]

Some traditional sports, particularly those involving cruelty to animals, were coming under attack in the eighteenth century, yet they still retained their hold in many parts of England. One unappetizing diversion advertised by enterprising promoters was 'riding for geese'. The landlord of the Bell at South Newton, in the culturally conservative Wiltshire downlands, offered fat geese as prizes on Whit Monday 1764: 'He who rides his horse a gallop, and pulls the head of the goose off, shall be entitled to the goose'. The Shrove Tuesday custom of 'throwing at cocks' – the nasty ritual of killing the birds by hurling sticks, stones, or cudgels at them – was more widely practised. But it was receiving increasingly unfavourable publicity by the late 1730s, and after mid-century it was more or less successfully suppressed, at first in the larger towns, and eventually in the villages. Cricket might encourage idleness, but at least it was less brutal. At Sheffield in 1757 reforming magistrates paid cricketers to entertain the populace on Shrove Tuesday, 'and prevent the infamous practice of throwing at cocks'.[20]

As for bull-baiting and cock-fighting, there was occasional criticism, mostly from urban sources – in 1776 a London newspaper called bull-baiting a 'cruel, inhuman practice'. By then it was banned at Birmingham, and at Romsey in Hampshire a reforming mayor had also tried to put a stop to it. But both sports retained their appeal in rural areas until well into the next century. In 1757 a newspaper contrasted the country folk's 'innocent sports, such as a cricket match or a game of cudgels, or some other laudable trial of manhood', with the less-desirable bull-baitings and cock-fights that were alleged to be more typical of London and other towns, but the truth is that these cruel exhibitions were just as popular in the countryside. There were bull-baitings at some of the same race meetings that promoted cudgel-play: at Marlborough in 1756, for example. Besides its goose-pullings, the Bell at South Newton offered bull-baitings and cock-fights during Easter and Whitsun weeks in 1760. Large numbers of people attended these exhibitions: the crowd at one near Bath in 1764 was big enough for a pickpocket to operate in it. Bull-baitings were promoted by at least one political club. The 'Friends of Liberty' held one at Newport, Isle of Wight, in October 1769, to celebrate John Wilkes's birthday, with a repeat performance at the same place in the following April. The Sussex craftsman John Burgess, who was also a Baptist lay-preacher and thus the kind of person who in earlier times would have abhorred such sports as the work of the Devil, entered his dog at a bull-baiting in 1788. The sport survived at many Berkshire forest villages until well into the nineteenth century: at Wokingham until around 1840.[21]

Cock-fighting had even greater resilience because it was so often promoted by members of the aristocracy. Viscount Weymouth and Sir William Napper fought a 'great cock match' for high stakes at the Weymouth Arms in Warminster in March 1738, with a return at the Ship Inn at Mere two months later. Lord Craven was another cock-fighting nobleman, taking on the cocks of William Willoughby, Esq., at Salisbury in 1739. This aristocratic patronage explains why admission (particularly at fashionable race meetings) was often by prior subscription only. Many cock-pits were at pubs, but some were private: an eighteenth-century Dean of Wells had one built at his country house, and widened the dining-room window so that he and his guests could watch in comfort. Many cockings, however, were open to people of all classes. In 1710 a German visitor noted that the audience at a cock-fight sat 'with no distinction of place', and that 'an ostler in his apron' might well win several guineas from a lord.[22]

There was great interest in cock-fighting among the betting fraternity. Newspapers printed the dates of forthcoming mains alongside the horse-racing calendar (as we have seen, the two often coincided), and sometimes reported the odds. Many cock-fights were advertised as being between the gentlemen of different counties – those of Dorset against Wiltshire at the Antelope in Dorchester in 1750, for example. These county contests may indeed have involved members of the elite, especially the 'subscription' matches at the race meetings. But we may well wonder about the pretensions to gentility of some of the contestants in matches between small towns or villages. Thomas Turner occasionally went to cock-fights, but he was sceptical of advertised claims that that they involved the gentry. In 1761, commenting on a cocking match in East Hoathly between the 'gentlemen' of his village and those of Pevensey, he asked, 'Is there a gentleman in either of the places that were concerned?' A year later he scornfully mentions one 'between the gentlemen (if any such there be) of this parish and the gentlemen of Lewes'. But with or without the gentry, there was, he tells us of another such contest, 'a great deal of money sported on both sides'.[23]

All these and many other leisure-time pursuits were promoted by entrepreneurs (especially publicans) shrewdly appraising the likely profits from the sales of food and drink that accompanied them. But the biggest sport, and the one most deeply affected by the commercial spirit, was horse-racing. Its origins go back at least to the sixteenth century, and in the seventeenth Newmarket, thanks to James I and Charles II, had become the virtual capital of the sport. After the Revolution of 1688 there was a rapid expansion. By the time the annual *Racing Calendar* began to appear in 1727 there were over a hundred courses up and down the land. Among them was Broadhalfpenny Down, where races were certainly being held in the 1730s. In Hampshire and the counties immediately to the west there were also important meetings at Basingstoke, Blandford and Marlborough, and particularly fashionable ones at Salisbury and Winchester, all assiduously reported in the local newspapers. Until 1740 there were many lesser meetings like the one at Broadhalfpenny, but in that year Parliament put most of them out of business by prohibiting races for stakes of less than £50.[24]

At the courses that survived, racing became more commercialized than ever. Yet as Wray Vamplew has pointed out, race meetings were still primarily social events, and not only for the privileged; they formed 'a high point of the social calendar for the bulk of the local populace'. At many county towns the races coincided with, or followed immediately upon, the Assize week, another important social occasion. Racecourses were mostly on common land, public space where admission was free, though on a few courses grandstands were built to provide more comfortable facilities for the affluent. At Lewes Races in 1771 John Baker watched from 'the Stand, a room or loft with sash windows all around'. The lower orders had to find what space they could. At Ludlow in the same year Caroline Powys observed a mound near the racecourse, 'cut into turf seats' for spectators, and a large tree in which others of 'the multitude' were precariously perched. Meetings attracted large crowds; some Cambridge travellers went to the races on Barham Downs, near Canterbury, in 1735, 'and lost some hours in staring at some hundreds of people, as idle, and foolishly employed as ourselves'. But the racing was only part of a bustling scene of carnivalesque enjoyment which provided lively entertainment for people of all social ranks.[25]

Gambling was always an important part of the proceedings, and a business for some, though the newspapers, doubtless reflecting popular feeling, always noted with glee whenever 'the knowing ones' were taken in. Ordinary racegoers were quick to take action against bookies who defaulted, as they did against 'one of the black legged gentry' at Andover Races in 1772; an angry crowd was about to administer 'the usual discipline of the horsewhip' when some of his fellows promised to pay the bet for him. No doubt a few people gambled more than they could afford, but ordinary country folk do not seem to have wagered large sums. A later enthusiast recalled that in 1830 betting 'at provincial meetings in the south was of small amount, merely taking the odds to a fiver or tenner', but even this kind of money would have been beyond the means of many spectators. A day at the races in 1787 cost an Essex farmer no more than £1.5s.6d.[26]

Gambling was not, after all, the only attraction; the spectacle itself was worth the journey. From about 1718 Thomas Marchant noted in his diary when he himself, or members of his family, went to 'Plate Races' – usually at Lewes, but also at Portslade, and at what must have been a very small meeting at Shermanbury – but he makes no mention of betting. Nor does Thomas Turner, who recorded his expenditures even more carefully than Marchant. But Turner was interested in the results at Lewes, and sometimes went to watch there himself. He enjoyed the excitement of a close contest – in 1758 he saw 'the finest horse-race that ever I see run on that down or any other' – and he too was happy when the 'knowing ones' were taken in. And there was always the drinking. Twice, in 1758 and 1764, Turner came home from Lewes 'very much in liquor'. The sale of drink was always a valuable by-product of any race meeting, and on the course it was carefully restricted. 'No booth to be erected on the course', the stewards of Blandford Races announced in 1756, except by persons subscribing half a guinea. Publicans in nearby towns, whose ordinaries were generally included in the advertisements of the race meetings, could also expect to do well out of them.[27]

There was plenty of gambling on other kinds of racing besides that of horses. When William Styles of Mitcham took on John Robinson in a foot-race over four miles on Epsom Downs in 1738, almost all the inhabitants of Mitcham, 'having a very great opinion of their man', bet on Styles. But he was beaten and, a newspaper reported, 'the ordinary people of that town are almost all stript'. Some wagers had much worse consequences. A Banbury barber laid a bet that he would run to Deddington and back (about six miles each way) in no more than two hours, and was only a hundred yards short of doing it with time to spare when he dropped dead, 'having drunk too freely of brandy and water'. Gambling was also a regular feature at cock-fights, with the usual results. When the gentlemen of Wiltshire and Dorset won a main at Oxford against Lord Craven, the sharpers were said to have been 'never so stripped in any match these seven years'. Among many other interesting wagers reported in the newspapers was one in which a man bet twenty guineas that he could drive six ducks five times round Epsom Common in under fourteen hours. He was said to have trained them 'like fighting cocks'; the result, unfortunately, is unknown. Eighteenth-century English men and women would bet on virtually anything. In 1715 Thomas Marchant had a bet of a shilling with his rector on the result of the next county election, and another for two bottles of wine on the subject of the parson's age; in the same year he bet a shilling that an acquaintance would not be indicted for poaching.[28]

Small-scale betting of this kind was fun, and the spice of excitement it provided mattered far more than the money. But in the case of horse-racing, both the size of the stakes and the amount of money circulating through betting rose dramatically around mid-century, in ways that transformed the sport.[29] Other forms of amusement also reflect the increasing importance of the money economy. The itinerant entertainers who so often turned up at fairs had always expected to be paid, but it certainly looks as if they were more numerous, that their offerings became more elaborate, and that people spent more on them, in the course of the eighteenth century. A menagerie with lions and tigers – 'an amazing collection', the county newspaper enthused – was touring Wiltshire in the autumn of 1767. It had been at Weyhill Fair, and was soon to move on to Devizes and Salisbury. Acrobats were always popular with both the middle-class and the country folk. A 'famous Italian artist and surprising balance master on the slack wire' was performing at Salisbury in 1755, and another one was there in 1766. Both of these events took place in the 'great room' at the Vine Inn, and were probably priced above the reach of ordinary people. But cheaper performances were also available: Thomas Turner paid only 1d. at Uckfield Fair in 1759 to see 'several curious performances on the slack wire'.[30]

There were many other miscellaneous entertainers, such as the dwarf Maria Theresa, less than three feet tall, on show at the Maidenhead Inn in Salisbury in 1771, admission 6d. for ladies and gentlemen, only 3d. for servants. And who could resist the talking dog who was touring the southern counties in the summer of 1755? – he could do sums, and answer questions from biblical, Roman, or English history. Or Mr Smith, with his 'mathematical statues', who was at Salisbury and Winchester a few years earlier? – his exhibit included a mechanical grocer who would supply 'sugar, tea, coffee, and all sorts of spices at the desire of the spectators'.[31]

*

So the cricket that by 1700 was rapidly growing in popularity among the peasants and artisans of southeastern England was part of a complex cultural environment. There were still the old, traditional May Games, Whitsun revels, and the like: ritual feasts which combined enjoyment with an affirmation of the ties that bound members of their communities. But with the inexorable advance of the market economy, many of these festivals were now being increasingly influenced by commercial sponsors such as the publicans who so often promoted, advertised and profited from them. Other forms of entertainment – cock-fighting, cudgel-playing – were also attracting players and spectators who came for fun or profit, or a mixture of the two. And some, like the itinerant shows just described, relied entirely on the admission-paying spectator for their existence.

At the beginning of the eighteenth century rural cricket was rarely compromised by the lure of money, though betting for very small stakes was common. For the most part this was a game of young men playing for fun. But there were some who saw it as dangerous and disorderly, perhaps even a pretext for Jacobite meetings. In 1726 an Essex JP thought the organizers of matches wanted only to 'collect a crowd of disaffected people in order to raise a rebellion' and dispersed what a newspaper described as some 'well-meaning neighbours who were innocently at play'. By the 1740s cricket was also attracting the attention of moralists who believed that the lower orders ought to be at work instead of idly watching or betting on the results. When nearly 6,000 people came to watch a match in Buckinghamshire in 1741, Ralph Verney lamented that 'these matches will soon be as pernicious to poor people as horse races', and described cricket's appeal as a 'contagion'. Two years later a pamphlet reprinted in the *Gentleman's Magazine* complained that the game 'draws numbers of people from their employments, to the ruin of their families', and that it encouraged illegal gambling and propagated 'a spirit of idleness'; the author particularly deplored the numbers of servants and apprentices who preferred watching cricket to looking after their masters' business.[32]

After 1700 cricket was spreading northwards into Berkshire and Buckinghamshire, but the southeastern counties remained its heartland. As late as 1745, when the landlord of a Norfolk pub advertised impromptu cricket for any 'gamesters' who cared to come, he had to tell them to bring their own bats and balls, 'there being none good to be had in the place'. Some southeastern matches, such as the one at Arundel in

1702 in which the first Duke of Richmond was a player, were obviously under aristocratic sponsorship. In 1705 a match at Malling, Kent, between teams from Chatham and West Kent was advertised in a London newspaper, and the size of the stake (eleven guineas a man) suggests that people of at least gentry status were involved, either as players or as patrons. The same is probably true of the match for a stake of £50 at Dartford Brent in 1709 between teams described as 'Kent' and 'Surrey', but more likely between Dartford and some unnamed Surrey town or village; as we shall see, Dartford was soon to be one of the most powerful of all the provincial teams. In between these dates, however, we know of at least two matches, both in 1708, that unquestionably fit the popular label of 'village cricket'.[33]

In that year a Kentish farmer named Thomas Minter noted in his diary that on 23 June 'we beat Ash Street at cricket'. Ash is in East Kent, between Sandwich and Canterbury; Minter lived there himself, so it sounds as if this was a match between one part of the parish and another. A month later, on 24 July, there was a match on Richmore Hill, on the North Downs near Sevenoaks. Robert Russell, a coachman from Shoreham, a village a few miles to the east, later gave evidence before a JP that he had been 'at a cricketing' on the hill on that Saturday; his place in society can be guessed at from the fact that he subscribed his deposition by making a mark. 'After the sport was over', he told the magistrate, he and 'divers other young persons' went to an alehouse and continued carousing throughout the night. Among the young persons who had evidently attended both the cricket and the drinking were a certain William Hammond of Knockholt, and a young woman from Cudham, Anne Wheelock; both Knockholt and Cudham are within a couple of miles of Richmore Hill. The party broke up around four or five in the morning and then, Anne Wheelock alleged, Hammond tried to rape her on the way home.[34]

If we move on from Kent into Sussex, we can learn a lot more about village cricket ten years or so later from the diary of the Hurstpierpoint farmer, Thomas Marchant. Between 1717 and 1727 Marchant mentions nineteen matches, most of them contests between 'our parish' as he calls it, and teams from within a few miles of Hurstpierpoint: such places as Henfield, Cowfold, Steyning and Newick. It looks as if Marchant himself had only a limited interest in cricket, largely confined to his son Will's involvement in it; he never gives the scores, though he does usually say who won, particularly if it was 'our parish'. In June 1721 he notes that

'Hurst' beat Steyning by an innings, which is the most detail that we ever get. He several times reports the frustration familiar to all cricket lovers, that the match was rained off, and once in 1727, when Hurstpierpoint went to play an away match at Patcham, that it was 'wrangled off', which sounds like a fairly serious dispute. Marchant occasionally went to a game himself, but most of the diary entries are there because Will has some connection with the cricket, either as a spectator or as a player. On 31 May 1717 Will 'went to see a cricket match' at some unspecified place; in May 1721 he and one of the farmworkers go to watch at Henfield; three weeks later Will and his brother Jack go to a game at Ifield Green, though it is washed out. By 1722 the phrase 'Will and our parish' becomes Marchant's normal description of the local team; the boy was now twenty-one and evidently a regular member of the village side. How good a player he was we shall never know.[35]

Marchant's diary shows how deeply embedded cricket already was in the life of Sussex villages. The diarist was a prosperous yeoman, with a large farm, Little Park, occupying 130 acres. He was one of the parish notables, on visiting terms with both the rector and the local squire, the Jacobite Henry Campion, and taking his turn in the usual parochial offices such as churchwarden and overseer of the poor. His daughter married the rector's son, Christopher Dodson, who later became rector in his turn in the good old eighteenth-century way. In October 1727 Marchant was appointed steward to the Duke of Somerset at Petworth at £100 a year, but he did not make a success of it and was sacked in the following March. Will, the elder son, was clearly destined to take over the estate, but Jack, the younger one, was bound for the church and was at Oxford when he died of smallpox only a month after his father's dismissal from Petworth. The two setbacks were too much for Thomas, who himself died at the age of fifty-two in September 1728.[36]

The Marchants may have been well-off, but they were still close to the soil. Will was no privileged, idle wastrel; he undoubtedly had more opportunities for cricket, shooting, coursing, and suchlike amusements than the other young men on the farm, but he did his full share of the work, ploughing, hop-picking, and repairing the parish roads with the rest of them. On 31 May 1717 he carted dung all morning before going to the cricket in the afternoon, and he, Jack, and one of the labourers brought in twenty-eight loads of the stuff from the 'home close' on the morning of the match against Steyning in June 1721. The temporal distribution of the nineteen matches recorded in his father's diary shows how completely cricket was bound up with the rural calendar. The earliest game was on 26 April, the latest on 29 June; all were played before the agricultural population became preoccupied with the harvest. The matches were also social occasions, at which members of the parish could enjoy each other's company, and several occurred on dates connected with the old festive calendar – on Holy Thursday or the day after, or during Whitsun week, for example. Thomas Marchant may not have cared much about the details, but he took obvious pride in the successes of 'our parish'. When he did go to watch, he sometimes encountered neighbours with whom he did business. One evening in June 1717 he ran into 'old Thomas Champion' at a match, and they discussed a payment due to Champion for work he had done on a neighbour's cottage. When 'Hurst' played Henfield in May 1722, Marchant was there and paid an acquaintance 28s. for a calf.[37]

Thirty years later cricket in Sussex had lost none of its popularity. We know more about it in the 1750s and 60s because Thomas Turner, the East Hoathly shopkeeper whose diary is by then our chief source of information, was much more keen on cricket than Thomas Marchant was, and occasionally played himself. Sometimes he watched when East Hoathly played rival villages, or rode to neighbouring places to watch other, perhaps stronger, sides. But even if the village team was without a game there was plenty of cricket on East Hoathly common. There were matches between teams drawn from within the parish, impressive testimony to the game's appeal, for the total population – men, women, and children – probably amounted to fewer than 400.[38] In 1756 and 1757 Turner twice played for the 'Street' quarter of the parish against the 'Nursery' quarter, each time paying his due as a 'gamester' – even in obscure matches like this one there were stakes, in this case of a shilling a man. Once he came down with a violent fever during a match and had to go home to bed, but he gamely paid his shilling. There were matches between the farmers and the tradesmen, between the married men and the bachelors, and one between an XI of men with the name John and the rest of the parish. But Turner also often played informally with a few friends, usually for small stakes. In 1755 he lost 6d. when beaten at single-wicket by the husbandman Thomas Cornwell, and three years later he and the blacksmith's son, Thomas Durrant, lost to the schoolmaster, Francis Elless, in a game played for a pound of gingerbread. The stakes in two single-wicket matches in 1763 were half a crown's worth of punch, and after winning one of them Turner had a serious hangover the next day. Even these single-wicket encounters for small wagers do not exhaust Turner's cricket, for he and his friends spent many a long summer evening playing; on a Saturday in 1760, for example, he played 'a little while with several more out before my door'.[39]

In spite of that memorable day when he 'struck the best ball in the game', Turner was not, I suspect, a very good cricketer. He never seems to have played for the village team, and in one of the Street vs. Nursery games, he just happened to be there to watch and only played when somebody failed to turn up. But he loved the game and would go a long way to see it. In August 1756 he rode the half-dozen miles or so to Cliffe Hill, near Lewes, to watch a match between Mayfield and an XI 'pretended to be chosen out of the whole county', a description which Turner decided was put about 'only to draw people together'. His scepticism about the 'Sussex' XI was duly confirmed when they were outplayed by Mayfield, but this did not prevent his going to the return game at Mayfield a few weeks later. Mayfield was probably the strongest side in the neighbourhood, sometimes travelling as far afield as Tenterden to play. The village lies about eight miles from East Hoathly, and in 1756 Turner went to at least one other match there, between Mayfield and Lindfield. His enthusiasm is also clear from his willingness, during a business trip to Lewes in July 1760, to go miles out of his way to watch a single-wicket match at Alfriston between two local champions.[40]

The list of villages whose matches Turner either watched or reported on (sometimes his brother went and told him the scores on the way home) is a lengthy one. Besides East Hoathly, Mayfield and Lindfield, it includes Framfield, Chiddingly, Laughton, Waldron, Isfield, Wadhurst, Uckfield and Ringmer, all of them quite small places within a ten-mile radius of Turner's home. Wadhurst and Lindfield, along with Burwash and Chailey, also turn up among Mayfield's opponents in the diary of the Mayfield schoolmaster, Walter Gale, who attended several of their matches in the 1750s.[41] Coupled with the earlier evidence about the prolific cricketing circle around Hurstpierpoint in the 1720s, all this confirms the game's vitality at the village level across eighteenth-century Sussex, in most places with no apparent elite involvement. Some teams, to be sure, did have genteel sponsorship. When Warehorne played Hawkhurst in 1727 the match was 'made' by George Baker, Esq., and Thomas Hodges, Esq., both of whom played for their villages.[42] We shall encounter a more famous example of a sponsored team, Slindon, in the next chapter. But even Slindon must have started as just another village team, before its brilliant success and the Duke of Richmond's patronage brought it national fame in the 1740s.

In the interval between the Hurstpierpoint matches in the 1720s and the ones recorded by Gale and Turner after 1750, there is much other evidence to show that cricket was routinely played in the Sussex villages, and it is surely likely that there were countless long-forgotten matches of which we have no record. But we get occasional glimpses: a Chailey player dying after a collision during a match at Newick in 1737, the Duke of Richmond's young son watching a village match on the Downs near Goodwood in 1744. There was cricket, too, at Midhurst. Father Thomas Hunt, the Catholic priest at Ladyholt, did some business with a lawyer he encountered at a match there in 1747, and a few years later Midhurst were beaten by nearby Easebourne in a game played in Lord Montague's park. The Wealden villages were still active: in 1749, for example, Rotherfield played East Grinstead at Town Row Green. In 1762 teams from Ripe and Arlington were opponents at the Dicker, near Herstmonceux, where cricket had been played in the previous century. We occasionally encounter regional as well as village teams. In 1749 Hastings and Pevensey Rapes twice played each other in what amounted to trial matches before the selection of an East Sussex XI to play West Sussex. By now the game had been established long enough for there to be elderly veterans who were willing to make fools of themselves: during Whitsun week, 1752, teams from the Wealden villages of Withyham and Hartfield played for half a guinea a man, the announcement stipulating that 'Every one of the gamesters to be [at least] 60 years of age'.[43]

Who played, or watched, these homeric encounters? The fact that even in the 1750s the vast majority of matches took place in the early part of the summer suggests that enough of the players were farmers or labourers to make it very difficult to raise teams during haymaking (which normally only began in July) or the corn harvest. At this level cricket was still a peasant game, its timing determined by the agricultural calendar. Besides the farmworkers, there were of course plenty of rural craftsmen and artisans among the players, especially in the clothworking and iron-manufacturing parishes of the Weald. As we have seen, Turner mentions teams of 'tradesmen'. In 1756 the East Hoathly ones were soundly trounced by the farmers, but the diarist was impressed by the performance of their counterparts in the Lindfield side when they played at Mayfield. Although the Lindfield men were beaten, Turner thought they batted and fielded better than Mayfield, and were only let down by their bowling; 'what is remarkable', he added, 'they was all tradesmen, and but one above 25 years of age, and I think eleven of very civil men'.[44]

These are general impressions: to identify individual players in the village sides is more difficult. The only one Turner mentions by name is Henry Dodson, who played for East Hoathly against Ringmer on Oak Apple Day, 1764; Turner is sufficiently respectful to give him the title 'Mr', though at about that same time he assisted Turner (who was the village undertaker as well as shopkeeper) as a mere 'underbearer' at a funeral. But Turner tells us quite a lot about the people with whom he played in the various pick-up games on the common and in front of his shop. They ranged from the husbandman Thomas Cornwell, the blacksmith's son Thomas Durrant, and the Fuller lads (sons of a local butcher and tallowchandler respectively), to men of somewhat higher status; the schoolmasters Francis Elless and John Long, and the local excise officer, George Banister. The people Turner met at matches or whom he accompanied to them as spectators were a similar cross-section of local society. They included his brother Richard, an apprentice at nearby Chailey, whose master they encountered at a game in 1756. In the same year Jeremiah French, the biggest yeoman farmer in East Hoathly, suggested that they hold a meeting of the vestrymen to do some parish business while watching the Framfield match, but in the event not enough of them turned up. Among other cricket-watchers were a second excise officer, Lawrence Thornton; two tailors, James Marchant and Charles Diggens; and a shoemaker, Thomas Davy. We tend to see more people from the middle rather than the lowest rungs of society because those are the ones with whom Turner naturally associated.[45]

Turner also sometimes tells us what went on after stumps were drawn. As in local cricket in our own time, the East Hoathly players generally adjourned to the pub when the match was over. Having helped the 'Street' beat the 'Nursery quarter' in 1757 Turner went with 'the rest of the gamesters' to the Crown and stayed until after eleven, though he insisted that he spent nothing on drink. After losing one of the single-wicket matches in July 1763 he again joined in the good fellowship at the Crown and this time had to pay his share for the punch, having lost the wager. But he came home, he claims, 'very sober'; that recent hangover was fresh in his memory.[46]

*

We are fortunate to know so much about village cricket in Sussex, for in none of the other southeastern counties were there diarists as prolific as Marchant and Turner. But we do know quite a lot about the cricket played by somewhat stronger teams in Kent and Surrey, and it is clear that the game flourished at the grassroots level in those counties too. By 1727 there were already old men in Kent, as there were in Sussex a few years later, who must have been playing for a long time: Cranbrook in that year staged one of those comical matches between teams of elderly men, whose ages in this case ranged from sixty-four to eighty-four. Marden, a village not far away in the Vale of Kent, had a famous team for a few years. 'All you that do delight in cricket,' ran a local jingle, 'Come to Marden, pitch your wickets.' There was cricket, too, at Milton, near Sittingbourne, whose team in July 1747 played Lynsted for the fairly modest stake of 2s.6d. a man. But they also played New Romney for a much higher stake – half a guinea a man – which suggests that gentry sponsorship may have been involved. The organizers certainly expected a decent crowd, announcing that no dogs would be allowed in the ground, and that food and drink would be available at a nearby pub. Another village with a good team was Bearstead, just outside Maidstone: in 1749 they were said to have trounced every other parish in their neighbourhood, though they were soundly beaten when they played in London. The list of early cricketing sites in Kent includes many more small towns and villages: Hawkhurst (more famous for its smugglers than its cricketers), Tenterden, Hadlow, half a dozen others. Wherever we look in the county, village cricket seems to have flourished.[47]

Bearstead and Marden had their moments of glory, but the greatest Kent team in the first half of the eighteenth century came from the small town of Dartford, nestling between the North Downs and the River Thames. It had a population of not much more than 1,000, yet as early as 1709 major matches were being staged there, and it has been suggested that the one ostensibly between Kent and Surrey in that year was more probably between Dartford and some unnamed Surrey local side: the newspapers often translated local teams into county ones, to make the match sound more impressive. Dartford's ground, 'the Brent', was unusually well looked after, being described in 1722 as 'a place as smooth as a London bowling green'. In the next year a group of travellers, including Lord Harley, visited Dartford. 'Upon the heath as we came out of the town,' Harley observed, 'the men of Tonbridge and the Dartford men were warmly engaged at the sport of cricket.' 'The Kentish folk' were the best cricketers in England, he was told, but within that county 'the men of Dartford lay claim to the greatest excellence'. In 1729 they easily defeated a London XI in a match on Kennington Common.[48]

Between 1747 and 1765 Dartford's opponents included Hadlow (for two guineas a man), Woolwich, the strong Surrey club of Addington, the even more celebrated London Club, and other well-known teams. Before 1760 they were, along with Slindon, the nearest thing to a professional team outside London, and their matches attracted big crowds, both on their home ground at Dartford Brent and in away matches in other parts of the county; nearly 4,000 turned up to see them beaten at Dover in August 1753. They often played in the capital, sometimes against teams labelled 'England'. In 1765 a crowd of 12,000 was reported to have attended their match against Surrey at the most famous site of London cricket, the Artillery Ground in Chiswell Street. In 1756 they played three games against Hambledon, the upstart new club in Hampshire, one of them on Broadhalfpenny Down.[49]

The Dartford team is the first provincial side in which we are able to name most of the players, though of only a few of them do we know enough to place them socially. They were, as we should expect, mostly of lower to middling rank. A very early player was William Beddel, a wealthy farmer and grazier, who must have played in the first years of the century. In their heyday in the 1750s the Dartford team contained two draymen and a clerk at a brewery: the owner, for whom all three of them worked, was a man named John Pettit, a patron of the club. One of the draymen, John Frame, was an outstanding bowler; he had a long career, and was still playing in the 1770s. The wicket-keeper was a shoemaker named John Bell, who later kept a pub called The Eleven Cricketers; when he died in 1774 a newspaper described him as 'the most noted cricketer in England'. His brother Thomas also turned out for Dartford. Frame, the Bells, the tanner William Hodsoll and several other Dartford players were often called up for important games in London. Thomas Brandon, a substantial shopkeeper who had been both constable and churchwarden in the town, was enough of an attraction to play a single-wicket match in 1754 against a Chatham player.[50]

Dartford's importance can be seen in the fact that their matches were played for relatively high stakes – as much as £50 a side when, with the help of a couple of Londoners as 'given men', they took on XXII of Essex at Woodford Row in 1761. As we have seen, there were other teams in Kent and Sussex who played for higher stakes than the odd shillings that were all that Thomas Turner had to put at risk in East Hoathly. In 1731 East Grinstead played 'Surrey' (more likely a village or town side) at Smitham Bottom near Croydon, for forty guineas a side, which means that the match was almost certainly under gentry auspices. Romney played Rye for five shillings a man in 1754, and a combined Tenterden–Rye team for half a guinea a man two years later. The numerous matches between teams described as Kent, Surrey or Sussex were also sponsored by members of the elite, as were some of those between more local combined sides. Lewes Rape, for example, played Pevensey Rape on the Downs near Lewes in 1743 for 'a considerable sum', and when Pevensey played Hastings Rape a few years later it was for 100 guineas a side. Large sums were also at stake in many of the frequent matches in Kent between teams from the Vale and the downlands. Ordinary villagers obviously could not play for this kind of money. When in 1743 one Suffolk village challenged another, their opponents would play for only a shilling a man, not the two guineas originally proposed.[51]

The young men who played these games no doubt enjoyed the fame as well as the small sums of money they earned, in a sport that was less likely than cudgel-playing to send them home with a broken head. They included a few who got into trouble, but that is only to be expected. A Slindon player, as we shall see, was had up for smuggling with firearms. He was not the only one to fall foul of the law. Richard Fellows, a butcher from Dawley near Maidenhead, was dragged off a cricket field one May day in 1723 and arrested on suspicion of involvement in a poaching gang. In September 1761 a player named Bry (better known by his nickname, 'Die-Game') from Headley, Surrey, was detained at East Sheen for horse-stealing; only a few months earlier he had had his moment of glory by beating 'the famous baker of Ewell' in a single-wicket game on Epsom Downs. He was sentenced to death at Kingston Assizes in the following April. Thomas Bell, one of the Dartford brothers, was also condemned to death, at Maidstone Assizes in 1762, for robbery on the highway. Happily, like so many eighteenth-century capital offenders, both Bry and Bell were eventually reprieved.[52]

So in the first half of the eighteenth century cricket was played by the delinquent as well as the law-abiding. It had a healthy foundation in the villages and small towns of the southeastern counties. So far we have talked about the game at this grassroots level. But before we can fully understand cricket's complicated social dimensions we need to look at its two other main components: the aristocracy and the commercial world of the capital. A Sussex team provides the link. Below the slopes of the South Downs, a few miles east of Chichester and not far from Goodwood, lies Slindon, a small enough place, but one deservedly famous in cricket history. To understand why this should have been so, we need to turn our attention away from the common folk and towards the aristocracy.

3

Peers, Patrons and Professionals

Every community, every society, has its own cultural systems in which it expresses and reinforces what it believes to be important truths about itself, or perhaps what it wants others to believe about it. In the eighteenth century, cricket was embedded in the culture of many English social groups. But for all of them it needs, as always, to be put into context. So let us leave cricket for a while and reflect on some features of the culture of the aristocracy of that period, and the rituals that were used to express it. At the heart of that culture were the processes through which the nobility and gentry publicly asserted their political and social authority, and also what they fondly believed was the popular nature of their rule. The strategies they employed were designed to portray themselves and their families – through sporting events, political occasions and great entertainments, but also through intellectual and artistic patronage – as regional and national leaders who nevertheless shared the habits and assumptions of their country neighbours.

There were, of course, countless ways by which the aristocracy could project their authority. One was through their leading role in the creation of new standards of taste and decorum. They were not unique in this – as John Brewer has shown, much of the support for the 'high culture' of the period came from the wealthy middle class, particularly in London.[1] But the aspirations of the bourgeoisie were in large part shaped by their desire to emulate their superiors. Noblemen were major patrons of all the arts, including music. 'The only agreeable entertainment' during a dull London December in 1739, John Caryll was told, was a concert sponsored by Lord Middlesex in the Haymarket, for which it was expected that the Earl would be 'above two thousand pound out of pocket'. By the mid-1760s well-to-do Londoners could hear concerts by Johann Christian Bach and Carl Friedrich Abel at Hickford's Rooms in Brewer Street; the nine-year-old Mozart performed there in 1765.

46

Besides the public concerts, the nobility also staged private ones for invited guests, and provided patronage for such groups as the Concert of Ancient Music, which performed for small, elite audiences.[2] Middlesex's role may have been unusual before 1750, though a good many noblemen were certainly patrons of the opera and of the singers, particularly the female ones. The third Duke of Bolton was so smitten with Lavinia Fenton, who played Polly Peacham in *The Beggar's Opera*, that he left his wife for her, though he was only able to marry her years later, after the Duchess's death.

Aristocratic patronage was even more conspicuous in the visual arts. Great noblemen had for years collected paintings and sculptures by the great continental masters: the early seventeenth-century Earl of Arundel is the most celebrated example. By the eighteenth century the Grand Tour, almost mandatory for blue-blooded youths, often laid the foundations for an interest in art and for the collecting habit. The Society of Dilettanti was originally a group of men privileged enough to have made the Tour. The society encouraged patronage of artists, though the sexual scandals which surrounded it sometimes obscured this aspect of its existence. But whether made by the virtuous or the profligate, the great collections contributed to the image of august, tasteful decorum which the Georgian aristocracy so assiduously cultivated. Classical sculptures, Renaissance paintings, the latest townscapes by Canaletto or his imitators: all found their way into the town houses or the country mansions of the wealthy. Sometimes those mansions had to be altered to make way for the new acquisitions, as was the case at Felbrigg in Norfolk when William Wyndham needed a more appropriate setting for his pictures and cabinets of prints. People just outside the higher reaches of this world of privilege began to develop a new kind of artistic tourism, with the genteel visitor travelling from one great house to another to marvel over the richness of their collections.[3]

The houses, and the immense parks which surrounded them, were themselves important elements in the visual projection of aristocratic pomp and power. Goodwood, Woburn, Stowe, Knole (to mention only the mansions of some of the cricket patrons we shall encounter in this book) dominated their rural surroundings both physically and metaphorically. A whole village might be knocked down to make room for a suitably impressive park – as happened at Sir Robert Walpole's Houghton, where the village was moved so as not to spoil the view. Ambitious landscaping, such as that undertaken at the Cokes' Holkham Hall (even before the great house was begun in 1734), was another component of the new image of the stately home; later in the century it was a poor nobleman who did not bring in Capability Brown to redesign his park. The essential thing was to provide a setting that combined impressiveness with good taste; long avenues, like the Duke of Beaufort's at Badminton, always helped, giving the visitor plenty of time to reflect on the awesome magnificence of the family he or she was approaching.

That magnificence was not merely passively demonstrated by the great houses and deer parks. It had to be actively asserted on great occasions through processions and public feasting. At the Sussex election in 1722, the Whig candidates, Spencer Compton and Henry Pelham, entered Lewes in a great procession that clearly asserted their status in the county. It was headed by the servants of the attending gentry, who were followed by the High Sheriff's pikemen and then a band. Next came the local clergy, the High Sheriff attended by six footmen, and at last the candidates, supported by the two great magnates who pulled the strings of Sussex politics, the Dukes of Newcastle and Dorset. Finally, a great crowd of gentlemen and freeholders brought up the rear – the voters whose job it was to give Compton and Pelham their majority.[4]

It did not need an election to demonstrate the prestige and quality of a local magnate. Many of the truly great aristocrats were by now becoming more remote, less inclined to indiscriminate entertainment of their inferiors, than in times past. But the ordinary local gentry were still close to their tenants. When Henry Campion, the Jacobite squire of Hurstpierpoint, returned in 1720 from a five-year absence (he had prudently disappeared after the 1715 rebellion), a delegation of villagers ceremonially welcomed him on his way from London. Another prominent Sussex Jacobite, John Caryll of Ladyholt, came home in September 1739 after his marriage; he was met at some distance from his seat, a newspaper reported, 'by all his tenants, and several hundreds of gentlemen and freeholders both of Sussex and Hampshire'. A group of men dressed like morris dancers, 'all in white, and ribbons', ran ahead of the coaches. After a great dinner at Petersfield at which 'several hogsheads of beer and all manner of other liquors' were consumed, the party proceeded somewhat unsteadily to Ladyholt, with the 'running-men' now carrying flaming torches and white wands. There was then 'a most sumptuous and elegant supper', which was followed by bonfires, salutes fired by the local militia, and other 'demonstrations of joy' going far beyond anything seen in the neighbourhood in recent years. The *Salisbury Journal* drew the appropriate moral:

As this gentleman has no power at Court, or seat in Parliament, it must be presumed the affection of the people is entirely owing to the charitable and generous behaviour of him and his ancestors, for these hundred years that they have been settled in this county, without place or pension.[5]

The Tory newspaper was of course using Caryll, and doubtless embellishing his reception, to construct the party's conventional image of the honest, liberally minded country gentlemen, independent of Court favour. However, this was not entirely a fiction, for the Carylls were indeed striving intermittently to live up to the old paternalistic ideal. As leading Jacobites they had, of course, obvious political motives for their displays of hospitality. A letter from John Caryll's mother in January of the previous year is worth quoting. The day before, she told her son,

I entertained the farmers and their wives, with some others of the neighbours, we were three and twenty at my table . . . They danced and drank till two in the morning, and seemed all very well pleased. Tomorrow I have all the workmen of all sorts, and my brother's servants with us, who are to have a ball also. They dine in their hall and afterwards are to dance and play in the drying room and new infirmary. On Monday I am to have the tradespeople with their wives and all the second rate gentry in the neighbourhood . . . I'm sure there never was such true merriment in this county before, the people are all charmed with it.

The proprieties of rank and status were being observed (the servants dine in *their* hall, and are allowed to dance only in the drying room), but this too was part of the accepted style of genteel entertainment. Lady Caryll could assure her son that he was 'the best beloved by all sorts of people from the highest to the lowest of any man in the county'. His popularity was, alas, an illusion.[6]

Among the nobility and the richer gentry this kind of old-fashioned hospitality was becoming less common. But it remained part of the self-image which members of the upper crust were supposed to aspire to, and which was received with suitable plaudits when they did. Part of the process, as in the Carylls' homecoming, was the ceremonial welcome after an absence, not in the new style of the enclosing landlord in the Dixton painting mentioned in the first chapter – in which only a handful of ingratiating servants greet the returning squire – but with appropriate public ceremony, followed by festive rejoicing. There were 'great doings', John Caryll was told, when one of his neighbours, Captain Batten, brought home his bride in 1754. They were met, as Caryll had been years before, by the 'running gentlemen', and there were the usual bonfires and bell-ringing. When the Duke and Duchess of Beaufort came home to Badminton in 1766 they were met at Calne by fifty of the tenants, substantial farmers all, who escorted them to the great house behind 'four huntsmen in green, with French horns'. The people of the neighbourhood were then entertained at Badminton with what a newspaper described as 'princely hospitality'.[7]

Another element in this theatrical show was the celebration of family events such as an heir's coming-of-age. When William Jones, Esq., of Ramsbury in Wiltshire, reached twenty-one, he had an ox roasted, distributed 200 half-peck loaves, laid on 10 hogsheads of beer, and gave 40 guineas to the poor. At Huntingdon in 1765 the coming-of-age of Lord Hinchingbrooke, the Earl of Sandwich's eldest son, was celebrated even more lavishly, as was fitting for a member of the aristocracy: an even bigger ox was roasted, 20 hogsheads of beer and 4,000 loaves given away. It was said that at least 6,000 people attended, and they were entertained with fireworks and illuminations, the firing of cannon, songs, and healths to the King, the Montague family, and other worthy causes. Some celebrations had explicitly political aims, such as the annual 'venison feasts' given by the Wiltshire MPs Sir Robert Long and Edward Popham, but others had no obvious purpose beyond the consolidation of the givers' local popularity. In 1767 the Hon. Thomas Fitzmaurice gave a 'grand entertainment' at Shanklin in the Isle of Wight, to which all the farmers and their families from four miles around were invited, and 'all the peasants near that would come'. A sheep was roasted and carried to the table behind musicians playing horns and violins, and there was dancing in the evening.[8]

In all this there is the expectation that the nobility and gentry will, as of old, earn the deference and respect of their inferiors by being generous and charitable towards them. Great men no longer kept open house as often as in times past, but there were those who still did so occasionally. The Duke of Newcastle held 'public days' for the people of the neighbourhood when he came down to his house at Halland for Lewes Races or the Assizes. Thomas Turner used to go to them, often complaining about the excessive drinking – in which, nevertheless, he himself participated. People of all social levels were welcomed, with dinner for the gentry, followed by what Turner describes as 'a very good supper' for the tradesmen of East Hoathly and the neighbouring parishes. In August 1757 the Halland throng contained 'a great company of people of all denominations from a duke to a beggar'. During the next few years the celebrations became increasingly hectic as the Seven Years War produced one British victory after another. At one in August 1759, Turner tells us, 'there was such huzzaing that made the very foundations . . . of the house to shake'.[9]

Turner was not rich, but he could have survived without Newcastle's largesse. For poorer people aristocratic handouts were more crucial, especially at Christmas. In 1768 Sir John Shelley of Michelgrove had a bull killed and its meat distributed to the poor of two nearby parishes. This sort of charity was less common during the rest of the year, but old ideals still lingered. Reporting on Maidenhead Races in 1750, a newspaper noted that the gentleman whose horse had won the Stakes, 'paid his rider genteely, treated the gentlemen and ladies elegantly that evening, and gave each poor man of the parish a part of the money his horse run for and bravely won'. Such examples of neighbourly goodwill were of course particularly necessary during hard times. In the harsh winter of 1740, Stephen Fox, MP for Shaftesbury, sent £30 to be distributed among the poor of the town, while the Duke of Beaufort ordered the weekly distribution of an ox, eight bushels of wheat and several loads of wood to the poor of Netheravon, a village where he had his hunting lodge. Periods of high prices caused by a previous year's bad harvest also inspired elite charity. At Knole in May and June 1757 the second Duke of Dorset paid over £26 for beef and at least £12 for bread for the poor of Sevenoaks, as well as £20 for the needy in the nearby villages of Kemsing and Seal.[10]

Sport was not the least important component of this aristocratic culture. It will not surprise the reader to learn that many of the gentry and nobility were firmly addicted to fox-hunting. The Charlton in Sussex was the most celebrated of the early eighteenth-century hunts, and it set the pattern for many later famous ones such as the Quorn and the Pytchely. Rich landowners such as Hugo Meynell in Leicestershire and Peter Beckford in Dorset spent lavishly to build up their packs: the annual cost of maintaining thirty couple of hounds at mid-century was estimated at around £245, more than the average gentleman's total income. Yet the chase was pursued with little regard for expense. Later in the century 'subscription packs', relying on members' contributions, become common. Thomas Ridge, of whom we shall hear more, established a hunt of this kind at Kilmiston in Hampshire in 1780, but it still brought him to ruin. The financial outlay ensured that most hunts remained under the patronage of great noblemen. They were often a major source of aristocratic influence in their region.[11]

Horse racing was another sport that, as we have seen, was deeply entrenched in local culture, and provided further opportunities for noblemen to project their power. Everywhere race meetings coincided with polite balls and assemblies; attending these events, Peter Borsay remarks, was 'a sign of one's allegiance to shire society'. The visitors from Cambridge whom we last encountered in 1735 at Canterbury Races spent the evening at the city's Assembly, where they spotted Lords Winchilsea and Romney, and many of the local gentry. Aristocratic swells like these were famous for their huge wagers, particularly at Newmarket, where many of them had stables, where attendance was virtually confined to the nobility and gentry, and where the authority of the Jockey Club, with its headquarters at the Star and Garter in Pall Mall, was first established. Formation of the Club may have been accelerated by events in April 1751, when 'a certain person in the sporting way', as the *Salisbury Journal* discreetly described him, was warned off at Newmarket by the noblemen, who agreed to 'prevent his wicked designs at every horse race, etc., where they have influence'. Although hunting was less likely than racing to spin-off urban festivities, it did so occasionally. At Dorchester in the autumn of 1738 there was a weekly 'hunting carnival' featuring plays and assemblies, to entertain the ladies and the gentlemen who had followed the hounds during the day. A correspondent of the *Salisbury Journal* felt that the carnival had achieved its purpose by reinforcing the bonds that existed 'amongst all the gentry here'.[12]

Those bonds, however, could be seriously strained by politics. Race meetings everywhere were likely to become highly charged political events. In 1750 Dorchester's absentee voters were urged not to commit themselves to any candidate until after discussions at Salisbury and Blandford Races. At Chippenham Races ten years earlier there was a large appearance of noblemen and gentlemen, presided over by the Duke of Beaufort, to support the two local candidates for Parliament in the 'country interest'. After a riot at Lichfield Races in 1747 feelings ran so high that for several years Whigs and Tories had to organize separate meetings.[13]

Racing and hunting were only two of many sports that were either played or patronized by 'the quality'. Bowls, or bowling as it was still called, may have been less popular than in the two previous centuries, but provincial towns such as Lewes, Tunbridge Wells and Winchester still regarded their greens as valuable civic assets, both for townsmen and for the neighbouring gentry, so it was still played virtually every-where. Two gentlemen played a match for twenty guineas in 1756 on the Bowling Green at Hampstead, and when the new Spring Gardens was opened near Gosport a few years later the proprietor thought it worth advertising its bowling green as an added attraction. Many other public gardens included bowling among their amenities.[14] Tennis (the less familiar 'real' variety, not the nowadays far more popular lawn tennis) was another genteel game; the Prince of Wales played it at the royal tennis court at Whitehall. As with other sports, London promoters were by now beginning to see profitable opportunities in it. A new court opened in Great Windmill Street in 1743, charging its patrons up to two shillings a set, with the use of a good billiard table if they had to wait. Another London promoter, Thomas Higginson, offered both tennis and fives at his court next door to a coffee-house in Lincoln's Inn Fields; he also gave lessons, and sold balls and racquets. Prize-fighting, unlike tennis and bowling, was not a sport fit for gentlemen to play. But it was one which some members of the aristocracy enthusiastically supported, either by attending and betting on fights, or as patrons of the leading pugilists. The Duke of Cumberland, the 'butcher of Culloden', was a major patron in the 1740s, though he had an irritating habit of with-drawing his support whenever he lost money, as he did to the tune of £10,000 in a wager on a fight in 1750.[15]

Cricket, on the other hand, was certainly a sport fit for gentlemen to play. Greatest among the early eighteenth-century cricketing aristocrats was the second Duke of Richmond, who lived at Goodwood, near Chichester. Richmond's ancestry was almost terrifyingly distinguished. His grandfather was King Charles II, his grandmother one of that monarch's numerous mistresses, Louise de Kéroualle, Duchess of Ports-mouth; in a book about sport it seems appropriate to mention that their affair was consummated during a race meeting at Newmarket. Richmond was devoted to the old lady, and regularly visited her in

France until her death in 1734. His father, the first Duke, was also keen on cricket. He played against the 'Arundel men' in 1702, spending 1s.6d. on brandy at the game.[16] Charles Lennox, Earl of March until he inherited the Richmond title as the second Duke in 1723, was born in 1701 and at the age of eighteen was married off to a daughter of the Earl of Cadogan, as part of the settlement of one of his father's gambling debts. An unpromising beginning, yet it turned out to be a remarkably happy marriage, and the Duchess was even willing to subsidize her husband's cricket, paying £19 in August 1731, for example, 'to Lord Duke for his cricket match'. Queen Caroline thought Richmond 'half-witted . . . bizarre' and too much the *grand seigneur*, but except for the smugglers he so ruthlessly pursued, most people found him genial and good-natured, and that is certainly the impression given by his correspondence.[17]

Richmond was strikingly eclectic in his interests. He was Canaletto's chief English patron, corresponded with Voltaire and Montesquieu, was president of the Society for the Advancement of Learning, and a lover of opera and the theatre. He was also interested in public health and civic improvement (especially of nearby Chichester, which was of course within his political sphere of influence), and had a menagerie in his park at Goodwood containing tigers and other wild animals. Close to 500 people, many from Chichester, came to see it one Sunday in 1730, an indication of how far England had come from the extreme sabbatarianism of the previous century. The Duke's steward was not impressed by the visitors. The staff were 'much troubled', he reported, 'with very rude company to see the animals'. They did all sorts of damage, and threatened 'to break John Horn's head' when that Goodwood employee tried to drive them away. Horn was then warned that he would be arrested for assault if he ever dared come to Chichester. Besides bringing undesirable people to Goodwood, the zoo was also pretty costly; in 1726 Richmond spent nearly £80 on an iron cage for the tiger.[18]

Like many noblemen of his time, Richmond was inevitably deeply involved in politics. His career in the public service included far more than the usual number of offices routinely collected by the average Georgian aristocrat. He was a privy councillor, Lord of the Bedchamber, Master of the Horse, and held military commands which took him to Hanover – and the battle of Dettingen – with George II in 1743. After the war's end he became Ambassador to Paris. Above all, in spite of his

Stuart ancestry, he was a passionate Whig, working in enthusiastic partnership with his friend the Duke of Newcastle (who controlled the eastern part of the county, as Richmond did the western) to manage the distribution of patronage and the conduct of parliamentary elections, thus ensuring that Sussex remained safely in Whig hands.

The Duke was also a great sportsman. The Charlton Hunt, of which he was Master, absorbed much of his energies, both physical and political. Besides galloping all over the countryside in pursuit of unfortunate Sussex foxes (he wrote a memorable account of one such chase in January 1739), Richmond carefully supervised the hunt's composition, ensuring that its hitherto largely Tory membership was swamped by the admission of a procession of his Whig friends. The Charlton deserved this attention; Timothy McCann describes its meets as 'possibly the most important social event in England outside the capital'. Yet Richmond could be accommodating to political enemies when he wanted to, telling the recusant John Caryll that he would be 'exceeding happy' to have his company at the next Charlton meet, and even inviting him to stay at Goodwood. There was, of course, an election in the offing, in which the votes of Caryll's dependants might be useful.[19]

Richmond was also very fond of cricket. He was certainly playing by 1725, when his team took on one raised by Sir William Gage of Firle in the first of several matches between them. Cricket was not as expensive as the zoo, but it still required a considerable outlay. Bats had to be repaired and bound, and the players fittingly attired: in 1726 the Duke paid £3.5s.9d. for 'waistcoats, breeches and caps for the cricketers', and two years later he bought them twelve 'yellow velvet caps with silver tassels' at 12s. each. The best known of Richmond's matches was one in July 1727 against a team led by Alan Brodrick of Peper Harow, heir to Viscount Midleton – famous in cricket history because it was played under 'Articles of Agreement' that in some ways anticipate the 'Laws' of cricket first promulgated in 1744. The articles also contain, however, some peculiar features that are not in the 1744 Laws – among them a twenty-three yard pitch, and an exemption of the Duke and Mr Brodrick from the usual prohibition of arguing with the umpires. Brodrick's team were given home advantage in Surrey for the first match, but there was provision for a return game in Sussex in August. Richmond was allowed to choose his side from 'any gamesters who have played in either of his Grace's two last matches with Sir William Gage', while Brodrick's men had to have lived within three miles of Peper Harow at least since the previous Lady Day. By later standards, the stakes were relatively modest: a mere twelve guineas a side.[20]

Richmond remained an enthusiastic cricketer for the rest of his sadly short life (he died in 1750). In April 1730 it was reported that he and other noblemen had 'diverted themselves at cricket in Hyde Park' and that they were shortly to play a match for 100 guineas – the stakes were already rising, unless this is an early example of the journalistic embellishment which was to lead to many exaggerated reports of the size of wagers. In July of that year the Duke's men lost to an XI raised by a Sunbury gentleman in a match on Merrow Downs near Guildford, and a month later they were allowed to postpone a match against Gage's team – to have been played at Lewes on a ground picturesquely known as the 'Dripping Pan' – because Richmond's star player, his groom Thomas Waymark, was ill. Waymark was already making a name for himself throughout the southeast, having in the previous year 'turned the scale of victory' by his 'extraordinary agility and dexterity' when playing against Kent at Penshurst. We shall have more to say about Thomas Waymark.[21]

Interest in these matches was not confined to the aristocracy and gentry. The talk in Chichester, Richmond's steward observed on 10 June 1730, was that 'his grace is to play a cricket match with Sir William Gage on Bury Hill'. And not all of them were conducted with the deference and decorum that one might expect when members of the aristocracy were involved. When Richmond's team played an XI raised by a certain Mr Chambers at Richmond, Surrey, in August 1731 it was for 200 guineas a side (again we have a further escalation of the stake-money), and a crowd of 'many thousands', including 'persons of distinction, of both sexes', as a newspaper described them, turned up to watch. Early eighteenth-century cricket matches were normally completed in a day, but in this one time was called at seven o'clock with Chambers's XI needing only a few runs to win and with four wickets in hand. There had been much betting on the match, not all of it by the quality, and there were loud protests at the lack of a conclusive result, even threats of a lawsuit (it would not have been the first one). When the Duke and his team were leaving they were 'greatly insulted by the mob . . . some of them having their shirts torn off their backs'. The Duke's men were probably not the only ones to have lost their shirts that day.[22]

*

For some years in the 1740s Richmond was patron of the village team at Slindon, not far from Goodwood. In some ways this is odd, because the place had long been a Tory, even Jacobite, stronghold, while Richmond was a passionate Whig. And although the Duke lived near by, he did not own the manor of Slindon, which for more than a century had been in the hands of a Roman Catholic family, the Kempes. Goodwood was in fact within the parish of Boxgrove, where cricket had been played more than a hundred years earlier. Members of Richmond's family usually went to church at Westhampnett, on the Chichester side of Goodwood; many of them, however, were buried in Boxgrove Priory. Slindon was at the very heart of the Sussex recusant network. There was a priest's hole in the manor house, and a Catholic mission in the village, endowed by one of the Kempes; it is not surprising that the 1676 religious census reported seventeen openly Popish families, an unusually large number for a small village. It is also not surprising that in 1742 the Anglican parish of Slindon still had a Jacobite rector. It was 'a corner of the county', the Duke of Richmond reflected, 'where a clever Jacobite parson might do us [the Whigs] a great deal of mischief'. Fortunately the present incumbent was not clever, and even more fortunately he was drunk most of the time.[23]

Slindon, clearly, was situated in an area where cricket was deeply entrenched. Precisely when they emerged from the common run of Sussex village teams is unknown, but by 1741 they were certainly attracting attention, for in that year they beat Portsmouth by nine wickets and 'Surrey' almost by an innings. A year later a London newspaper reported that Slindon had played forty-three matches and had lost only one of them; not surprisingly, they were now invited to perform in the capital. Their first match at the Artillery Ground was on 6 September 1742, against the London Club, and was advertised as 'the greatest match at cricket that has been played for many years'. London won a close game, but in a second match on the 10th, rescheduled after a rainout, Slindon were routed, beaten by the huge margin of 184 runs – perhaps some of their players had gone home to Sussex to go back to work. When they next came to the Artillery Ground, to play Kent in 1744, Slindon were strengthened by the addition of several well-known players from London and elsewhere.[24] During the next few years they played against most of the leading southeastern teams – Addington, Bromley, Dartford, Hadlow – but they were no longer the power they had been earlier in the decade. By 1754 they had retreated to the narrower horizons of Sussex local cricket. But cricket long continued at Slindon; in the early nineteenth century one of their players, a game-keeper named Francis Mellersh, was a well-known stonewaller.[25]

The most famous of the earlier Slindon players was Richard Newland, a yeoman, whose two brothers, John and Adam, also represented Slindon. There had been Newlands in Slindon at least since the beginning of the previous century, when a certain John Newland served as steward to the landlord, Sir Garrett Kempe. Richard Newland the elder, father of the cricketers, was a solid member of the village community, often a churchwarden; in 1704 he married a young woman from nearby Eartham. Richard the younger, the first of his three cricketing sons, was born at Slindon in 1713; he married the sister of another Richard Newland, a surgeon with whom he has often been confused. In 1733 his own sister, Susan, married yet another Eartham resident, a certain Richard Nyren. Their son was the famous Richard Nyren, captain of the Hambledon Club. Richard Newland was sufficiently well known to have been invited to play in important matches even before Slindon made their first appearance in London. He was, apparently, 'the Sussex man from Slindon', who in August 1742 played twice for combined teams against the Gentlemen of London; once at Dubber's Hill, near Croydon, and once at the Artillery Ground. He may have been still playing in major matches as late as 1759.[26]

The other Slindon player about whom something is known was the village tailor, Edward Aburrow, popularly known as 'Curry'. He played in several matches at the Artillery Ground in 1744, and again appeared there (for 'England' against Kent) in May 1751. We know more about him, beyond his reputation as a bowler and some undistinguished per-formances with the bat, because he got into serious trouble. In 1745 he was one of a group of men who were following the familiar local trade of smuggling, landing 'prohibited goods' at Elmer's Sluice, on the Sussex coast; worse, he or some others of the gang were armed. The incident reminds us that Slindon, like other Sussex villages, was a violent place. Richard and John Newland were among a group of men indicted in 1749 for assaulting a certain Griffith Hughes. All were discharged, but the trouble may well have been connected with some smuggling affray. By this time the Elmer's Sluice business had come out and Aburrow was imprisoned at Horsham. The Duke of Richmond, whose enthusiasm for cricket was surpassed only by his determination to wipe out the Sussex smugglers, was unsympathetic. Aburrow's 'whole family', he told the

Duke of Newcastle, were notorious villains (one of Curry's brothers was hanged for agrarian violence in Hampshire), and even though Curry was 'a famous bowler at cricket' Richmond was in favour of making examples of them all. Curry, however, saved his neck by turning king's evidence and returned to Slindon, where his second son was born in 1750. Soon after that he moved to Hampshire, either to West Meon or to Hambledon, and he may have been wise to do so, for Sussex smugglers had a nasty way with informers. His son, another Edward, also known as 'Curry', was to be yet another Hambledon cricketer.[27]

Slindon's was a village team all right, but in the early 1740s it became the next provincial side after Dartford to make its mark at the Artillery Ground, and thus helped to bring rural cricket into the orbit of the commercialized sport that already entertained the teeming population of the capital. The team's rise to metropolitan fame was made possible by something else besides its brilliant playing record: the patronage of the second Duke of Richmond. The Duke's lack of sympathy for Aburrow the smuggler is in some ways remarkable, for Slindon was by this time *his* team. When they played at the Artillery Ground in June 1744 he took the matches seriously enough to keep the full scoresheets (the first ones surviving from anywhere that give the batsmen's individual scores) among his papers. Slindon's matches were also important in the West Sussex election campaigns which the Duke managed so carefully.

There can be no doubt about Richmond's passion for cricket; nor can there be about his zeal for politics; and the two often overlapped. 'You'll think me mad with elections, and 'tis true I am so,' he admitted to a friend in 1733, during the hubbub over Walpole's Excise Bill, 'but all England at present is the same; it is epidemical.' A good deal of the preliminary manoeuvring before elections took place at race meetings and other such gatherings. As we have seen, besides being sporting contests horse races were social events which, like sessions of the Assizes, brought the gentry together in convivial settings. They presented obvious opportunities for political intrigue. In June 1733 Newcastle noted that Lewes Races and the Assizes were to be held during the same week, so that 'when the gentlemen are together we may know their sentiments as to the next election'. Newcastle was talking about the Whig gentlemen, but his statement could have applied equally to the Tories: two months later he was warning Richmond that their opponents would probably 'set up somebody at Steyning Races' as a candidate.[28]

As another election approached towards the end of the decade the opposition leaders again went to the races. In August 1739, just after the end of race week, the Tory gentry met at the Star in Lewes, to pursue, as the sympathetic *Salisbury Journal* gushed, 'their COUNTRY'S INTEREST', and to oppose 'all Pensioners and Conventioners', in other words all agents of Walpolean corruption and supporters of the peace policy which had led to the recent Convention of the Pardo. Just a few weeks earlier the paper had reported that 'No Conventioners!' was an almost 'universal cry' in Sussex. Nearly another year passed before the election campaign actually began, but again it was at Lewes Races that the 'Country interest' made their move, adopting Samuel Medley of Buxted Place as their candidate. Richmond was already at work, organizing a rival meeting at Horsham, to which he promised to bring 'besides the gentry, . . . some of our top farmers, that we call yeomanly men'. Among them, he told Newcastle, were 'Sam Row the smuggler' (Richmond was apparently not yet totally hostile to members of that trade, as long as they had votes), and 'John Newland that you must remember' – probably the uncle, rather than the younger brother, of the famous Slindon cricketer. He also got the Duchess to go to Westhampnett church to listen to a long and boring sermon ('and to commend it mightily') so that the parson there would use his influence on behalf of the Whigs. He was, Richmond thought, 'a mad Welsh enthusiast', but was 'vastly followed by the people'. All these careful preparations ended in anticlimax: Medley gave up the fight, and the Whigs James Butler and Henry Pelham (Newcastle's famous brother) were returned unopposed for Sussex in May 1741. But then, only ten days after the election, Butler died and there had to be an unwanted by-election.[29]

Richmond was an astute observer of public opinion, and he well knew that middle-class voters had to be courted, not commanded. And not all voters were even middle class. Sir William Gage told Newcastle that many in the Lewes area could not come to one of his election meetings because, although freeholders, they were no better than labourers who 'could not leave their mowing and haying'. Such people were obviously vulnerable to aristocratic pressure, as was the case near Petworth, where a lot of the voters, Newcastle was told, were 'tenants or copyholders, traders or workmen' dependent upon the Duke of Somerset, and this was bound to have 'its natural consequences'. The outcome of canvassing was necessarily limited, in other words, by social realities. Still, even men as great as Richmond could never take the electorate for granted, which is why so much money had to be spent on entertaining them. Shortly before the first election the Duchess bought 36 hams, 118 pounds of cheese, and forty dozen glasses, at a total cost of just over £18, for the 'election treat' at Goodwood. Something surely must also have been spent to fill up the forty dozen glasses.[30]

Like race meetings, cricket matches were obviously useful arenas for political action, especially for people with sporting interests. One of Horace Walpole's friends noted that after the gentlemen of Sussex had beaten Kent on the Downs near Lewes in 1735 they were 'as much pleased as if they had got an election'; they celebrated far into the night, laying bets about the return match at Sevenoaks. The Duke of Newcastle had nothing like Richmond's enthusiasm for cricket, but his agents nevertheless canvassed at matches in East Sussex almost as energetically as Richmond's did in the west. But it is Richmond's sponsorship of the Slindon team that most dramatically illustrates the association of sport with politics. The new opposition candidate Thomas Sergison made an appearance at Stansted Park when Slindon played Portsmouth in June 1741 but found few supporters and promptly left. 'All our friends,' Richmond gloated, '. . . were in great spirits especially as Slindon beat Portsmouth, and had nine men to go in.' We may well wonder which aspect of the victory meant more to him – the cricketing or the political.[31]

Confrontations like this were not accidental. The expectation that Sergison would use the Slindon–Portsmouth match to demonstrate his strength made Richmond vow to 'face him there with fifty staunch freeholders all engaged to us'. In the event Sergison had no more success in drumming up support at Stansted than his predecessor, Samuel Medley, had had at earlier cricket matches. But he did better a few weeks later when Slindon played at Portslade. Both political factions were there in force. Sergison treated his supporters lavishly, and there was trouble when they chanted insults at the Whig candidate, Charles Sackville, Earl of Middlesex, scion of another prominent cricketing family, for his alleged attendance at a 'calves-head' dinner years before. According to Richmond, 'a bloody battle' ensued in which a lot of heads were broken. The Slindoners were driven from the field, but they returned with a fresh supply of cricket bats and were eventually victorious. Sir William Gage showed that as usual he had his priorities straight when he told Newcastle about the disturbance: 'I am glad the cricket match was over before this happened.'[32]

Richmond was not always so successful in his efforts to use cricket to promote the Whig cause. There was a disappointing attendance at one election meeting in July 1741 because it coincided with a great cricket match at Wisborough Green. When Richmond's two great passions collided, however, politics did not always take precedence. In September 1741 he had to miss a strategy session with Newcastle because he was promoting a match on Merrow Down between his 'poor little Slindon' and a powerful Surrey county side. But his use of the game, as of virtually everything else connected with elections, was far more systematic than that of the opposition, and made a considerable contribution to his control of West Sussex. Like Newcastle in the eastern division, he sent his steward around to work the crowds: at one match in June 1741, the man found much discussion of the election. The spectators, he reported, were 'almost all hearty for us', and the talk was that the Duke of Somerset would after all be neutral. The Tories were amateurs by comparison. When Sergison promoted a match in his own park at Cuckfield he drummed up a good crowd by having it announced in all the neighbouring parishes on the previous Sunday, but then neglected the most basic rules of ritual hospitality by failing to invite the players to eat and drink with him, and did not even canvass votes from the spectators.[33]

Throughout the campaign the Whigs had shown themselves to be more attuned to the outlook of the rural population, and they owed much of their success to Richmond. The Duke was the first of the great noblemen who used cricket to enhance their reputations and their popularity with their rural neighbours. Of course, this was not the only reason why he and his like were involved in the game. Serious-minded sports historians sometimes forget that people who played games may have done so not just to make money or to act out some hidden agenda – a symbolic affirmation of class or national or regional identity perhaps – but because they actually enjoyed them. For many eighteenth-century noblemen cricket was almost as much fun as hunting and horse-racing, like those other sports an occasion for friendly competition and for socializing with friends and neighbours, a source of satisfaction if they or their teams did well. It was also one of the many excuses for the compulsive gambling for which members of the English aristocracy were famous. But the serious historians are right that for such people cricket was ultimately more than a game. Promoting, attending, and playing in matches with their neighbours was part of the process of 'theatrical show' by which they demonstrated the benign nature of their authority. On the cricket field the Duke of Richmond's very presence proclaimed that, however grand and blue-blooded, he was still a Sussex man, sharing the rustic pleasures of his neighbours. Richmond's letters to the county's other great Whig nobleman, the Duke of Newcastle, show that he knew how to play that role when it suited him – to adopt, tongue-in-cheek, the independent tone of a local yeoman. 'As a Sussex freeholder,' he once told Newcastle when he wanted a favour from him, 'I have a title to be troublesome.'[34]

But the Duke of Richmond was not the only great person to share the growing passion for cricket. In the 1730s the example was set by the then heir to the throne, Prince Frederick, who used the game to demonstrate his new-found English identity (he had lived entirely in Hanover until he was twenty-one). It was his son, George III, who later 'gloried in the name of Briton', but Frederick must also have realized how much he had to gain by distancing himself from the reputation of his father and grandfather, the first two Georges, as boring Germans. Nothing could have been more English than cricket. Frederick was reported to have first 'diverted himself' at the game in Kensington Gardens in September 1735; his playing days were to end tragically when he died from the delayed effects of being struck by a ball, apparently while fielding. He had played fairly often for both Surrey and the London Club, nominally as captain; the newspapers are always delicately silent about his actual performances. But he was well-enough known to be a cricket lover for a match to be played in his memory at Saltford, near Bath, soon after his death in 1751.[35]

The Prince had been a patron of the game long before he started playing it. When Surrey met Middlesex at Moulsey Hurst in July 1733 he rewarded each player with a guinea, 'for their great dexterity', and at the same ground a few days later he gave a silver cup as the prize in a match between his XI – 'the Prince's men' – and a team raised by Edwin Stead, at this time an important patron of Kent cricket. Special tents were provided when Frederick attended: at a match on Kennington Common in 1737 a 'pavilion' was erected for him and his party. His appearance always attracted large crowds, for people in those days liked to gape at royalty as much as they do now. 'The conversation of the town', James Collier told his father in July 1745, was not, as we might perhaps expect, about any possible threat from the Young Pretender, but about the impending match between Kent and Frederick's 'All England' XI on Bromley Common: 'The Prince of Wales and all the nobility in town will be present.' After this kind of publicity it is not surprising that the Prince's arrival on the Common led to total chaos; the crowd surged around his carriage, people were thrown from their horses, ridden over, and one man 'carried off for dead'. At another of his matches the crowd was so thick that a poor woman was knocked down and suffered a broken leg; the Prince gave her ten guineas.[36]

Many other 'persons of distinction' were involved in promoting cricket matches during this period. The newspapers regularly report that 'the noblemen and gentlemen' have arranged matches in which the leading players could demonstrate their skills. After the London Club had narrowly beaten an XI from the Weald of Kent at the Artillery Ground in 1743, 'the noblemen and gentlemen concerned in this match' were so pleased by the exciting finish that they promptly arranged another one between the same teams in the following week. Two years later William Hodsoll of Dartford, Valentine Romney of Sevenoaks, and Richard Newland of Slindon were 'appointed by the noblemen' to play a single-wicket match against three other well-known players, and the next day 'the noblemen and gentlemen present' made another match between two XIs of the same sort.[37]

Who were these 'persons of distinction', these 'noblemen and gentlemen' who were regarded as the great patrons of the game? It will not surprise us to know that besides the Prince, the second Duke of Richmond figured prominently among them. Richmond was still actively promoting matches long after his Slindon lads had left the London cricket scene. In August 1747 there was a single-wicket match at the Artillery Ground between three of the Duke's 'servants' and three prominent London players, and the next day the noblemen arranged the first of two five-a-side matches in which the same players and four others participated. Until he went off to Paris as ambassador in 1748 and then became preoccupied with his war against the Sussex smugglers, Richmond was always a major patron of the game.[38]

Among the other great cricketing families were the Sackvilles of Knole. Lionel Cranfield Sackville, created first Duke of Dorset in 1720, was mainly engrossed by his political career, but he still had time for cricket. He gave the famous Sevenoaks Vine ground to the town, and also established a 'cricketing place' in the Park, which was regularly mown and rolled. He died in 1765, and by then two of his sons had established reputations as cricketers. A third one, Lord George Sackville, is better known to history than either. He had already gained swift promotion in the army when, home at Knole in October 1757, he led the defence of the great house when it was attacked by a mob of unarmed and ungrateful peasants, who were rioting against the recent Militia Act. Two years later he found the French at the battle of Minden to be of sterner (as well as better armed) stuff, and was court-martialled for cowardice. Long afterwards (having changed his name to Germain) he made an important contribution to American independence through his misman-agement of the British side of the war, as Secretary of State for the Colonies. Americans, though not Kentish peasants, have cause to be grateful to him.[39]

Of Dorset's two older, cricket-playing sons, we have already encoun-tered the eldest, Charles, Earl of Middlesex, as Richmond's candidate in the Sussex by-election of 1741, and as an extravagant patron of music. Middlesex was a close friend of the Prince of Wales, who appointed him his Master of the Horse. They were also friendly rivals on the cricket field. In a great match on Bromley Common in 1735 Middlesex cap-tained Kent against the Prince's team, in the process making an impress-ive demonstration of his family's territorial influence and showing that a Sackville had no intention of being intimidated by a Prince of Wales. The Earl arrived at Bromley a couple of hours before Frederick, it was reported, 'at the head of the Kent gamesters, and attended by a great number of people of that county'. We know that he continued his patronage of cricket after he succeeded to the dukedom in 1765, because he bought eleven bats for his team for 2s.6d. each, and two balls for 3s.6d: the comparative prices show how primitive eighteenth-century bats still were. The same bundle of 'cricketing bills' in which this pur-chase is recorded contains an account for wine 'delivered to His Grace of Dorset's Booth' on 11 June 1766: ten bottles of white, and a dozen of red port. There must have been a fashionable party at Knole for the match. Middlesex had also been one of 'the rivals of the bat' (Sir William Gage was the other) in the match between Sussex and Kent in 1735 at which Horace Walpole's friend was a spectator.[40]

Walpole, who was an intellectual snob and disliked cricket, was probably unimpressed by this news. When the younger Sackville brother, Lord John, visited him at Twickenham, 'certain games called *cricketalia*', Horace sniffed, were held in his honour in a nearby meadow. By that time Lord John was an experienced player, better than his older brother.

He and Middlesex first turn up in cricket history when their Kent team beat Sussex at Sevenoaks in 1734; the return match in Sussex was cancelled because many of the players had decamped for the softer pleasures of Bath. In 1738 Lord John skippered Eastbourne in a local game in Sussex, and a year later he and his brother sponsored one of the matches at Coxheath between the 'Hills and the Dales' of Kent, for £500. In 1743 we find him leading a Kent side on Bromley Common and getting beaten by a team chosen by Lord Mountfort, in front of a distinguished crowd which included the Prince of Wales and Lords Waldegrave and Baltimore. By 1739 Lord John was already playing in major matches in London, being described as one of three 'very good gamesters' who were brought in to strengthen a London XI for a game on Kennington Common. On 18 June 1744 he appeared for Kent against 'England' at the Artillery Ground, in a match which we know a good bit about both because Richmond's copy of the scoresheet still exists and because a certain James Love, alias Dance, wrote a light-hearted poem about it. Sackville made only 5 and 0, but he did make a brilliant catch to dismiss Richard Newland at a critical stage of the game.[41]

Lord John's appearance at the Artillery Ground is an astonishing development, in the light of eighteenth-century assumptions about social hierarchy. Nothing could better illustrate the blurring of class lines which cricket could sometimes permit: a blue-blooded Sackville playing on a public ground, with and against professionals, and in front of a paying, plebeian audience. Another striking feature of this match is that in spite of Lord John's presence in the side, Kent were captained by Valentine Romney, a well-known professional who was the Sackvilles' head gardener at Knole. No wonder some people worried about the disorderly implications of this sort of thing. In 1743 'The British Champion' pointedly questioned the nobility's 'right to invite thousands of people to be spectators of their agility, at the expense of their duty and honesty' – especially in matches in which the elite had made 'butchers, cobblers or tinkers their companions'. Yet the Lord John Sackville who accepted a gardener as his captain was also one of the few people who could put the Duke of Richmond in his place. 'I wish you had let Ridgeway [a professional] play instead of your stopping behind' (playing long-stop), he protested to Richmond in September 1745, 'it might have turned the match in our favour.'[42]

The list of eighteenth-century noblemen who were in one way or another connected with cricket by no means ends with Richmond and the Sackvilles. Horace Walpole sneered that Lord Mountfort, whose team had beaten Kent in 1743, was guilty of many 'absurdities', including 'making cricket matches and fetching up persons by express from different parts of England to play matches on Richmond Green'. He was also addicted to the turf, sending his servants to place bets for him at country race meetings. The fourth Earl of Sandwich, John Wilkes's drinking companion (and later persecutor), was well known for both his cricket and his gambling. Cartoonists regularly depicted him with a cricket bat; in a 1757 print he is shown with one over his shoulder, remarking 'I love deep play; this or nothing.' But age or dissipation eventually caught up with him. In 1766 he was playing cricket with his two sons and another relative; Sandwich was out for o, and when fielding, 'was not able to run or move, but paid his money and went to bed'. Lord Temple and the Duke of Bedford were also patrons of the game. Temple's men were victorious when their teams met at Wotton in Buckinghamshire in 1741, but Bedford's 'Woburn Club' had a more regular existence during the next few years, winning several matches against the well-known London Club. They also twice played a team from Northamptonshire and Huntingdonshire, raised by the Earls of Sandwich and Halifax.[43]

Most of these matches were between teams which included paid, plebeian players as well as the aristocratic sponsors. But sometimes the noblemen preferred to play among themselves, just in case they were made to look foolish by their inferiors. In 1733 the Prince of Wales attended a match in Hyde Park between 'several persons of the highest rank', and at Kew in 1737 he and ten gentlemen played an aristocratic team led by the Duke of Marlborough. In 1751 there were several aristocratic matches. At Newmarket, Sandwich led a team of Old Etonians in three matches against an XI raised by Lord March, for £1,500 a side; March's team could be drawn from anywhere in England, but could not include 'professed match players', in other words plebeian professionals. The Etonians bet heavily on their performances – to the tune of 'some hundreds of pounds', it was said. The nobs were to be 'dressed in the handsomest manner', a newspaper announced, 'in silk jackets, trousers, velvet caps, etc.', and the side bets were alleged to have reached the sum of £20,000. A huge crowd of celebrity-watchers turned up, and were entertained with the usual popular diversions. Besides the cricket there was 'cocking, smock-racing, camping or foot-ball, wrestling and cudgelling', which altogether attracted over 6,000 spectators. Soon afterwards, when the less-fashionable players of Dartford met Bromley they offered to pick a combined XI from their two teams and play the Newmarket winners 'for any sum'. The noblemen wisely did not accept the challenge, though they seem to have had no objection to playing each other again in the Duke of Bedford's park at Woburn, or to a match at Moulsey Hurst against the 'gentlemen' of Ripley and Thursley, for £100 a side. However, the nobility, who were less tied to particular localities than the gentry, were by now beginning to spread the game more widely. There were contests in the same year in Yorkshire and Durham between the Earl of Northumberland's and the Duke of Cleveland's teams, and at Fakenham in Norfolk between the teams of Col. Townshend and Lord Orford.[44]

It would be nice to know more about these games, but the results are rarely reported. We can get something of their flavour from the memoirs of that unrepentant young rake, William Hickey. In August 1768 Hickey played for an XI of 'gentlemen who had been educated at Westminster', against the Old Etonians. The match was arranged by the most distinguished Old Westminster cricketer of the day, Lord John Frederick Sackville (son of Lord John Sackville, and soon to succeed his uncle as third Duke of Dorset), and was played at Moulsey Hurst for twenty guineas a man. The required generosity towards the lower orders was not forgotten: the winnings were to be donated to the poor of the neighbouring parishes. The players, Hickey tells us, were 'young men of the best connections, several of fashion and large fortune'; besides Sackville they included Lord Francis Osborne, Lords Bulkeley and Molesworth, and Sir Watkin Williams Wynne, 'not one of my London acquaintances being likely to be present'. This was lucky, for Hickey had fallen into bad company and was fast wasting away what little fortune he had. The Westminsters took the match seriously and held several practice sessions. Hickey, confident in his abilities as a left-handed batsman and 'a famous stop behind wicket', did not attend them, but he was determined to do his best for the team. Alas for good intentions; on the day before the match he ran into two of his old drinking companions, got utterly plastered and had his pocket picked. Yet he still managed to get to Moulsey Hurst in the morning, arriving just in time to avoid forfeiting his twenty-guinea stake. The Westminsters won 'a hard match', but Hickey was honest enough to admit that the victory would have been easier if he had not still had a huge hangover:

'I was so ill all the time that I let several balls pass me . . . by which our adversaries gained a number of notches.'[45]

The Westminster–Etonians match is one among many in which members of the governing class played within their own social circle. But as we have seen, the game did bring together people of quite different social classes. The Richmonds and the Sackvilles played and promoted cricket because it reflected many of the values central to the aristocracy's conception of itself. Nobility meant the willingness to engage in friendly, 'manly' sports with friends and neighbours; to provide leadership and a model of uncomplaining integrity that lesser men might follow; to offer generous hospitality to players and spectators alike. It was through the involvement of great aristocrats that the game was transformed from a peasant sport into an organized, professionalized one. It is easy to see how it happened: a nobleman whose team was beaten in a game for high stakes might strengthen it in the rematch which honour required him to demand, by including the gardener or the groom alongside his friends and relatives. It is only one step from this to the actual employment of people in the households of the nobility because they were cricketers, whatever their skills at gardening or the care of horses. There were other kinds of professionals – players who were in effect independent contractors and were paid a match fee by the promoter, yet spent most of their time at their own crafts or trades. But the players retained by the great men were the nearest thing to full-time professionals.

The first retained professional that we know anything much about is Thomas Waymark, groom to (can we be surprised?) the second Duke of Richmond. The Duke paid several other cricketers to play for his teams – among them a Reigate barber named Stephen Dingate, and a certain Joseph Budd – but Waymark was the only one to be employed at Goodwood. He played for Richmond as early as 1727, in the match against Alan Brodrick's team, but the Goodwood accounts only record his employment between 1729 and 1732. At Christmas 1729 he was given 10s.6d. 'to buy shoes and stockings', and was paid seven shillings a week, plus board, from then until the following midsummer. After that date he seems to have been employed less regularly – he worked, for example, for only nine days between Christmas 1730 and Lady Day 1731. But he remained on the staff at Goodwood for at least another year. That his job as groom was more than a nominal one is indicated in the accounts by a payment of over £2 for looking after two of the Duke's horses.[46]

We have already noted the admiring references to Waymark's performances in 1729 and 1730, and that he was so important to the Duke's side that they were allowed to postpone a match when he was ill. We then lose sight of him until the 1740s; by then he is described as being from Bray Mills, near Maidenhead, working for a certain Mr Darvile. But he was still regarded as one of Richmond's servants, and played for his team in the two matches in June 1744 about which the Duke was sufficiently excited to keep the scorecards. From this, and the poem by James Dance, we know that Waymark batted respectably in the first game (13 and 16 – scores were low in those days) but missed a crucial catch in the second one. Between 1746 and 1749 he played in numerous single-wicket matches at the Artillery Ground, in one of them partnered by his 'young master', presumably Darvile's son. The Goodwood connection still existed, though, as in 1749 he went back to umpire a boys' match in which Richmond's two sons were playing; a newspaper report describes him as 'one whom the Duke formerly kept on purpose to play at cricket'.[47]

There were other retained players in this period, but we know little about them, apart from Valentine Romney, the head gardener at Knole. He must have been a good cricketer, often picked for important matches at the Artillery Ground; as we have seen, he skippered Kent against 'England' in 1744, and was one of those 'appointed by the noblemen' to play in a single-wicket match in June 1745. By 1768 his playing days were long since over, but the Sackvilles still rewarded the old family retainer with a Christmas gratuity of two guineas.[48]

Besides the retained players there were also more independent paid players: part-time-professionals or 'free agents', to borrow a modern baseball term. Many of the men who performed intermittently at the Artillery Ground, such as those from Slindon and Dartford, undoubtedly come into this category, though it is not clear exactly how much they were paid. From a few matches in the 1740s we can infer that at that time it was probably between a guinea and two guineas a man. For a match in Buckinghamshire in 1741, Earl Temple's share of the players' pay came to £21, this being half the total for the match, paid, Temple says, 'out of my winnings in play purse'. He was, in other words, paying ten men two guineas each, he himself or some other gentleman being the eleventh (unpaid) member of the side.[49] In 1745 the Duke of Rich-

mond, Lord John Sackville and other notables shared the expenses of
three Sussex matches against Surrey at the Artillery Ground, Moulsey
Hurst and Bury Hill, respectively. For the first two, twelve 'gamesters'
were paid three guineas each, in other words £1.11s.6d. per match; for
the decider on Bury Hill on 9 September, ten gamesters received one
guinea each. But it looks as if Richmond had to strengthen the Sussex
team at the last minute, for Adam Newland, one of several of that family
who worked at Goodwood, was sent scurrying off to fetch 'Martin of
Henfield' – and Martin was paid two guineas for playing, twice the sum
received by the other professionals.[50]

'Martin of Henfield': here we have yet another link between the village
game and the cricket patronized by the aristocracy. Henfield was one of
the teams against whom young Will Marchant of Hurstpierpoint had
played two decades earlier, and Martin was now their star player. This
is clearly how the early professionals were recruited: a young player
makes a name for himself in village cricket, and is snapped up by a
nobleman anxious for his team to win. There must have been many
others like Martin, and they suggest, as Slindon does, that the teams
wearing the colours of great noblemen such as Richmond depended for
their existence on the vitality of the game in the villages. When John
Fuller of Uckfield wrote to Richmond in 1746 to propose a Sussex
'Cricket Plate', he obviously assumed that enough of the country gentry
would be able to raise teams from their neighbourhoods to make the
competition worthwhile. The scheme, Fuller suggested, would 'pay each
man that played a guinea, and eleven black velvet caps for the con-
querors'.[51]

For the ordinary player not fortunate enough to have been enlisted
into the household of a Richmond or a Sackville, the rewards of professionalism were still fairly modest. A guinea or two was a useful
supplement to the earnings of a craftsman, and even more of an agricultural labourer, but it still left the lower-class cricketer with the need to
earn his living at his trade. On the other hand, the lure of the gambling
which attracted many of the aristocracy to the game was becoming ever
more insistent. On both the horses and the card tables the stakes were
steadily increasing. Richmond won 174 guineas from his brother-in-law
in 1723–4, and another £390 from Lord Albemarle; but a few years
later, after hoping to pay off some of his debts with the £200 or so he
had won at Tunbridge Wells, he then had a run of bad luck on the
horses. Newspapers always claim that a cricket match is being played

for 'a considerable sum'. After the Gentlemen of London had won a narrow victory at Sevenoaks Vine in 1743, it was announced that 'several very considerable bets' had been laid on the match by the noblemen and gentlemen involved. When Stanstead beat Hertford a few years earlier, the match was played for a stake of 200 guineas, and 'upwards of £1,000' was said to have changed hands in the betting. Yet the suspicion remains that these stakes were greatly exaggerated by the newspapers, and that they concerned only the nobility. If we look at the accounts of the gentry we see no sign of such profligate sums. John Bridger of Lewes kept a careful record of his winnings and losses at cricket and other amusements, but the entries are mostly of small sums, a shilling here and there, though on a couple of occasions (in 1759 and 1763) he records winning as much as 7s.6d. Such sums may well have been his share of the stakes of matches in which he played.[52]

What in the end are we to make of the nobility's involvement in eighteenth-century cricket? We can take it as a given that for many of them cricket was interesting primarily because it gave them something else to bet on. This explains their willingness to promote matches and pay the players out of their own pockets. But it is clear that many of them also enjoyed the game for its own sake, and that they played in those matches at Newmarket and Moulsey Hurst for the fun of it. That they might win or lose twenty guineas added additional spice to the contest, but there were plenty of other ways to gamble – at cards, on the horses, and so on – without going to the trouble of exerting themselves in front of a large, possibly derisive, crowd. Playing in matches restricted to members of their own class protected them from the danger of losing their dignity at the hands of better, but less exalted, players. But for noblemen such as the Sackvilles who could only be satisfied by playing with and against the best, there was no substitute for the cricket which brought players of all social levels together.

Cricket, as we have repeatedly seen, was a peasant sport which was taken up by the aristocracy and gentry, and in the process transformed and professionalized. But there was a third social force which was increasingly affecting it in the 1730s and 40s: the force of commerce. It was in London, with its huge concentration of wealth and population, that the eighteenth-century 'commercialization of leisure' occurred most dramatically. The process inevitably touched cricket, as it touched most other leisure-time pursuits. The great days of Lord's and the Oval lay far in the future. But we have already heard a lot about a ground in the metropolis where cricket was played to entertain a mass audience: the Artillery Ground. That too now needs to be put into its historical setting.

4

Cricket in Metropolitan Culture

In comparison with the rural areas we have been exploring, London seems like another country. There were plenty of conflicts and tensions lurking behind eighteenth-century England's placid green fields, conflicts which sometimes erupted into violence. But in spite of the stresses, rural society was relatively stable, and could slowly adapt to the inexorable growth of a market society, even as it undermined the traditional certainties of Old England. But in London the transformation of the old order had already happened. At its clattering Thameside wharves more than half the country's exports and imports were loaded and unloaded. In its teeming streets and shops and markets goods of every possible description were sold and exchanged. In the quieter streets of the City, monied men underwrote the financial transactions that made all this trade profitable or unprofitable. London was the centre of government, the arbiter of fashion, the heart of the nation's cultural life, the hub of its economy, the axis – or so its inhabitants believed – around which the rest of England revolved. It contained enormous wealth and lavish scenes of conspicuous consumption. It also contained a greater concentration of crime and desperation and poverty than any other city in Europe.

London was huge, overwhelming, intimidating. Its population of roughly half a million people in 1700 had, by mid-century, grown to 750,000 or so, in spite of a death-rate well in excess of the rest of the country. London was a magnet for great numbers of people naïvely hoping to better themselves; all too often it killed them. Yet thousands of these optimistic immigrants survived and created a city whose prosperity and vitality astonished all who came there. Out of this vast population perhaps four or five per cent were at the very top of the heap (in the families of the aristocracy, gentry and merchant princes); roughly a quarter were what we should call 'middle class' (smaller businessmen, traders, professional people); the remaining seventy per cent were the working population (artisans, wage-earners, labourers) and the poor, whose numbers fluctuated widely according to the state of the economy.[1]

Not everyone in London was prosperous; still, there was plenty of money around. Everything was for sale: necessities, luxuries, frivolities; political influence, sex, entertainment. There was beginning to be more leisure time, certainly for the middle and upper ranks of society, and even for many of those lower down. The commercialization of leisure which we have observed in the countryside was naturally even more pronounced in the capital. By the end of the seventeenth century the most important cultural centres were no longer the royal Court and the houses of the nobility, but were more likely to be found in the urban coffee-houses, clubs and assembly rooms of London and a few other great cities. 'Ceasing to be the handmaiden of royal politics', John Brewer has observed, culture was now 'the partner of commerce'; the arts had become 'commercial enterprises'.[2] The entrepreneurs who catered to this market for leisure naturally pitched their appeal in different ways according to the social group they were aiming at. For the quality, leisure had to be combined with respectability and good taste: there were polite theatres, concert halls, art galleries. The upper ranks of the middling sort shared much of this polite culture, emulating the tastes of their superiors and providing the mass market which enabled Handel, for example, to make a living from his composing rather than by depending on royal or aristocratic patronage. The lesser folk were still somewhat more attached to traditional forms of entertainment, though these too were being affected by the pull of the market.

Both the separation between polite and popular tastes and the social mixing which some forms of leisure encouraged could be seen in the pleasure gardens which were such prominent features of metropolitan life. They provided opportunities for strolling through artificially constructed 'natural' (and after dark fetchingly illuminated) surroundings, with places for eating, drinking, listening to music or watching firework displays, as well as for sexual intrigue and dalliance. Vauxhall, the oldest, had been founded after the Restoration, when the rule of the Puritan saints came to an end and London citizens began to demand more secular forms of relaxation than they had previously been permitted. By 1700 it had acquired a bad reputation as a place of assignation for people of loose morals, but it was cleaned up in George II's reign. The Prince of Wales (who owned the ground rent) liked it sufficiently to make it fashionable again, and a 1753 guide book proclaimed that even bishops could be seen there without 'injuring their character'. It had magnificent gardens which were beautifully illuminated on summer nights, and attracted middle-class Londoners as well as members of the elite. The music was excellent, too: in 1745 the celebrated Thomas Arne was one of its composers. Vauxhall's pavilions were decorated with paintings of English popular amusements by Francis Hayman, one of them of a cricket match.[3]

Ranelagh Gardens in Chelsea, with its famous Rotunda, came later. It was founded in 1742, at a cost of some £16,000 – or so Horace Walpole was told. To recoup this huge investment it naturally had to be more expensive than Vauxhall, charging 2s.6d. for admission as against Vauxhall's one shilling. This probably shut out the lower end of the Vauxhall patrons, and Ranelagh certainly appealed to people who were self-consciously genteel. But the attractions Ranelagh offered were not significantly different from those at Vauxhall. The music was good (the eight-year-old Mozart performed some of his own compositions on the harpsichord there in 1764) and the masquerades often brilliant. One interesting feature of Ranelagh was that like some of the theatres it was a corporate venture of a more modern type than the other pleasure gardens, most of which were owned or leased by individuals: Ranelagh was owned by shareholders who subscribed £1,000 each.[4]

Another reasonably respectable place of entertainment was Marylebone Gardens, well known for its bowling green. At one time it had offered free admission, but in 1737 it began to charge a shilling, inclusive of refreshments, and thus to move up market. It always had a good band and good soloists. In 1769 the composer Samuel Arnold took over the lease, perhaps so that he could have somewhere to have his music performed. A few years later he needed a new conductor, so he lured Arne away from Vauxhall. Besides the music, the pleasure gardens also offered dramatic recitals and conjuring displays, as well as splendid fireworks. Marylebone had large, beautifully laid-out gardens and was famous for its confectionery (in 1760 it was offering almond cheese cakes, and 'rich seed and plum cakes'), but in spite of all these attractions it lost popularity and had to close in 1778.[5]

Among the places whose appeal was to people lower down the social scale was Cuper's Gardens, on the south bank of the Thames opposite Somerset House. Cuper's, like Vauxhall, charged a shilling for admission, and in the 1740s its owner, the 'widow Evans', briefly succeeded in making it fashionable. The Prince of Wales might be seen there as well as at Vauxhall, and other members of the aristocracy were also frequent visitors. But Mrs Evans wanted to increase the number of paying customers, and tried to get them by improving the fireworks. Her spectacular new display, she announced in 1744, would include 'a fiery dragon, which flies from the bottom of the gardens to the top of the orchestra'. A few years later, alas, there was an explosion when the fireworks were being prepared, and several of her workmen were badly injured. Cuper's also offered ambitious musical performances which included Mr Handel's 'grand choruses out of several of his oratorios' and a concerto on the 'chromatic horn' (presumably an early version of the valve horn) by a certain Count Messing and his son, 'they being the only persons that perform on that instrument'.[6]

Londoners also flocked to many similar smaller places of entertainment. Some of them, such as the Adam and Eve in Tottenham Court Road and White Conduit House in Islington, started as pubs which in the course of the century added tea gardens and other attractions; as we shall see, White Conduit also had a cricket field. Others began as spas. Both Sadler's Wells and the New Wells in Goodman's Fields, Clerkenwell, went in for pantomimes and acrobatic displays. One summer night in 1744 over 600 people crowded in at the New Wells to watch 'Mr Dominique's flying over twenty-four men's heads with drawn swords, a thing never done in England before'. The night after this risky venture a performance by a woman who danced on stilts on a tightrope was promised, and another by a man who was also going to dance on the tightrope, in this case pushing a wheelbarrow from which fireworks would be launched. A couple of years earlier Monsieur Brila, a famous 'equilibrist', performed on the tightrope along with his three-year-old son. The New Wells also saw commercial possibilities in more traditional entertainments, promoting the 'famous Bath morris-dancers' after they had come to the capital to perform at Bartholemew Fair.[7]

Pickpockets, prostitutes and other undesirable people naturally mingled with the crowds at these places. This is the world that Ned Ward's *London Spy* describes earlier in the century: the world of cheats and sharpers, of knaves and projectors, of pimps and cuckold-makers. For years the Middlesex Grand Jury had been regularly denouncing the theatres as lewd and disorderly. In 1744 their presentment was against 'places kept apart for the encouragement of luxury, extravagance, and idleness' – places such as Sadler's Wells and the New Wells, which were especially to blame for attracting throngs of loose and idle persons. Subsequent newpaper reports show that the popularity of such dens of iniquity was not much affected by the disapproval of moral reformers. There was probably little that the magistrates could do about them until in 1752 Parliament at last took action and required that any establishment offering either music or dancing had to be licensed. This did in some of the more notorious places, and even Cuper's Gardens, which declined into a mere tea-garden. The New Wells had also closed by 1752, becoming a Methodist place of worship, thus purging itself of past sins.[8]

The smaller gardens and the variety theatres of the Sadler's Wells type attracted less genteel audiences than did polite places such as Ranelagh and even Vauxhall. The social complexion of the audience was obviously partly determined by the price of admission. Sixteen hundred people piled into the Mulberry Gardens in Clerkenwell for the fireworks one August night in 1744: admission was free, the proprietor relying on the sale of food and drink for his profits. Perhaps to keep the numbers down an admission charge of 2d. was soon afterwards instituted, but the place openly advertised itself as being suitable for 'the honest sons of trade and industry'. Sadler's Wells was a bit more expensive, but not much: in 1746 you could get in to watch the tumblers and rope-dancers from either the pit or the gallery on buying a pint of wine. Earlier in the century its typical patrons were described as 'strolling damsels, half-pay officers, peripatetic tradesmen, tars, butchers' and suchlike people.[9]

The pleasure gardens were only the tip of the iceberg in a dizzying sea of entertainment. There were dozens of more ephemeral attractions. You could admire Mr Perrott's 'Luminous Fountains' or illuminated grotto at Chelsea, to which, it was said in 1742, 'an incredible number of all ranks of people daily resort'. You could gape at 'the wonderful buffalo from Asia' at the Rummer Tavern at Charing Cross, or the ostriches at the Crown in Kensington. You could marvel at the 'Swedish Giant' on show outside the Mansion House, who was a big attraction in the summer of 1742. There were jugglers and fire-eaters, and the inevitable talking dog, advertised as being fluent in French and German as well as English.[10]

Some diversions were less innocent. The St James's Fair, or May Fair, famous for drinking and sexual licence, had been suppressed in 1708 after the usual complaints by the Middlesex Grand Jury. But the almost equally raucous Bartholemew Fair survived all through the century. Brutal sports abounded, and attracted elite as well as plebeian audiences. Cock-fights were frequently advertised, and were watched by spectators from all social classes. A main in 1742 charged half a crown, which would have kept out all but the moderately affluent, and its advertisement was addressed to 'all high bloods'. Just to make sure, it ended with the injunction, 'dear ragamuffins, you are desired not to attend, it being for the diversion of gentlemen only'. Bears were still baited, as were (less frequently) more exotic animals. When a leopard was baited to death at the Bear Garden off Soho Square in 1716 the cheapest seats were priced at 2s.6d., far above the reach of servants or artisans: some of the better ones went for 5s., others for half a guinea. On another occasion a pathetic tiger was the victim. Bull-baiting was also still alive and well in London as late as 1776. In October of that year at a baiting in Tottenham Court Road the bull managed to pull up the stake to which it was tethered and charged the spectators, several of whom were injured.[11]

Londoners also paid to watch human beings injure each other. There was sword-fighting, with plenty of blood flowing, at the Amphitheatre near Cavendish Square run by the hard-bitten James Figg, who was himself a regular performer. Figg's also offered cudgel-play (with lessons for any gentlemen rash enough to try it), wrestling, and prize-fighting. In the early years of the century the fighters used to parade through the streets behind a drum, 'exquisitely plaited, and adorned with ribbons', challenging all comers. Later the big sword-fighting and boxing matches moved to a more lavishly furnished booth in Tottenham Court Road owned by Cumberland's client, Jack Broughton. Like Figg's, this booth also offered fencing matches and sometimes cudgel-play, 'to divert the gentlemen till the house fills'. A fight there in 1739 drew 'a prodigious crowded house of nobility and gentry, at five shillings a ticket'; one of them wagered 300 guineas against 200 on the result. When Broughton fought the Bristol butcher, Jem Slack, in 1750 the betting among the quality was for even higher stakes: this is the fight on which Cumberland is said to have lost £10,000 when Slack was victorious. Two hundred reserved tickets at £1.10s.6d. each had been sold and £130 taken at the door, all of which Slack won, plus another £100 from a wager with a gentleman at the same odds: once again the interaction of different classes at sporting events is strikingly apparent. Prize-fighting also took place at the Tennis Court in James Street; in 1760 Slack was beaten there by 'Stephens the nailer' in front of 'many noblemen and persons of distinction'. Again Cumberland lost heavily.[12]

But the most popular exhibitions of violence were free and open to all: the executions of criminals. Most of the London ones took place at Tyburn, near Hyde Park Corner, but there were others within easy reach of the capital: for example at Kennington Common, which we have already encountered as a cricket ground. The association of public spaces with both executions and sporting events was entirely natural: not many other such arenas were available. Some of the slang phrases describing hangings show how the terror that they inspired could be deflected by their being treated as sporting events or public holidays: an execution took place at a 'hanging match', a 'hanging fair', or 'Paddington Fair'. Huge and often disorderly crowds watched the processions that brought the condemned from Newgate and the operation of the 'fatal tree' itself. Even for routine hangings the crowds were probably far greater than for any sporting event: an estimated 30,000 spectators thronged Tyburn one day in 1776, and in really sensational cases, such as that of Lord Ferrers in 1760, many times that number found vantage points to watch either the procession or the execution. There was much drinking, the boisterous exchange of macabre humour, the spectators' yells that marked the final drop – and afterwards the critical response to the conduct of the ceremony, the judgements whether the victim had made a good end.[13]

The crowd's involvement in these gruesome rituals reveals many ambiguities, differing according to the public attitude to the condemned. Often there was sympathy, but if the hanging followed an especially odious crime, the crowds would be determined to see justice done. In Somerset in 1740, the High Sheriff tried to spare a well-connected woman and her daughter from the indignity of being hanged before a large crowd by holding the execution at an unusually early hour of the morning. But the women had been condemned for a particularly brutal crime (they had beaten a servant to death), and the local people were 'very much irritated' by the timing; some of the early arrivals cut down the gallows to delay matters, but even so the ceremony was completed by six o'clock, 'to the great disappointment of several thousands of people, that came from far and near to see a public example of two wretches that so much deserved it', a newspaper reported. Whether in London or in the provinces, executions were high on the list of spectator sports.[14]

*

So Londoners were not squeamish about their amusements. And competition drove entrepreneurs to offer ever more sensational contests. Violence involving men was profitable: why not violence involving women?
Some sword-fights were advertised as being between couples, a man and
a woman on each side; there was one at Islington in 1727 between two
Londoners, James and Elizabeth Stokes, and a couple from Ireland,
Robert Barker and Mary Welsh. Prize-fighting between women was less
common than between men, but took place occasionally right down
to the early years of the nineteenth century. Advertisements for such
exhibitions were pitched to largely male audiences in unashamedly
voyeuristic terms, stressing both the scanty clothing of the contestants
and the apparently titillating promise of feminine violence. At one such
event in 1722 the women wore 'close jackets, short petticoats, white
stockings, and pumps', and were said to have 'maintained the battle
with great valour ... to the no small satisfaction of the spectators'.
Fights were held in other places besides the boxing amphitheatres. In
1765 two women fought in Islington Fields for the prize of a new shift
worth half a guinea, exchanging blows 'with prodigious masculine
vigour and ability for above twenty minutes'. Nell Draper, the 'victorious
Amazon', got the shift, but only, a newspaper reported, 'at the price of
her left eye'.[15]

London also offered plenty of sporting spectacles for the more fastidi-
ous, though those too could often be pretty violent. Some of them
had a regional flavour, appealing to nostalgic exiles trying to recover
treasured memories of the pleasures of their youth. At Streatham Wells
in Surrey in August 1743 there was a match at 'Long Bullets', a north-
country sport in which leaden balls were thrown at ninepins. The contestants were teams from Yorkshire (to whom familiarity no doubt gave
an advantage) and Surrey; a 'sharp match of cricket' was also part of
the day's attractions. In 1764 two Irish teams played 'a great hurling
match' in a field behind Bedford House. It ended in a riot, but the
participants tried again and eventually finished the game; the winners,
Leinster, marched away in triumph behind drummers and a band. A
more regular spectator sport, at least for a time, was Prison Bars, which
we have already heard about in Cheshire and Staffordshire. The game
enjoyed a brief period of popularity in London in the 1740s, with
matches between teams from Cheshire in Tothill Fields and at the Mitre
in Highgate, and there was even a pub called The Ten Prison-Bars-
Players. The contestants obviously took the game very seriously. When

two 'Cheshire champions' played ten of the rest of England in 1744, the Cheshire men walked off after an argument, and would only agree to a rematch if their opponents promised to accept the umpires' decisions, 'honourably play the right and accustomed way of playing, and not to make trifling disputes on purpose to gain time'.[16]

The list of the sports to be found in eighteenth-century London is almost endless. In the bitter January of 1740, besides the conventional winter sports, the frozen Thames also supported the inevitable refreshment booths, and a sheep-roasting, while both football and ninepins were played on the ice near Brentford. The Thames had long been the site of races between the watermen, but in the 1750s the sport became fashionable higher up the social scale, and crews of young men competed for wagers of 100 guineas or so. William Hickey boasted of being 'an uncommonly expert and skillful rower'. In 1768 he and seven other young men bought a 'rowing cutter', and with a liveried waterman as coxwain rowed from Lambeth to Gravesend, from there to Richmond, and back to Lambeth – 130 miles, he claimed – in thirteen hours. Later that summer they invited themselves to a fashionable regatta at Hampton Court organized by the Earl of Lincoln, and, Hickey assures us, their boat was acclaimed as the most elegant one in the procession.[17]

Cricket was more widely played in London than any of these other sports, but it exhibited some of the same features: their coarseness, their commercialism, the varied social character of their patrons. Virtually nothing is known of cricket in the capital during the seventeenth century, except as a game for schoolboys, but by the early years of the eighteenth it was certainly growing in popularity. The first newspaper reference occurs in *The Post Boy* in March 1700, when a series of matches on Clapham Common was announced, the first of them on Easter Monday. Some affluent people must have been involved, as the matches were to be played for '£10 a head each game (five being designed) and £20 the odd one': the language is very similar to that in which cock-fighting mains were advertised.[18]

The site of this series – Clapham Common – suggests that apart from the stakes financial considerations must have been secondary, for admission charges could not have been levied in such a public space, and there is no sign of the involvement of publicans looking for profit. Several other London commons were soon to be used for cricket, among them Chelsea, Walworth and the famous Kennington Common, the last-named being the one on which big matches were most likely to be played, and where the most elaborate provisions for the sale of refreshments probably existed. But the publicans were soon moving into the cricket scene in other parts of London, as they were in the country. Regular matches were played on Tuesdays, Thursdays and Saturdays in a field next to the Duke of Ormond's Head, a pub near Lamb's Conduit Fields, and the owner of White Conduit House in Islington was also soon trying to cash in.[19]

In 1718 there was a match in White Conduit Fields for half a guinea a man between a London XI and a team ostensibly representing Kent, but actually drawn from the 'Punch Club Society' of Rochester. After play had been going on for four hours in front of a large crowd the Londoners were clearly winning. At this point several of the Punch Club players walked off, 'hoping thereby', the Londoners sneered, 'to save their money'. The Punch Club indignantly replied that it was just the weather; they had left because of 'the violence of the rains, which fell so heavy it was impossible to continue the game'. The Londoners sued to recover their stakes, and the case was heard before Lord Chief Justice Pratt. His lordship confessed that he did not understand the game, but ordered it to be played out, which was done in July of the following year, London winning by some twenty runs. This was not the only match to be decided by a lawsuit. In 1724 a Kent team sponsored by Edwin Stead met Chingford at Dartford. When Kent were in sight of victory the Essex players refused to continue, and again the issue came before an exasperated Chief Justice, who as in the case of the London–Rochester match ordered it to be played out – two years after it had begun.[20]

It is also apparent that cricket was never insulated from the violence and vulgarity which was always so much a part of the London leisure scene. In 1764 the magistrates complained about the 'swarms of loose, idle and disorderly people' who gathered to play cricket in the fields surrounding the capital. Many of the participants, the JPs noted, were 'gamblers and thieves' and the games often ended in brawls. Pickpockets did well at more organized matches, as they always did in large crowds: in 1763 a visiting countryman had been relieved of over £20 while he was 'looking on the cricket players'. But the forces of law and order were never popular with freeborn Englishmen, and there are several reports of crowds protecting people from arrest. When Surrey were playing Kent on Kennington Common in 1736 three soldiers arrived and tried to apprehend a deserter, but, a newspaper reported, the crowd rescued him and inflicted 'a severe discipline' on the soldiers. Not all deserters were so lucky. In 1755 a press-gang went into Tothill Fields in Westminster, 'where several men were playing at cricket', and arrested nineteen, some of whom were found to be soldiers or sailors who had gone AWOL.[21]

Disputes involving both players and spectators were common. At a match on Kennington Common in 1737 stones were thrown and a man killed when people entering the ground became angry at others who were jumping the queue. When the London Club played Brompton on Chelsea Common in July 1731 two players came to blows after one of them tore the other's ruffles off his shirt, 'swearing he had no property to them'. Team-mates from both sides joined in, and the Brompton men eventually had to retreat, some of them, it was reported, 'with black eyes and broken heads'. This began as a fight over a status symbol, but often enough the trouble resulted directly from incidents in the match itself. In 1738 Kent played London at the Artillery Ground in front of a huge crowd – 10,000 according to one estimate – and the match ended in confusion after an argument over 'whether one of the Londoners was fairly out'. At Carshalton in 1762 a disputed catch brought an abrupt end to a Surrey–Kent match. The conflict moved from words to blows, several heads were broken, and there was a challenge between 'two persons of distinction'. All bets on the match were duly called off – an indication of how completely things had got out of hand. But it was even worse when Essex played a Kent team at Tilbury in 1776. Guns were seized from the Fort after a dispute on the field; an Essex player was killed, as was a soldier who tried to stop the carnage.[22]

Violence inspired by disappointed gamblers was a regular feature of cricket in the London area. It will be recalled that the Duke of Richmond's team were manhandled after a game in 1731, and we may suspect that this was also the cause of the trouble when Brentwood played Hertford at Ware a few years later. The match was for stakes of £200, but it was said that the total amount wagered came to over £2,000. Brentwood were winning easily when they were attacked by 'a mob of bargemen', and after order was restored they only just scraped home by six runs. Disorders often erupted at the Artillery Ground. In 1732 Middlesex claimed that time was up when London needed only a few runs to win, even though by the scorer's watch six minutes remained. Over £100 was at stake in the match, so the subsequent threat of another lawsuit is not surprising. There was serious trouble at a big match on the same ground in 1744, and in 1765 when Surrey were playing Dartford, allegedly with nearly 12,000 spectators present, play had to be suspended because of violence by the mob, 'many of whom had laid large bets'. A number of spectators were seriously injured, and the final stages of the match had to be put off until the following day.[23]

As in limited-overs matches today, additional diversions were sometimes provided for those who craved a little more spice than they expected to find in the cricket. At Tothill Fields in 1762 two butchers played each other, the wickets having been pitched on either side of a pond into which the naked contestants regularly and hilariously fell. Some years earlier, in 1744, the organizers of a match on Walworth Common between a Southwark XI and another from the Kent Road advertised a smock race to bring in the crowds. Two 'jolly wenches' (one a 'handsome broom girl' known as 'the Little Bit of Blue', and the other 'Black Bess of the Mint') were to race for a Holland smock worth a guinea. 'They are to run in drawers only', the promoters announced, 'and there is excellent sport expected'. Not surprisingly, they expected an unusually raucous crowd and promised to employ their own security forces: 'Captain Vinegar, with a great many of his bruisers and bulldogs' would control the ring, 'that no civil spectators may be incommoded by the rabble'.[24]

Another innovation was the introduction of women's cricket. As with the men, we first hear about women's matches in rural settings, but by 1747 there was sufficient interest in them for a match to be put on in London, at the Artillery Ground. This was between women's teams from four Sussex villages – Charlton and Singleton on one side, and West Dean and Chilgrove on the other, and was followed by another the next day between the women of the Sussex downs, wearing orange ribbons, and those of the dales, wearing blue. It is hard to know how seriously these and other rural matches were taken by the spectators, but from the language of newspaper reports it looks as if they were seen as less comical than the smock races and other such exhibitions that were so popular in both London and the countryside. In 1745, on Gosden Common, near Guildford, the women of Bramley were narrowly beaten by a team from Hambledon (a Surrey village near Godalming, not the famous Hampshire one). A large crowd was impressed by the quality of the play: the women were said to have 'bowled, batted, ran and catched as well as most men can do'. Upham, in Hampshire, was another place where women played. In 1765 the married women of the village played the spinsters, with prizes of a large plum cake, a barrel of ale and a 'regale' of tea, and this was repeated three years later. Matches between married and single continued in many villages until well into the nineteenth century. There was one at Moulsey Hurst in 1775, another at Bray Hill in Sussex in 1793: the women of that neighbourhood, which is not far from Goodwood, were said to be especially good at the game. Eighteenth-century Englishwomen clearly had more opportunities for physical exercise than their Victorian successors.[25]

By the 1730s an astonishing amount of cricket, reputable or disreputable, was being played in the London area. The victuallers played the coachmen at Highgate in 1740, and two teams of watermen met at the Green Man and Horns on Kennington Common in 1752. There were matches between brewery teams, no doubt well lubricated, on Walworth Common in 1749 and 1754. On the famous Moulsey Hurst ground in 1755 teams of constables from two different parts of Surrey fought it out. Some of the matches between parishes in London and the suburbs must have involved pretty affluent people. When the Gentlemen of St James's met those of St Margaret's, Westminster, in Tothill Fields in 1729 it was for fifty guineas a side, and the match on the same ground in 1756 between the Westminster Gentlemen and those of St George's, Hanover Square, was another one almost certainly confined to members of the elite. Yet in many other games the stakes were not very high, indicating that the players came from further down the social scale. Harrow played a combined team from Brentford and Acton on Willesden Green in 1735 for a guinea a man, and we find the same stakes in matches involving Mitcham and the Shacklewell Club in Stoke Newington a few years later. When the 'Gentlemen of London' played those of Southwark and Lambeth on Kennington Common in 1743 the stakes were only half that sum.[26]

These were all obscure local matches, but there were plenty of others which involved well-known players. Major matches were played on Kennington Common, Dubber's Hill near Croydon, Bromley Common, Laleham Burway at Chertsey, and Moulsey Hurst near Hampton Court. One September day in 1759 David Garrick and his friend John Baker – the Sussex lawyer – crossed the Thames in Garrick's boat to watch a single-wicket match at Moulsey Hurst.[27] But by far the most celebrated London ground of its day was the one lying between Chiswell Street in Finsbury and the nonconformist burial ground in Bunhill Fields: the

Artillery Ground. We have already encountered it as the site of many important matches, but it is now time to look at it more closely.

The Honourable Artillery Company, the fashionable militia unit for the sons of wealthy London citizens, had owned the field in Finsbury since before the civil wars. They held their drills and parades there, which must have been desultory affairs, for the Company was more famous for its food than its exertions. Ned Ward describes people strolling 'as lazily as an Artillery captain before his company', and a 1744 poem by James Love, alias Dance, comments on the members' lavish feasting. The 'city-warriors', he sneered, were 'wisely determined not to fight, but eat': they promptly threatened to sue. For many years the Company's field had been the site of archery and shooting contests, and the Finsbury Archers continued to use it long after archery had lost its military function and had been transformed into a sport. Early in the eighteenth century the Company ran into financial difficulties and, to raise money, started letting out the ground for a variety of purposes; in the 1720s they were collecting £30 per annum for the grazing rights. They also took part of it adjoining Chiswell Street for building, leaving an entrance to the ground (which is still there) between the houses. Cricket was already being played there in 1725, as in that year the Company's minutes deplored 'the abuse done to the herbage of the ground . . . by cricket players'.[28]

By the early 1730s the Artillery Ground had become the principal venue for 'public' (that is to say, commercial) cricket in London. Some 'private' matches were still played there: two spectators were injured at one in 1734, and there are occasional references to a 'Club of the Artillery Ground'. In 1732 the ground was being managed by Christopher Jones, landlord of a neighbouring pub, the Pied Horse, and the connection with this hostelry was to be an enduring one. Cricket was not the only diversion on offer. In 1759 the field was let to a Mr Ladd, so that he could try out his newly invented 'carriage without horses'; he was not, however, allowed to charge for admission. Among the sports held there were hurling matches between Irish teams, and regular foot-races. At one in 1750, a newspaper reported, 'there was the greatest concourse of people present ever known'. For a few years around mid-century, occasional horse-racing meetings were held there; in 1754 the Company complained about the unauthorized use of a track 'for horses and foot people to run races round the Ground'. And lest we should think the Artillery Ground was above such things, in 1765 there was a race from the Bunhill Row gate to the Bunhill Fields gate between a 'little gentleman' less than four feet tall, and three 'blooming young ladies'.[29]

But the Artillery Ground was best known for the top-class cricket it staged. Its most successful manager was George Smith, Jones's successor at the Pied Horse. Smith himself played occasionally. In 1748 he took part in a single-wicket match, partnering 'Little Bennett' against Thomas Waymark and Darvell; he was allowed a substitute fielder, which suggests that he was not particularly agile. But his chief importance is for his entrepreneurship, for he was prominent among the numerous London businessmen who offered organized entertainment to the public, for money. Smith was less famous than Jonathan Tyers, the proprietor of Vauxhall Gardens, but he was in the same line of business. He quickly saw the possibilities of profit from the sale of cricket prints, and in July 1748 was advertising an engraving of the Vauxhall Gardens painting of a cricket match by Francis Hayman. It would be a limited edition, with only 300 impressions, and a bargain at five shillings. From Smith's activities at the Artillery Ground we can learn a good deal about the promotion and financing of mid-eighteenth century cricket.[30]

Smith at first charged 2d. for admission, even to big matches. This surely tells us something about the character of a cricket crowd in this period, for it is the same amount that the Mulberry Gardens, appealing to 'the honest sons of trade and industry', charged in 1744. A few much more expensive reserved seats, in 'the rooms and gallery that front the ground', were sold, but even these probably cost no more than the cheapest seats at the opera (see Plate 2). The crowds thronging the Artillery Ground may have included a few fashionable people, but according to the author of 'The British Champion' they were primarily apprentices and servants. To encourage such people to neglect their own or their masters' business, this critic thought, was indefensible in 'a trading country'. Yet cricket's promoters were only too happy to do it.[31]

The ground was always crowded and uncomfortable. There was trouble because of overcrowding at the big match between 'England' and Kent on 18 June 1744 – the one that was important enough for the Duke of Richmond to keep the scoresheets. For years Smith had been complaining about people who avoided paying by climbing on the Bunhill Fields walls, warning offenders that they would be prosecuted and that the only legal entrance was through the yard of the Pied Horse. He also repeatedly appealed to spectators not to encroach on the playing area, and announced that it would be roped around to prevent them

from doing so. According to James Dance's poem, Smith himself dealt
with the pitch invasions, wielding 'with strenous arm the cracking whip'.
But the Company was enraged by the riot as well as by Dance's slurs:
Smith was severely reprimanded and made to cancel his next fixture
when a special parade was deliberately arranged for that day.[32]

Smith's remedy for the violence was worse than the disease. The
ground, he decided, would in future be surrounded by 'a complete ring
of benches' holding at least 800 spectators, there would be additional
stewards armed with whips, and to exclude the rowdy element the price
of admission would be increased to 6d. This higher price was charged
for the match between the London Club and the Duke of Bedford's
team, but it led to a disastrous fall in attendance: either at this or at
another July match, a newspaper reported, there were only 200 spectators, 'when before there used to be 7,000 to 8,000'. Within a few
weeks Smith restored the 2d. admission. Later events confirmed the
depth of consumer resistance to the higher price. In July 1747 Smith put
on the match between the two women's teams from Sussex. For this he
again put the price up to 6d., explaining that he needed to take at least
£80 at the gate to cover his costs. But in the following year he went back
to 2d., admitting that tripling the charge had been 'very prejudicial' to
him. It was too late, for before 1748 was out Smith declared bankruptcy,
and both the Pied Horse and the remaining nine years of his lease of the
Artillery Ground were put up for sale. However, Smith had influential
friends (he was by now himself a member of the Company), so somehow
he got out of it and retained control of the ground until the early part of
1752. The Company even let him borrow their cannon when he organized a celebration for the Prince of Wales's birthday. He eventually
moved to Marlborough to manage an inn, and died there in 1761.[33]

Smith's statement that he needed the 6d. admission charge because
his costs for the women's match came to £80 is worth examining. If
true, this means that it would take a crowd of 3,200 if he was just to
break even – though his profits would of course have been increased by
the sales of food and drink at the Pied Horse. He was almost certainly
exaggerating, but it is still clear that he would have needed to attract a
very large crowd if he was to make a profit at the lower, twopenny
admission charge. This makes some of the newspapers' estimates of
Artillery Ground attendances – 10,000 for the match between Kent and
'England' in 1738, for example – a bit more plausible, though doubtless
still on the high side. After Smith put in the benches as a result of the

1744 disorders the spectators standing behind them must have been uncomfortably crammed in. No wonder there was trouble.

Smith's management of the Artillery Ground is a striking sign of the commercialization of cricket that was well under way by the 1740s. Other signs of this are the advertisements in which he and other promoters tried to build up the importance of their matches by insisting how exciting they were going to be. There were complaints that the advertisements were published by 'Alehouse- or ground-keepers [Smith of course was both] for their own profit'. A good example is the *Daily Advertiser*'s announcement of Slindon's encounter with the London Club in 1742. This was billed as 'the greatest match at cricket that has been played for many years', and was expected to attract 'the greatest number of people that ever was known on the like occasion'. Slindon's recent successes were noted, as were the large bets that had been laid, including one that a Slindon player, probably Richard Newland, would himself score forty 'notches'. This kind of publicity is not surprising at the Artillery Ground, but even matches on public grounds where admission could not be charged were widely advertised, presumably for the benefit of the local victuallers. When Bromley and Chislehurst played a combined team from Dartford, Woolwich and other places on Bromley Common in 1743, it was announced that this was the deciding game of a series, each team having won one previously. The second game had been decided 'by one notch only', and both of them had been 'allowed to be as good ones as have been played anywhere this season'.[34]

What the takings were at the Pied Horse on match days we do not know, but they must have been considerable. The right to sell refreshments at matches played on common land was obviously much sought after, and as at country race meetings, it was often restricted to local victuallers. When Bromley played Addington in 1744 outsiders were warned that nobody would be permitted to sell liquor on the Common except those 'who belong to the parish'. The rule was relaxed in the following year, though, for a Kent–England match, when George Williams, landlord of the White Lion at Streatham, was allowed to set up his 'Red Cap Tent' at Bromley. Williams was another of the entrepreneurs cashing in on cricket's growing popularity. In 1745 he took his 'grand tent and flying squadron of Red Caps' to Moulsey Hurst for a game between Surrey and Sussex, and soon afterwards he was advertising his tent at Addington Hill when Addington were at home to Dartford, at Chislehurst Common when Kent played Surrey, and also at Ascot Races. With his tents and his uniformed waiters he sounds like a professional caterer in the modern style. But Williams was also a player, and indeed skippered the local Streatham team.[35]

So there was money to be made out of cricket. Much of it was made by gamblers, and the newspapers often focused almost entirely on this aspect of the game, treating the actual scores as of only secondary interest. A report on a London–Surrey match in June 1735 is a striking example. Before play began the odds were six to four on Surrey. When London batted and their opening pair put on 22, the odds swung dramatically the other way to six to four on London. But London collapsed and were all out for 67 (not as poor a score in this period as it sounds to us today). Surrey then went in and got a lead of about 30, the odds, at four to one, now heavily favouring the county. Batting again, London lost four wickets before they cleared off the arrears, and at this point the betting on a Surrey victory was 'more than a guinea to half a crown' – over eight to one. Ah, the glorious uncertainty of cricket: needing only 43 to win, Surrey lost four wickets for 10, which, we are told, 'reduced the bets equal, and so continued till the time agreed upon was expired, when two hands were to come in and 9 notches to tie'. Surrey, in other words, finished on 33 for seven. The terms under which eighteenth-century matches were played often specified that the match would be 'played out' by continuing it into a second day if necessary, but no such rule seems to have operated in this case. So it ended as an exciting draw, but one in which the attention of a good many punters must have been on the odds rather than the scores. James Dance's poem notes the 'buzzing murmurs' around the ring at such matches: 'I'll hold you ten to four, Kent – done sir – done.'[36]

The newspapers tell us a good deal about cricket's appeal to those who watched (and played) it. The great noblemen who sponsored the teams could no doubt afford their stake money, which as we have seen often amounted to as much as £1,000. But for lesser folk the loss of far smaller sums must have been serious. When the London Club played Chertsey at Moulsey Hurst in 1737 the Chertsey folk were confident of victory and bet heavily on their team. But, a newspaper reported, 'the countrymen went home with empty pockets'. Where there were losers there must also have been winners, though these were often the professional bookmakers. However, ordinary folk did occasionally beat the odds. Before a match between Twickenham and Kingston on Twickenham Common in 1768 the odds were six to four on the home side. But

Kingston won comfortably, one of their players (a corn chandler) taking home 'upwards of 30 guineas'.[37]

How can we account for the obvious popularity of cricket, a rural, peasant sport, in the totally different setting of the capital? We should first remember the huge migration into London that was occurring during the century before 1750. London was on the edge of the region – the southeastern counties – in which cricket had developed during the previous century, and many people must have brought childhood memories and experiences of it with them when they moved to the great, sprawling city. And this is precisely the time when leisure, like everything else, was becoming commercialized, and amusements of every possible kind were being sought after by people of all classes. It was also the time in which cricket was being professionalized even in the countryside. Great men such as the Duke of Richmond and the Sackvilles wanted to play and promote cricket in their rural strongholds. But, like the rest of the landed elite, they were increasingly being drawn to London – by political, legal, social and cultural forces – and it is not surprising that they wanted to enjoy there, and bet on, some of the same leisure-time pursuits familiar to them on their estates. You could not hunt in London, but you could play or watch cricket. There were plenty of other fields in or near the capital on which cricket could take place: Kennington and Bromley Commons, Moulsey Hurst and so on. But in the heart of the City George Smith served as the commercial catalyst who linked the patronage still provided by the aristocracy, the interests of the professional players who could sell their skills and make at least a part-time living out of the game, and the great mass of London residents – artisans, apprentices, tradesmen – who were willing to pay to watch it. Smith's role was almost exactly that of Thomas Lord fifty years later.

Like Lord, Smith must have worked closely with cricket's great aristocratic patrons. As we noted in the last chapter, newspapers of the day contain many references to the arrangement of matches by 'the noblemen and gentlemen'. One between the London Club and a team from the Weald of Kent in 1743 was made 'between several noblemen and gentlemen for very great sums of money', the nobs having been encouraged to promote it by an exciting finish in a previous match between the same two teams. In July of the following year the Prince of Wales and 'several persons of distinction' ordered that a rained-out match should be replayed on the following day, and a group of noblemen and gentlemen arranged for an unfinished match at Moulsey Hurst to be finished, also at the Artillery Ground. Great men of this kind wanted matches between teams that were evenly matched, to make the results unpredictable and their wagers correspondingly more interesting. Sometimes this could be achieved by inviting strong provincial sides such as Dartford or Slindon to take part; if not, teams were artificially chosen with this in mind. A match at the Artillery Ground on 19 September 1744 was 'between twenty-two of the best players, picked by the noblemen and gentlemen present at yesterday's great match'; about a fortnight later the same patrons chose what they thought would be two evenly matched teams for a three-a-side single-wicket game.[38]

No direct evidence has survived that would enable us to see exactly how George Smith's relations with the great men functioned. It was probably not a one-way affair that operated only from the top down. The noblemen are unlikely to have bothered themselves with the details of all the matches that were included in the Artillery Ground's increasingly hectic programme. It is more likely to have been a collaborative process, with the noblemen and gentlemen picking some of the players, and Smith filling up the teams so as to ensure an even contest – and also paying them. Sometimes the players themselves made the initial arrangements. In 1748 two of the leading ones – 'Long Robin' and Tom Faulkner – played each other at single-wicket, first on Long Robin's home ground at Bromley, then at Faulkner's on Addington Hill, each winning one. Smith got the decider for the Artillery Ground, though whether the initiative came from him or from the players is unknown. Of one thing we can be certain: that George Smith was the indispensable middleman in the organization of London cricket at mid-century.[39]

Who, then, were the people who played all this cricket in the capital? It seems clear that, as in the countryside, many ordinary people played cricket for relaxation: in the teams of victuallers, coachmen, brewery workers, watermen, for instance. The lawyer John Baker went to a three-a-side match at Moulsey Hurst in 1758 in which the players included a butcher, an ostler and a parson. Further up the scale were those who played in more widely publicized matches without being paid for it. The Earl of Middlesex and Lord John Sackville are striking examples, but we get occasional glimpses of less-exalted 'amateurs'. In 1731 the Gentlemen of London were captained in a match on Kennington Common by a certain Mr Littleboy, described as 'a bookbinder in

Creed Lane', which is yet another reminder that the term 'gentleman' could be an exceedingly loose and inclusive one. Two distillers named Wheatley and Wakeland played in big games at Moulsey Hurst and Kennington Common in the mid-1730s, presumably without being paid for it. In London no less than in the rural areas, amateur cricketers were drawn from a broad cross-section of English society.[40]

So too were those who regularly performed at the Artillery Ground for money. As we already know, they were of quite diverse origins and occupations: Thomas Waymark was a groom, John Bell of Dartford a shoemaker and his team-mate, John Frame, a drayman. The Slindon stars included the yeoman Richard Newland and his brothers, and the tailor Curry Aburrow. Valentine Romney was head gardener at Knole. All these were familiar faces during the 1740s on London and other grounds in the southeast. Others often seen there included a Maidstone clockmaker named Cutbush, who was in the Kent team for the big match against England in June 1744, and in the previous year had been one of a Kent trio in a single-wicket game against Richard Newland and two players from the London area. Another Dartford player, William Hodsoll, was a tanner by trade, but of many other Artillery Ground regulars we do not even know that much. All we know about Stephen Harding, for example, is that he came from Thursley in Surrey, and was a bowler, but also a big hitter. In a match at the Artillery Ground in 1751 he hit a ball 'out of the ground against a house in Bunhill Row' (this was before the laws were changed to allow six for such a hit, so he only got four for it). In 1765 he, or someone of the same name, made 24 in four strokes during a match on Richmond Green; presumably in this case a local rule allowed the six hit.[41]

Two of the Artillery Ground performers stand out because of their unusual backgrounds. Tom Faulkner, a prominent player in the ten years or so after 1748, was from Surrey, a member of the strong Addington team, but was also well known as a prize-fighter. Like many of that trade he had a colourful, perilous career. At the end of a particularly brutal fight near St Albans in 1758 both Faulkner and his opponent, George Taylor, had to be carried from the ring; Taylor died soon afterwards. Faulkner recovered, and a year later won an obviously fixed fight against a certain Joe James at Putney. There is no sign, however, that this kind of corrupt behaviour affected his cricket. Faulkner was one of the many professionals in these and other sports who ended his days as landlord of a pub, in his case at Clerkenwell.[42]

Among Faulkner's friends was Robert Colchin of Bromley, usually known as 'Long Robin' because of his height. He had some dubious pretensions to gentility, but he played as a professional and was said to have 'cultivated an intimacy' with prize-fighters, hackney coachmen, and other such disreputable characters. Presumably to disguise his relatively modest origins, Long Robin affected to be one of those eighteenth-century gentlemen who deliberately dropped out of his class, having 'studied and practised all the vulgar arts under the best masters'. He was a hard drinker, a smoker, and – a nice touch, this – liked to eat black puddings at Bartholemew Fair, 'for the humour of the thing'. His favourite diversion, however, was attending executions at Tyburn. Robin's friends naturally thought him 'a mighty good-natured gentleman and without the least bit of pride in him'. He was certainly a good batsman, and his bogus gentility also enabled him to be a successful promoter of matches. In the 1740s he was a familiar figure at the Artillery Ground, playing for London and Kent as well as for his native Bromley, and he regularly appeared in single-wicket games. In 1745, for instance, he was one of a trio who played Hodsoll, Romney and Richard Newland, and three years later he and Waymark twice played Faulkner and a leading London player named Joe Harris, winning both times.[43]

So cricket was obviously flourishing in the London area by the middle of the eighteenth century. Teams from Putney, Brentford, Fulham, Southwark and other suburban parishes provided young men of the middle and lower classes with ample opportunities for playing, and their friends and elders for gambling on the results. At a higher level of skill, great matches were there to entertain the crowds who flocked to the Artillery Ground and Kennington Common, or, for people willing to go a bit further afield, at such places as Moulsey Hurst and Bromley Common. However, something was missing, especially at the Artillery Ground: the sense of local identification with the teams which gave the rural matches so much of their vitality. No doubt when Dartford or Slindon came to play in the capital they had some local support, either from Kent or Sussex exiles or from people who came up from the country to watch, and the same was probably true of the teams from Addington, Bromley, Sevenoaks or the Weald. But the matches at the Artillery Ground were all too often artifically arranged to increase the chances of a close contest, with players being shunted about from XI to XI, or being made part of smaller combinations in single-wicket matches which changed bewilderingly from day to day.

The public appetite for this kind of cricket was bound to slacken, except no doubt among the inveterate gamblers who were, admittedly, a significant proportion of the spectators. When Long Robin and Waymark played Faulkner and Harris, who, beyond the contestants and the gamblers, can have cared very much? – especially if tomorrow the same players were likely to be deployed in different combinations at the behest of George Smith or his aristocratic backers. A century later William Clarke's famous All-England XI encountered the same problem, as the public's interest began to wilt after years of watching famous players monotonously destroying the local teams who tried their luck against them. Professional skills at a high level of perfection might be on display, but eventually spectators wanted something more: the sense that the game mattered in ways that transcended the individual performances of the players, or even the amount of money to be won or lost from betting on them. This could only happen in places which had a deeply rooted idea of community – real or imagined, parochial, county or regional. It was difficult for this to develop in London, with its highly mobile population of recent arrivals – people with no strong roots in either the metropolis as a whole, or its component parishes.

But it was a different matter when Slindon played Portsmouth, or Dartford played Dover, or, at a less-exalted level, when Hurstpierpoint played Henfield – Thomas Marchant's refrain of 'our parish' when he recorded his village team's victories echoes through the century. There is much that we do not know about the meanings that eighteenth-century people attached to the cricket they played and watched. If Dartford or Bromley or Addington had been lucky enough to have their own historians we might have a very different understanding of the significance of their matches. Fortunately we do have one such village – not a typical one, to be sure – about whose cricket we have plenty of information. Thanks to the marvellous John Nyren, we are for once able to glimpse how a cricket team could become the focus of passionate local loyalties, and the game they played take on a meaning far beyond the runs scored in a contest of twenty-two men with bat and ball. It is time for us to travel down from London into rural Hampshire, and to the famous village of Hambledon.

5

Hambledon: the Players and
the Community

Hambledon still has much of the air of an eighteenth-century village. Sheltered beneath the Hampshire downs, with their softening 'hangers' of great beeches, the place contains all the required ingredients of the imagined English past: a fine medieval church with the remnants of a yew tree of almost unimaginable antiquity in the churchyard, a couple of old inns, two satisfying village streets with a post office and a few shops, all surrounded by a green countryside dotted with farms and cottages. It seems an appropriate home for that legendary cricket team, with their famous ground at Broadhalfpenny, a few miles up the road towards Clanfield. If it is like this now, what must it have been more than two hundred years ago? Romanticized by the nostalgia so many of us feel for simpler, less-mercenary times, our constructed image of Hambledon is likely to be that of the ideal rural community.

The truth was very different. In the years before its cricket brought it undying fame, Hambledon was a divided, contentious place, on the edge of an even more violent, crime-ridden region, the Forest of Bere. Gilbert White, who lived not far away at Selborne, said in 1774 that he greatly disliked Hambledon 'on account of its morals and dissipation'.[1] The village had its local tragedies and disasters – a terrible fire which destroyed many of the houses in 1726, for example. And it had more than its share of poverty and lawlessness, as well as of political antagonisms. Yet during the 1760s it produced a cricket team far overshadowing all possible competitors. In the two following decades Hambledon played teams described as 'England' fifty-one times, winning twenty-nine of these matches. Of course 'England' meant something different from what we understand by the term today: the England teams were usually drawn mainly from Kent and Surrey. But these were after all the counties that still formed, along with Sussex, the real heartland of the game. Besides these 'England' matches, Hambledon regularly played each of the three counties separately, with equally impressive results. No other local team – not Slindon, not Dartford – even remotely approached the pinnacle of fame which Hambledon attained. Before we can begin to understand this, a brief review of its earlier history is required.[2]

Hambledon was a large parish of over 9,000 acres, containing several other hamlets or tithings – Chidden, Denmead, Ervills and Glidden – besides the main village, and stretching from the stiff clays of the vale in the south to the lighter soils of the hilly northern parts. It was in other words an almost classic example of the mixed type of settlement described in our first chapter, containing a nucleated village at the centre, surrounded by an area of small hamlets and detached farms: just the sort of place in which we might expect to find cricket, or some other bat-and-ball game, at a pretty early date. By 1750 much of the village was enclosed in small farms, but there were still extensive commons on which the inhabitants had grazing rights, Broadhalfpenny being one of them. In 1725 the vicar estimated the total population of the parish as 700 'and upwards'. By the time a century had passed that population had more than doubled.[3]

The village had for centuries been owned by the bishopric of Winchester. There were the usual manor courts and a weekly market, from which tolls accrued to the Bishop, inevitably causing friction with the inhabitants. The Bishop's ownership of the manorial rights ensured that there was no resident squire, though in the seventeenth century the powerful Nortons of Southwick had had much influence in the parish. The Nortons were gone by 1700, but a few prominent yeomen farmers stood out above their neighbours, and some of them – the Lands, for example – were eventually to move up into the gentry class.

In the mid-seventeenth century the manor contained thirty freehold tenants and fifty-five less-secure copyholders whose only title to the holding they leased from the Bishop was a copy of the manor court roll. There must also have been a landless population of some considerable size. By 1716 113 people paid their shares of the parish poor rate and there were probably approximately another forty families who were too poor to be assessed. Some of these poor people must have received parish relief, but unfortunately our sources do not tell us how many. The ratings are no more than a rough guide, but at least they suggest that the distribution of wealth in Hambledon was more or less what we should expect in a place of its size. Just under a quarter of the families did not have to pay

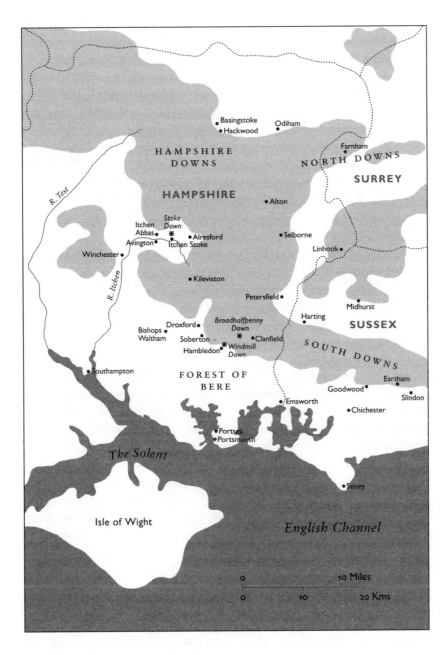

The Hambledon Neighbourhood

at all, and another quarter were assessed at small sums, 1s. or less. Just under another quarter were somewhat better off, but still scarcely affluent, at between 1s. and 3s. Another quarter might be termed the 'middle class' – people who were rated at between 3s. and £1. A tiny handful had assessments of over £1 – Henry Barlow, Henry Binstead (both from families which regularly held such village offices as overseer and church-warden), Peter Cleverly, and the wealthiest of all, John Ring, the only one to be assessed at over £2. The parish contained the usual sprinkling of craftsmen – shoemakers, bricklayers, carpenters, blacksmiths and the like – as well as the more numerous farmers and labourers.[4]

Apart from the absence of a resident squire – and many other English villages were without one – Hambledon's social structure appears very similar to that of its counterparts elsewhere in southern England. Politically, however, it was unusually divided, at any rate in the early part of the eighteenth century. A century earlier, during the civil wars, it had been a Roundhead stronghold, supplying numerous recruits for the Parliament's armies. In November 1643 Col. Richard Norton marched from Southampton with his 'Hambledon boys' to join Sir William Waller's army at Farnham; in March 1644, still under Norton's command, they took part in the battle of Cheriton. The 'Hambledon boys' gained a considerable reputation during the fighting in the region. Like most Hambledon people they were no doubt glad to see the back of the Bishop after Parliament had won the war. But the village contained Royalists as well as Parliamentarians. Among the King's adherents was a yeoman farmer named Thomas Symons, whose wife was the sister of the Sussex Cavalier George Gunter of Racton. One October day in 1651 Gunter arrived at the Symonses' house, bringing with him a mysterious group of gentlemen and their servant, a certain Will Jackson. Some of the gentlemen had spent the day coursing hares on Broadhalfpenny Down, and they now enjoyed the Symonses' hospitality – a convivial evening and a night's rest before journeying on to Brighton. Symons was too drunk to recognize that Will Jackson, the servant, was no less a personage than King Charles II, a disguised fugitive fleeing to France after his defeat by Cromwell at the battle of Worcester.[5]

In 1660 both king and bishop came back, but the village's political divisions lingered long after the civil war had become a distant memory. Even after 1700 political allegiances were still, as they had been in the seventeenth century, largely determined by religious affiliations. A Baptist congregation met fortnightly in William Luff's house in Denmead tithing – the very 'frontier of the parish', the vicar described it – but it numbered only about a dozen people. More serious was the presence of a score or so of Roman Catholics, always potential Jacobites, adherents of the exiled Stuarts, and some thought that there might be influential people lurking behind them. In 1725 the vicar dismissed them as being 'of little consequence as to their estates', but the Jacobite presence in the village always worried the local Whigs. Trouble erupted at a race meeting on Broadhalfpenny Down in April 1716. Two of the Whig Binsteads joined a group of army officers in drinking a round of Whig healths – to King George, the Duke of Marlborough, the Hanoverian succession and suchlike causes. A mob headed by the vicar, William Harby, a known Jacobite, approached and there was a noisy confrontation. Stones were thrown and Harby pulled the younger Binstead's nose, threatening him with a stick and denouncing him as an 'informing dog'. More volleys of sticks and stones followed, allegedly from the Catholic recusants present, one of whom, the well-known John Caryll of Ladyholt, loudly condemned the Glorious Revolution, saying that the Whigs 'had breached into the laws of the nation'.[6]

This was far from being the end of Whig–Tory conflict at Hambledon. The Pretender's birthday, 10 June, was a favourite date for Jacobite demonstrations, and on that day in 1723 John Collins, one of the Hambledon churchwardens – 'a poor, tricking, shuffling fellow of no visible substance', his enemies described him – ordered the church bells to be rung both morning and evening. When they had finished he joined the ringers at one of the inns and was said to have 'drunk plentifully' with them. The Whig–Jacobite conflict also had its parish-pump dimension. Churchwarden Collins was embroiled with the local Whigs on other, less obviously political matters. During his year of office several 'improvements' in the church were made: the walls were whitewashed, a new window created in the south wall, stained glass removed from other windows, and part of the venerable yew tree in the churchyard cut down. All this, apparently, was done to meet the claims of members of the church choir that they needed better light, but the parishioners were sharply divided over the matter. It was said that when he did not get his way, Collins encouraged the singers to go on strike and to sing comic songs ridiculing their opponents. Those opponents once again included one of the Whiggish Binsteads, as well as Collins's successor as churchwarden, Henry Barlow.[7]

*

More dangerous for local people than these echoes of national contro-
versies were the troubles caused by the royal forests – Bere, Woolmer,
Alice Holt – on their doorstep, and from their resentment at the power
of the Bishop of Winchester over them. The two things were connected,
for the see had important holdings in the forests, and increasingly tried
to exploit them. The royal forests had existed time out of mind to protect
the King's deer, though control over them had by now been generally
handed over to local gentlemen as a reward for services to the crown or
its ministers. For the general population the forests were a useful source
of timber even when many of the trees had been cut down, as well as
providing the tempting prospect of bringing poached venison to their
tables. Gilbert White thought that the forests benefited their surrounding
parishes in other ways, including the provision of peat and turf as fuel,
wood for burning lime, ash as fertilizer, and space in which to pasture
the borderers' geese and cattle.[8]

In the early decades of the eighteenth century the forests, in Hampshire
and elsewhere, were the scene of a dramatic collision between two very
different concepts of the agricultural economy. On the one hand was
the traditional respect for ancient custom, for longstanding grazing
rights, for 'use rights' to wood, peat, and so on, for the local inhabitants.
On the other was the newer emphasis on property rights, under which
the products of the forests belonged absolutely to the King or to whom-
ever he had assigned them, and which defined any intrusion on them as
unlawful theft or trespass. The former attitude prevailed among the
common folk; but the latter was held by many of their superiors, and
was protected by the formidable power of the state. To people in
authority the inhabitants of the forests and those who lived near them
were, as a later Hampshire historian sneered, 'the worthless from all
parts of the country', attracted by the irreligious character of such places
and their general exemption from the forces of law and order.[9]

Deer had always been poached, keepers assaulted, and authority
flouted in the royal forests. A century earlier there had been serious
trouble in Wiltshire and Dorset when King Charles I sold off parts of
the local forests to favoured courtiers who showed no respect for the
population's customary rights. After the Revolution of 1688–9 the site
of the violence shifted to Windsor Forest, and then, around 1720, to
Bere, Woolmer and Alice Holt Forests in Hampshire. Hambledon lay at
the centre of these latest conflicts.[10]

The disorders in Hampshire were provoked by the more aggressive attitude of the Bishop and his officers after Jonathan Trelawney's translation to Winchester in 1707. The death of the previous Bishop, the aged Peter Mews, had been followed by an interregnum during which the local inhabitants showed their customary ingenuity in cutting timber and stealing the deer that the empty bishopric could no longer protect. Winchester had always appointed many of the officials who administered the local courts: in 1663, for instance, we find the Bishop nominating Charles Cranley and William Gammon as bailiffs of the manors of East Meon, Hambledon, Fareham and Alverstoke. But as they and their families settled into the neighbourhood – a Cranley was still serving the Bishop fifty years later – such people were likely to become too friendly to the tenants. In the forests this comfortable continuity was especially likely to affect the subordinate officers – the keepers and their like. Gilbert White knew an old man whose family had been keepers in Woolmer Forest for over four generations, spanning more than a hundred years.[11]

All this changed when Trelawney arrived. His first steward launched a vigorous campaign to end the inhabitants' recent encroachments on the Bishop's rights. He enraged the tenants by attempting to abolish old manorial customs that had only cost the Bishop a few shillings here and there, and offended many of the old forest bureaucracy – the woodwards and their deputies – by his arrogance. The national courts usually sided with the Bishop in the many subsequent lawsuits over customary rights, but a suit begun in 1717 went against him. It involved a group of Hambledon residents and shows the villagers' characteristic tenacity in defending their interests. At issue was the question whether beech trees in the forest were 'timber' or merely 'wood'. If the former they were the property of the Bishop; if the latter they could be cut by the tenants for their own purposes. In spite of expert testimony on the Bishop's behalf by officials from the Portsmouth dockyards the Hambledon men won the case, both at Winchester Assizes and later in the Court of Exchequer.[12]

Timber was a troublesome issue, but the real problem was the deer. Many parts of the forests were weakly administered and ill-guarded, and the deer naturally provided a constant temptation to a local population for whom meat was a rare luxury. The most celebrated of the poaching gangs was one at Bishop's Waltham, only a few miles from Hambledon; they were known as the 'Waltham Blacks' from their habit, followed by their counterparts in other places, of blackening their faces to reduce the chances of detection. Later in the century Gilbert White noted that the fame of this and other poaching gangs had not been forgotten; there were still old men in the neighbourhood who 'over their ale . . . used to recount the exploits of their youth'. In the 1720s, White recalled, deer stealing was an essential test of masculinity: 'Unless he was a *hunter*, as they affected to call themselves, no young person was allowed to be possessed of manhood or gallantry.' A newspaper made a similar observation, speaking of 'the manly exercises of deer stealing'. The Waltham Blacks drastically reduced the number of deer in the Hampshire forests, and even after 1723, when several of their leaders were executed, sporadic violence continued.[13]

Some of the violence occurred at Hambledon. Among the leading inhabitants was a wealthy yeoman named Thomas Land, from one of those families who were climbing the social ladder towards gentility. He had been John Collins's colleague as churchwarden but was on the opposite side in the lawsuit over the alterations to the church, and it is possible that he disliked Collins's attempt to curry favour with the young men of the church choir. Young men were particularly vulnerable to the lure of deer-stealing, and Land may also have been unpopular with the poaching fraternity because of his apparently Whiggish politics – the Blacks tended to have Jacobite sympathies. At all events, not long after his breach with Collins a group of men broke into Land's coppice, collected straw and kindling, and set fire to the stacks of wood there. The suspects included at least two Hambledon men: Richard Martin, a shoemaker, and Thomas Taylor, a blacksmith. A third suspect was a tailor from Bishop's Waltham, John Collins, junior, presumably a relative of the Hambledon churchwarden.[14]

All this suggests that there were people in Hambledon who were inclined to resist authority, even if they did not go out into the forests with the Blacks – or at least were not caught doing so. In 1737 there was further violence, caused by food shortages, as a report from Winchester noted: the city was still 'alarmed by the rioters from the forest, who have plundered the farmers of their malt and corn'. Three years later a Hambledon man, Edward Smith, was sentenced to transportation at Winchester Assizes for assaulting a gamekeeper's servant in Bere Forest. Smith claimed that he was peacefully passing through the forest when the keepers apprehended him, thinking that he was one of a gang of poachers they were pursuing. More than a score of Hambledon villagers testified to Smith's good character, but to no avail. Whatever the truth of the matter the case shows that gangs of deer-stealers were still at work in the area. In 1746 Blacks were again said to be terrorizing the forests, and shortly afterwards the blacksmith Henry Aburrow (a brother of the Slindon cricketer) was condemned to death for outrages against the property of a gentleman at West Meon, another place bordering on the Forest of Bere. Only when the deer were drastically reduced in number (the last of the Woolmer Forest ones were carted off to Windsor by the Duke of Cumberland after 1750) was there a temporary reduction in the violence. Even then the footpads continued to follow their trade in the Forest and on the local highways.[15]

So Hambledon was in a region where there was a good deal of conflict during the first half of the eighteenth century, and the parish had its share of the disorders. The strong local traditions of independence and resistance to authority were later to be expressed (even if mediated by respect for the laws) on the cricket field. None of the evidence we have been surveying, however, offers any clue as to why the village should have had so brilliantly successful a cricket team. Before we can consider this question further we need to investigate the origins of the game in this region – to explore, in other words, the pre-history of Hambledon cricket. When did the village first have a team? It is a murky subject which has caused much debate among cricket historians, but a few leads are worth pursuing.

The earliest date at which we can be absolutely certain that there was cricket at Hambledon is 1756. By then the village team was strong enough to be able to take on the famous Dartford side in a series of three matches. One of these took place on Broadhalfpenny Down on Wednesday, 18 August, and we know about it because a 'yellow and white spaniel dog, of the setting kind', answering to the name of Rover, got lost on the Down. Rover's owner, a clergyman named Keats from Chalton near Petersfield, was sufficiently distraught to put an advertisement in the *Reading Mercury* offering five shillings for the dog's return. There must have been a good crowd at the match, and some of them – certainly Mr Keats, and presumably others in whose villages the Reading paper circulated – evidently came from some distance away. The last of the three matches between Hambledon and Dartford took place in London at the Artillery Ground, and was billed as 'the deciding match between the two elevens', for £50 a side. Two days before it took place, five members of the Hambledon team played a single-wicket match, also on the Artillery Ground and for £20 a side, against a five which included such celebrated players as Faulkner, Frame and Tom Bell.[16]

No ordinary village side could have taken on the mighty Dartford team at this time, nor would an ordinary village side have been invited to play at the Artillery Ground. A London newspaper confirms that the Hambledon players were already well known outside their immediate area, referring to them as 'the famous Hampshire gamesters'. It also looks as if Hambledon must by now have had some fairly wealthy backers, as the £50 stakes would have been beyond the means of the average village team. That Hambledon could compete at this level must surely indicate that cricket had been played there for a good many years: good teams do not emerge miraculously out of nowhere.

So we have to go back to the dark ages before 1756 if we are to discover when a cricket team first sprang up in the village. One possible clue is the ancient bat still preserved at Winchester College, said to date from 1742 and to have been used by a certain John Miles in the first match ever played on Broadhalfpenny Down. There is no possible way of confirming this story, though that cricket was played on Broadhalfpenny by this date is likely enough. The Down had been the site of an annual race meeting for many years – as we have seen, there was a political altercation at one in 1716 – its dates listed in the *Racing Calendar*. In 1739 we hear of a horse which had recently won the Plate 'on Broadhalfpenny course, near Hambledon'. The enforced ending of the Broadhalfpenny meeting in the following year, when races for stakes lower than £50 were outlawed, deprived the local publicans of their accustomed profits from the racegoing crowds. Cricket would have been a natural substitute, especially if there was already a local team of some quality.[17]

There are some further leads in the 1740s. In 1744 a London newspaper announced a forthcoming match at the Artillery Ground, in which one of the teams would include four Slindon players, and two others 'from Hamilton in Sussex'. There is no such place as Hamilton in Sussex, but Hambledon is close to the Hampshire–Sussex border, and a few years later the Hambledon Club was often mistakenly referred to as 'the Hamilton Club'. Another possible sign of a Hambledon team's existence occurs in a 1747 letter from Dr Thomas Hunt, the Roman Catholic chaplain at Ladyholt, to his patron John Caryll. One Friday morning that summer Father Hunt – having performed his religious duties for the day, he hastily assured his patron – went to a cricket match on Windmill Hill at Harting in Sussex, in which the contestants were Harting and 'Hampshire'. Now there is absolutely no evidence for a representative county team in Hampshire at this date, but, as we have seen, local teams were often given the name of their county to make them sound more important. In later years, during the great days of the club, the names 'Hampshire' and 'Hambledon' were virtually interchangeable: in 1771 the *Salisbury Journal* spoke of 'the Hampshire lads, known by the name of the Hambledon Club'. Harting lies only a couple of miles from the Hampshire border, Hambledon no more than seven or eight miles further on. What could be more natural in these circumstances than to label Hambledon as 'Hampshire'? Unfortunately Father Hunt gives no more precise evidence about the Hampshire team, but he does tell us that this was the second match between the two sides, that Harting had lost the first one 'very foolishly' and were consequently allowed two 'given men' for the return match, chosen 'from where they would except Slindon'. This second encounter, Hunt reported, 'was a fine match and all played extremely well' – by which he appears to mean that Harting won comfortably.[18]

'Hampshire' may have lost this particular match, but by now cricket was certainly beginning to flourish in the eastern part of the county. In August 1749 there was a match at the Artillery Ground between Long Robin and 'a gentleman from Havant' on one side, and two gentlemen 'from below Winchester' on the other, for forty guineas. 'Below Winchester' is a vague term that could apply to any of a dozen Hampshire villages, but it certainly refers to an area that includes Hambledon. One further clue is that in August 1750 a match arranged at the Artillery Ground between London and 'Hampshire' had to be put off until after the harvest, a sure sign that plebeian rural players were involved.[19]

In the light of later events it seems unlikely that there were no Hambledon players in any of these 'Hampshire' matches. But whether there were or not, cricket must have been spreading more widely in Hampshire than ever before. Accepting this, we are at once thrown back on the historian's insistent question: why? Why did cricket take off in Hampshire just before, or just after, 1750? One answer is obvious: county boundaries are permeable and have never been barriers to cultural exchange. There had been cricket in the adjoining parts of West Sussex for years – Slindon is after all only just over twenty miles from Hambledon, as the crow flies. The game must have spread slowly westwards, though it would have taken some years before any village team played it well enough to achieve any sort of prominence outside its own immediate area. The movement of individuals surely helped to spread cricket more widely: the elder Curry Aburrow's move to Hambledon soon after 1750 is an example. Economic conditions may also have had something to do with it. The first half of the eighteenth century was a good time for the rural population. Real wages were rising, and a series of good harvests led to particularly low food prices – bad news for farmers, but good news for labourers, who in these circumstances were never short of employment, and who as consumers benefited from the lower price of bread. Both the labourers and the many craftsmen who populated rural villages had more time and inclination to play or watch on the numerous holidays that, as we saw at Hurstpierpoint in an earlier chapter, enabled even quite poor people to enjoy their own forms of leisure. Moralists complained bitterly about it all: the higher standard of living was undermining the work habits of the English people, and seducing them into idleness and vice – watching cricket, for example.[20]

Broadhalfpenny was a cricket ground, but it was also Hambledon's 'sheep common'. In 1756, the same year as the match at which poor Rover went missing, the manor court wearily gave one of its regular warnings that 'any man that shall oppress the Sheep Common called Broadhalfpenny with any more than two sheep to an acre' would be fined £1. The Down was also a place of public assembly, the site of earlier race meetings, and of the now declining 'Toy Fair' on the first Tuesday in May. It is no coincidence that the first cricket practice of the year was regularly held on that day. Next to the open common on the bleak, windswept hillside, just where the roads (not much more than tracks in the eighteenth century) from Chidden and Clanfield met, stood an unimpressive hostelry with the equally unimpressive name of The Hut. In 1762 it was taken over by a new landlord, Richard Nyren, formerly of Eartham in Sussex, and nephew of the great Slindon cricketer, Richard Newland. It is better known by its later name, The Bat and Ball.[21]

Like the Newlands, the Nyrens had deep roots in the Sussex countryside. There had been Nyrens at Eartham, the next village to Slindon, for centuries. Jasper Nyren was vicar there in James I's reign, and his descendants were always people of consequence in the village: a second Jasper Nyren used the description 'gentleman' when he married in 1672, though the family might more properly be described as yeomen. It will be recalled that Richard Nyren the elder married Richard Newland's sister at Eartham in 1733; their son Richard, the Hambledon cricketer, was born there two years later. The younger Nyren was still there in 1758, when he married a Catholic woman, Frances Pennicud, at Slindon. He must have moved to Hambledon soon afterwards, for he cannot have taken over The Hut immediately after his arrival – he must have been there long enough to be able to get a certificate of his good character from local residents before his licence was issued. Exactly why Nyren made the move from Sussex is unknown. But he was in his early twenties, had been carefully coached by his uncle, Newland, and must have been in his prime as a player (he was still a good one twenty years later). So it may well have been the lure of an already established cricket team that attracted him. As we shall see in the next chapter, the Hambledon Club had some wealthy backers, and they may have encouraged Nyren to move to the village.[22]

Even in the 1760s records of Hambledon's performances are still scanty and uneven, for the newspapers were at that time extremely erratic in their reporting of cricket outside of London. But we know that on 10 and 11 September 1764, they narrowly beat Chertsey at the famous Laleham Burway ground, in the first of a series of three matches. It was an eventful contest. Chertsey had three players 'much hurt' and Hambledon two, one them suffering a broken finger and a sprained knee. There was also some high drama, when, as a newspaper reported, a constable tried to arrest 'a gentleman of fortune' from near Weybridge for being the father of a bastard child. The 'gentleman' drew his sword, aimed a pistol at the unfortunate officer, and 'went off in triumph'. The cricket was exciting, but this confrontation was even more so, causing 'a great deal of diversion'. The newspaper describes Hambledon as 'Squire Lamb's Club', presumably a misprint for 'Land'. There was of course no real squire in Hambledon at this date, but the Lands were prominent residents – it will be recalled that Thomas Land had been the victim of an arson attack by the 'Blacks' in 1723. This Thomas died in 1767, and the patron of the cricket club is more likely to have been his son, also named Thomas, who was born in 1714. However, it may be that Land's role in the club was being exaggerated by a newspaper unable to comprehend all the intricacies of the local social order.[23]

There may have been other Hambledon matches at about this time in which the name of the local team is concealed behind that of the county. In June 1764, two months before the Chertsey games, 'Hampshire' had comfortably beaten Sussex, and two years later another match between the two counties was played during the race week at Winchester. There was racing on the Tuesday and Wednesday, followed by cricket on the 'Race Down' on Thursday, and then more racing on the Friday. The willingness of the organizers to interrupt the horse-racing is a striking illustration of the game's appeal, for Winchester's race week was an important part of the local calendar for high and low alike. Hampshire made a great recovery to win this match (after the first innings the odds were 40:1 against them), but the experiment of playing during race week was not repeated. Other teams were active in Hampshire by this time – matches are recorded, for example, between Bramshott and Odiham in 1764, and Bramshott and Guildford in 1765 – but it is still hard to believe that Hambledon players were not present in the Hampshire sides, if indeed they did not comprise the whole of them. Once again we should be alert to the newspapers' common habit of labelling as a county team what was in fact a strong club side.[24]

By the late 1760s reports of Hambledon's matches become more common, though there are still a few years in which only one or two are recorded. In 1768 Hambledon beat Kent at Broadhalfpenny, and split a pair of matches against Sussex, who were captained by the third Duke of Richmond. We begin to encounter the names of prominent individual players: the famous John Small, for example, who made more than 140 runs in the two innings of the Kent match, and 80 not out against Sussex. As batting skills improved scoring steadily became heavier, and matches routinely went on into a second, or even a third day. The Hambledon team by now drew large crowds wherever they played: nearly 20,000 spectators were said to have attended when they beat 'Surrey' (actually the Caterham Club) at Guildford in 1769. Cricket was now so popular in Hampshire and Surrey, a newspaper reported, that people would ride forty miles to watch it. Guildford tradespeople were delighted by the profits they were making from the vast crowds, and naturally wanted more matches in the town.[25]

In 1770, for the first time, we are fortunate in having a brief description of a Hambledon match written by a spectator: our old friend John Baker, the Sussex lawyer. Early in October of that year (the season went on late in those days) Baker was visiting his brother at Chichester, and decided to ride to Broadhalfpenny to watch Hambledon play a team from near Croydon, the Coulsdon Club. It was a journey of close to twenty miles, but Baker and his young nephew bravely got themselves up at five o'clock and set out at half past six, arriving at Broadhalfpenny at a quarter past ten. Hours later, after the waning light had ended play for the day they rode on to Petersfield under a bright moon, and spent the night there. They were back at Broadhalfpenny the next day and stayed until Hambledon had won the match, though before it actually ended Baker and a group of acquaintances crossed the road to The Hut – 'Nyren's house', he calls it – for dinner.[26]

Baker tells us little about the spectators on this occasion, but he says much more about them at other Hambledon matches. In July 1772 he rode from Horsham to Guildford with a parson friend to see Hambledon play 'England' – actually a mainly Kent team raised by Sir Horace Mann. Hambledon were already batting when Baker and his friend arrived at Merrow Down. It was a cheerful scene. The 'Basin' was ringed by a great crowd of spectators, while the local publicans were doing good business in their booths, some of them rented by members of the nobility, and thus the equivalent of present-day sponsors' tents or boxes. As in our own times, the occupants often seem to have been more interested in the food and drink than in the cricket. Guildford was crowded with company for the match, so that night Baker had to make do with accommodation at the house of a local haberdasher. A bowl of punch, with lobster and cheese, seems to have consoled him.[27]

Hambledon won this match by 62 runs on the second day, but the next time Baker saw them play, against 'England' at Sevenoaks Vine in June 1773, they were comprehensively beaten. It was miserably cold, and Baker was so disgusted by their performance that he did not stay for the single-innings match that was hastily arranged to fill up the expected third day. Still, his journey was not altogether wasted. On both evenings he had the good luck to pass by the inn where the Hambledon players were staying, and heard them 'merrily singing catches (and very well too)'. They were famous for their singing as well as for their cricket, but Baker was somewhat offended to hear them enjoying themselves after they had been 'so shamefully beat'. He also had an interesting conversation with one of the Hambledon players, William Barber, in the shop of a local cricket-ball maker.[28]

By the 1770s cricket was thus a familiar part of the social scene throughout southeastern England, and it was spreading among people of all sorts and conditions. There may even have been women's cricket at Broadhalfpenny. In 1768, just over the Sussex border, the women of Harting and Rogate played three matches against each other; close to 3,000 spectators were said to have attended the third of them. One of the umpires, a newspaper reported, was 'a principal in the Hambledon

Club' and he was so impressed by the women's skill that he offered them the chance to play at Broadhalfpenny, which they eagerly accepted. Whether the match ever took place is unknown, but four years later, after Hambledon had conclusively beaten Hampton at Moulsey Hurst, some of the Club's players tried to arrange a match between a Hampshire women's XI and XXII of the Hampton men. The betting, it was reported, was 'considerably in favour of the female professors of that noble exercise', but the Hampton men prudently refused the offer.[29]

The Hambledon Club were clearly an attraction wherever they played, in away matches as well as on those wonderful days of 'high feasting' at Broadhalfpenny. Several of their players soon attained national fame. One who did so was the Petersfield shoemaker John Small. As we have seen, he was certainly attracting notice by 1768, when his batting dominated a game against Kent at Broadhalfpenny. He was over thirty by then, and it is surely likely that he had made plenty of runs before that date, in a period in which we know almost nothing about individual performances. Year after year Small was the mainstay of the Hambledon batting, and it caused something of a stir when he was for once actually bowled out, in an away match against Kent in 1772. His greatest innings was against Surrey at Broadhalfpenny three years later. After an evenly contested first innings, Hambledon lost five wickets cheaply when they went in again, causing (as we shall see) some hedging by the betting fraternity, who were now giving long odds on Surrey. Small and Richard Nyren then came together in a massive partnership which, to the consternation of the gamblers, put the game so far out of Surrey's reach that they conceded defeat. Small's contribution was an unbeaten 136 – and not many centuries were scored in those days.[30]

Another famous Hambledon victory was the one over 'England' (a combined Kent–Surrey side) at Sevenoaks in June 1777. The first three batsmen – Pattenden, Miller and Minshull – gave England a respectable start, Minshull eventually reaching 60 not out. But Tom Brett, Hambledon's fast bowler, swept away the tail, and England were all out for 166. Hambledon began their innings at about five o'clock on that Wednesday afternoon. The Sevenoaks carrier, with his load of parcels to be delivered to neighbouring towns, passed the ground and stopped to watch just as the Hambledon left-hander, James Aylward, began his innings. On Friday morning the carrier again came by the ground during his return journey, and was astonished to see that Aylward was still there, having batted, slowly but formidably securely, throughout the whole of Thursday. He was eventually out for 167, the highest individual score ever made at that time. Hambledon's total, 403, was another record, and their demoralized opponents were then skittled out for 69, Hambledon winning by the huge margin of an innings and 168 runs.

Victories like these make it easy to understand how the Hambledon team achieved such prodigious fame, both in their own time and in the eyes of posterity. They were a country team, but their success inevitably drew them into the commercialized world of the capital. Between 1773 and 1777 Hambledon played several times at the Artillery Ground, often opening their season there with a five-a-side single-wicket match, though also on occasion playing in matches between full XIs. John Baker twice attended the single-wicket games, watching the cricket after pursuing his other passion, the law – he observed trials at the Guildhall in the mornings before going up to the Artillery Ground in the afternoons. In May 1775 he got caught in a riot, an incident which again demonstrates the plebeian nature of eighteenth-century cricket crowds. Hambledon's opponents, Kent, were bowled out for 37, and in response the great John Small plodded his way to 42 in two and a half hours. At this point the fielding side claimed that they were being obstructed by the overflowing crowd (Baker says that he 'never saw so many people together') and walked off. Hooligans who had climbed on the wall of the adjacent Bunhill Fields then began pelting spectators with brickbats; according to a newspaper report, several people were 'terribly wounded'. Baker was not one of them, as he had sensibly decided to leave, though there was such a crush at the exit that it took him three-quarters of an hour to get out into Chiswell Street.[31]

Baker's diary confirms the newspaper reports that huge crowds attended these London matches as well as the rural ones at places such as Guildford. The Artillery Company was by now becoming uneasy about the disorders that occurred and announced that no more cricket would be permitted on their ground. They must soon have rescinded this decision, but in 1777 Baker noted that the price of admission had gone up to sixpence, on the pretence that the space for spectators had been reduced by the building of a new wall. We already know what had happened when George Smith put up the price to this level in the 1740s. Later in the 1777 season Hambledon were again at the Artillery Ground for a match against an 'England' XI raised by the Earl of Tankerville, but that seems to have been the virtual end of major cricket there. In

1780 the Corporation of London prohibited it permanently because of the recent violence.[32]

Enough of cricket matches. Others have written eloquently about the Hambledon team's exploits, and we have (can I be pardoned for this heresy?) other, more important, historical questions to explore. One set of such questions concerns the make-up of this great side, the social position of its members, and their relationships both to the wealthy men who sponsored them and to the community which cheered them on. We should always remember that we are heavily dependent – too heavily, perhaps, but there is no alternative – on John Nyren's wonderful reminiscences of the great heroes of his distant boyhood. And we should read *The Cricketers of My Time* critically, taking due account of its author's assumptions and prejudices. In Nyren's case the prejudices are those derived from his rural upbringing, and the sense (which he shared with William Cobbett and many others) that by 1830 the simpler, happier England of his youth had been corrupted by the growth of an unrestrainedly commercial society, and by the malign influence of London, Cobbett's 'Great Wen'. With these caveats in mind, what can we learn from Nyren about the cricketers of his time?[33]

First of all we should note the obvious fact that this was rarely just a Hambledon village team. There were, to be sure, occasions when teams described as 'Hambledon Parish' or 'Hambledon Town' took the field, as they did in one match against 'Hampshire' and two others against Surrey, all at Broadhalfpenny in the summer of 1773. In 1778 Hambledon Parish (with one given man) completely outplayed the rest of the Hambledon Club in a match on Stoke Down – certainly not a mere practice match, as it was played for a purse of fifty guineas put up by the Club. One Hampshire farmer, John Thorp of Preston Candover, thought it worth recording the match in his diary, presumably because he had attended it. Throughout the years of Hambledon's greatness a few similar matches, some against local sides such as Petworth and Alresford, occasionally appear in the fixture list.[34]

But for the 'grand matches' against 'England', Kent and other major teams, Hambledon increasingly called on men from outside the parish. Tom Brett came from Catherington, the next village, Aylward from only a little further away at Corhampton, near Droxford. But John Small lived ten miles away, at Petersfield, Tom Taylor and Richard Veck somewhat further, at Alresford. Noah Mann came from North Chapel in Sussex, and had to ride some twenty-five miles to get to Broad-halfpenny. In the 1780s there was a marked increase in the number of outsiders. The great bowler David Harris, from Odiham in the north of the county, was recruited in 1782; later in the decade other famous players such as the Wells brothers and Billy Beldham, all from Farnham, and the Walkers from Hindhead, also in Surrey, appeared regularly for Hambledon.

Still, until the 1780s, Hambledon teams were composed predomi-nately of men from the village or from within a radius of ten or twelve miles of it (Noah Mann is the exception). Most of them were from the middle ranks of village society. William Barber and Buck Stewart were both shoemakers who turned to pub-keeping; Barber was Richard Nyren's successor at The Hut. Nyren must have been becoming prosper-ous by 1772, when he took over the more upmarket George Inn in Hambledon village. Curry Aburrow was a tailor like his father, the wicket-keeper Tom Sueter a prosperous builder. Sueter (like his father) was regularly sworn as a juror in the manor court; he was constable in 1778, sang in the church choir, and was always in demand when building work had to be done – on the church, the poor house, the cricket club's 'lodge' at Broadhalfpenny or Windmill Down. Among the outsiders, John Small was another pillar of his church and its music, accompanying the Petersfield choir on either bass or violin for over seventy years. He and Mann were among the numerous shoemakers who played, though Small soon began to capitalize on his fame by manufacturing cricket bats and balls on the side. Aylward and Brett were both farmers. Brett's family had been at Catherington for generations, and were so numerous that they virtually ran the village; earlier in the eighteenth century they had owned the impropriation of the parish living.[35] Of the two Alresford men, Taylor was landlord of the Globe Inn (which, happily for his business, adjoined the local cricket ground), while by 1783 Veck, who had grown up there, was able to raise sufficient capital to buy a draper's business at Bishop's Waltham.

Men of this type were sufficiently prosperous to be fiercely indepen-dent. They might accept whatever favours were on offer from the Club's aristocratic backers, and they were sensible enough to use appropriately respectful language to them. Nyren's story about the Club's slow bowler, Lamborn, is significant. Lamborn, it will be remembered, was the simple shepherd who invented a devastating new spin: the off-break. He had learned it by practising bowling while tending his father's sheep on the

Downs. In one match Lamborn repeatedly beat the Duke of Dorset with it, and after just missing the Duke's leg stump was so carried away that, Nyren tells us, 'forgetting the style in which we were always accustomed to impress our aristocratical playmates with our acknowledgment of their rank and station', he shouted in his thick Hampshire accent, 'Ah, it was *tedious* near you, Sir!' There was general laughter, but it may have been a shade uneasy, for Nyren makes it clear that Lamborn ought not to have addressed Dorset so familiarly. It was all right to use his crafty bowling to make a duke look a fool, but Lamborn ought still to have used the proper form, 'your Grace'.[36]

Respectful they might be, but while they remained at Hambledon the players were nobody's clients. John Small may have been a shoemaker, but he certainly did not kow-tow to the aristocracy. John Nyren tells a revealing story:

The Duke of Dorset having been informed of his musical talent, sent him as a present a handsome violin, and paid the carriage. Small, like a true and simple-hearted Englishman, returned the compliment, by sending his Grace two bats and balls, also *paying the carriage*.[37]

It sounds, on the face of it, like a straightforward exchange of gifts, but the subtext – Small's refusal to be patronized, even by a duke – is clear. At this time the carriage charges on packages were normally paid by the recipient. Dorset ostentatiously sees that the much less-affluent Small does not have to pay anything; Small responds in exactly the same way, with a present that he knows Dorset will value, likewise with the carriage paid.

Independence: this was a quality at the very core of the self-image of freeborn Englishmen of whatever social class, and especially of that now vanishing breed, the yeoman. Through the nostalgic mists of fifty years, the younger Nyren saw the ideal superbly exemplified in his own father:

I never saw a finer specimen of the thoroughbred old English yeoman than Richard Nyren. He was a good face-to-face, unflinching, uncompromising, independent man. He placed a full and just value upon the station he held in society, and he maintained it without insolence or assumption. He could differ with a superior, without trenching upon his dignity, or losing his own.[38]

Two of John Nyren's other stories throw some further light on the relationship between the Hambledon players and the great men who played alongside them. One involves a curious episode in which the elder Nyren expressed the wish to see what Nancy Parsons, the Duke of Dorset's current mistress, looked like. The lady often came to Hambledon matches, but always modestly stayed in her carriage. The Earl of Tankerville offered to help and succeeded in getting her to put her head out of the coach window while Richard Nyren was close by. John Nyren suggests that the incident shows the 'easy footing' on which relations between the noblemen and the commoners were based; it is also, surely, a striking example of the flouting of social conventions – in this case the ones by which upper-class people protected their privacy – to which cricket could sometimes lead.[39] Nyren's other story concerns an argument, presumably over some interpretation of the laws, between his father and the two great aristocratic patrons, Dorset and Sir Horace Mann, nephew of Horace Walpole's great friend. When Nyren was proved to have been right, Sir Horace (but perhaps not the Duke?) crossed the ground and heartily congratulated him on his firmness.

Richard Nyren and his like did not need to wait for the approval of great noblemen when they expressed their views on what was cricket and what was not. In 1771 Shock White of Reigate came in against Hambledon at Laleham Burway with a bat wider than the wicket. There were loud protests, but the existing laws were frustratingly silent on the bat's maximum width. The Hambledon players wasted no time. Two days later they legislated on the matter: four and a quarter inches was to be the limit in future, and just to make sure they had an iron gauge made of the correct width, which was for many years kept at The Bat and Ball. The entry in the minutes recording this decision is signed, not by any of the Club's aristocratic patrons, but by Richard Nyren, Tom Brett and John Small. In the absence of any central authority, the laws were being made by Hambledon's own elder statesmen. Three years later the noblemen and gentlemen of the Star and Garter Club incorporated the regulation limiting the bat's width in the next printed edition of the Laws of Cricket.[40]

John Nyren is adamant that the Hambledon players were, almost without exception, absolute paragons of virtue, uncorrupted by the gambling which in the early 1800s was to undermine much of the integrity of the game. We may suspect that he was perhaps a little naïve about this, for there was a match against Kent in 1783 that certainly sounds suspicious. Runs were still officially recorded by making notches on sticks. On this occasion the Hambledon scorer 'accidentally' mislaid his stick just after an exciting game had ended in a tie. The Kent scorer then claimed, too late, that there had been a mistake and that Kent had actually won by one run. 'High odds' had been laid on the result, and it may be that the Hambledon notcher knew somebody who would have lost a lot of money if Kent had won. But the account in the *Hampshire Chronicle* seems to imply that if there was anything suspicious about the match the culprit was the Duke of Dorset, who was playing for Kent and would undoubtedly, as usual, have wagered a large sum on the result. 'The odds ran greatly in favour of the Hambledon Club', the paper says, 'and had not the Duke of Dorset missed two easy catches, the knowing ones would have been deeply taken in'.[41]

These suspicions may be unjustified, for we have no positive, cast-iron evidence of cheating, and this is the only Hambledon match in this period about which there seems to be any doubt at all. Nyren speaks of an unnamed player who 'sold the birthright of his good name for a mess of pottage', but claims that he was alone in having done so. The rest of the team were, he says, 'staunch and thorough-going. No thought of treachery ever seemed to have entered their heads . . . what they did, they did for the love of honour and victory.' If anyone put money first it was more likely to be the Club's gentry backers. This was certainly the case in the famous match against Surrey at Broadhalfpenny in 1775. Hambledon's second-innings collapse made two of the Club's most faithful members – the Revd Charles Powlett and Philip Dehany – so certain of the outcome that they hedged their bets and put their money on Hambledon's opponents. After the massive partnership between Small and Richard Nyren had added enough runs to win the match, the two gentlemen ruefully complained of being deprived of their expected winnings. Nyren's scathing reply has become part of Hambledon legend: 'Another time don't bet your money against such men as we are!'[42]

The Hambledon men valued their independence, yet in the end the huge disparity in wealth and status between them and their aristocratic backers was bound to undermine it. Several, including John Small, got jobs as gamekeepers for one or other of the Club's members, though this seems only to have begun to happen around 1780. In 1784 the innkeeper Thomas Taylor was appointed gamekeeper to the Duke of Bolton at Itchen Stoke. It was no doubt a useful supplement to his income, but Taylor assuredly made less money from it than from his inn and the refreshment booths he was allowed to erect whenever Hambledon played on Stoke Down. Richard Nyren must also have benefited financially from the support of the gentry and aristocracy; they would have spent lavishly at his booths on match days, as well as at The Hut and, later, down at the George. The Club's annual meetings at the George were always advertised well in advance (including the time that dinner would be on the table) to ensure a good attendance of members. But, as we have seen, Nyren was never in the pocket of the gentry. The only regular Hambledon player from the early years (before 1780) who was totally bought up by any of the Club's wealthy patrons was James Aylward. Sir Horace Mann was sufficiently impressed by his marathon innings at Sevenoaks to lure him away from Hambledon to become Mann's bailiff at his Bishopsbourne estate. A fine batsman, Aylward made a rotten bailiff, Nyren gleefully reports.[43]

The Hambledon players were also dependent on the Club more generally because they were in effect part-time professionals. Exactly how much they were paid we do not know, for the Club's accounts survive only for a few years in the 1790s. When they appeared in major matches they must have been paid by the promoters, who may or may not have been Club members. In the 1780s, according to William Beldham, players customarily got five guineas for a win, three guineas if they lost, but the rate may have been lower in the previous decade. Players also won or lost money from wagers, and were sometimes rewarded with special bonuses if they had done well. In 1777, after Hambledon had beaten 'England', the owners of the Artillery Ground divided £50 between the two sides, 'as a proper encouragement for another year'.[44]

The players were also paid by the Club for attending the weekly practices at Broadhalfpenny. Even the younger players ('the boys') were paid, though at a lower rate than their elders. Some of the men also got travel expenses, as Richard Purchase did for 'horse hire' from Liss beyond Petersfield in 1773, and the Wells and Beldham brothers from Farnham twelve years later. In May 1775 it was ordered that Small, Brett, Sueter and some others were to be paid for special practice at single-wicket, as preparation for the five-a-side match at the Artillery Ground a few weeks later. How much they got at this time we do not know, but by 1782 the leading players received 4s. on practice days if they were on the winning side, 3s. for the losers. After 1790, when we have better accounts, the weekly totals of payments to players varied from as much as £6.15s.6d., presumably for a match against another club, to as little as one guinea – but there is no way of knowing the number of players sharing these sums. Accounts dating from 1808 and later suggest that the scale was not much different from the three or four shillings paid in 1782.[45]

What did this all mean for the Hambledon players? The agricultural writer Arthur Young estimated that the average weekly wage of an agricultural labourer at this distance from London was about 7s.6d. However, the only labourer among the Hambledon regulars – and he played only from 1777 to 1781 – was the shepherd, Lamborn. In 1798 it was reported that Richard Swaine, a Sussex labourer, had been able to retire on his savings, having been a famous cricketer in his younger days. It seems unlikely that he would have had much to save on only 7s.6d. a week, so it is possible that his cricket had added substantially to his income.[46] Craftsmen such as Small and Aburrow would undoubtedly have made a good deal more than a labourer, and the yeoman/innkeeper Richard Nyren more still. But even for them the five guineas for a win or three guineas for a loss would be a useful contribution to earnings, while to young Lamborn they must have seemed princely sums. Players themselves bet on their performances, but on balance that is unlikely to have added much to their incomes. Nobody could make a living simply from playing cricket – there were not enough lucrative matches – but the additional income the players derived from the game may have made some of them think twice about offending the Club's wealthy backers.

The Hambledon men played for money, but that is not all they played for. They played for fame, for honour, for the love of the sport, and not least because they played for a cricket club that so strikingly expressed the identity of their neighbourhood – the rural communities of Hampshire and the adjacent counties. John Nyren's wonderfully evocative depiction of the 'high feasting' on Broadhalfpenny cannot be entirely dismissed as the expression of a nostalgic longing for the lost innocence of his youth. Those 'fine brawn-faced fellows of farmers' drinking to Hambledon's success, intently watching every great match 'as if the event had been the meeting of two armies to decide their liberty', and 'baying away in pure Hampshire' whenever one of their heroes made a good hit, evoke the powerful sense of local identity that still pervaded eighteenth-century England. In earlier chapters we have seen how places such as Hurstpierpoint and East Hoathly took pride in their cricketers. With a much more famous team, Hambledon was bound to excite even more powerful local loyalties. 'Silver Billy' Beldham recalled how years later, after their best players had been lured away to play in London, the inhabitants of rural counties would still closely follow their achievements, with 'many a flagon of ale' wagered on their performances.[47]

As we have seen, many of the Hambledon players were respected members of their communities, and that too bound the Club closely to the region. They sang in their church choirs, they accompanied them on fiddles or other instruments, they responsibly performed whatever civic duties it was their turn to undertake. The younger Curry Aburrow, son of the Sussex smuggler, was constable of Hambledon in 1786, and in 1793 was appointed Overseer of the Poor for the first of several times. This does not mean that his conduct was always above reproach. In April 1778 Aburrow and another respectable pillar of society, the wicket-keeper Tom Sueter, were convicted of having in their possession a deer which had been unlawfully killed. The escapade may not have diminished their reputation in the village, given the strength of the poaching tradition in those parts. Aburrow and Sueter both played in Hambledon matches that summer, at Sevenoaks and Broadhalfpenny, respectively, while the poaching charge was under appeal. They were acquitted on 14 July, when by a curious coincidence one of the JPs hearing the case was the Hambledon Club's patron, the Revd Charles Powlett.[48]

So the Hambledon men were moulded by the culture of their region. We can see this in the singing for which the team was famous. Contests between local groups – 'singing-matches', as they were called – were much in vogue in eighteenth-century Hampshire: we find them advertised at Wickham, Romsey, Fareham, Bishop's Waltham and other places. They were usually promoted by publicans, as at the Globe in Andover during Whitsun week, 1756, where each competing group had to sing three songs in two or more parts, and one 'catch'; 'none to sing but those who dine at the ordinary'. Admission cost one shilling, though this also entitled the holder to sixpennyworth of liquor. One can imagine the Hambledon cricketers doing well in these 'musical meetings'. Tom Sueter had a fine tenor voice, John Nyren tells us; besides singing in the church choir he used to entertain his cricketing friends with hunting songs in the club room after practice, or join the long-stop George Leer in a glee at The Bat and Ball. When in 1782 Hambledon played a combined Odiham–Alresford team (strengthened by the inclusion of several of the Hambledon stars) at Odiham, there was a singing-match between the players at an inn on the first evening of the match – a striking sign of the team's musical reputation.[49]

It was not only through their singing that the Hambledon players shared in the familiar rural customs. Nyren describes how Noah Mann, a brilliant horseman, used to entertain the crowd at Broadhalfpenny after his long ride from North Chapel. Handkerchiefs would be thrown down on the ground, 'and these he would collect, stooping from his horse while it was going at full speed'. This sounds like a humane version of the barbaric sport of 'riding for geese' described in an earlier chapter. Cricketers were apparently more civilized.[50]

Cricket, at Hambledon or elsewhere, was still part of that vibrant, if violent, rural culture. Some thought that country sports were becoming less brutal in the latter part of the century, and according to the Baptist preacher James Spershott, the excessive drinking that had prevailed before about 1750 had also much diminished. In the old times, Spershott tells us, farmers coming to Chichester market would be drunk for days on end, 'till their wives came to fetch them home'. Spershott also observes that cock-fighting was becoming less popular by the 1780s, though this is contradicted by the continuing frequency of newspaper advertisements for it. I know of no specific evidence that cock-fights were ever among the additional attractions at cricket matches as they still were at race meetings, but it seems likely enough. Cock-fighting was certainly advertised as taking place at Winchester Races in 1766, when the cricket match between Hampshire and Sussex also formed part of the programme. The Hampshire JPs were still worrying about the demoralizing effects of 'revels, horse races, cock fightings, bull baitings' and suchlike diversions; in 1781 they again ordered the local constables to prosecute the publicans who organized them.[51]

The village of Hambledon, the Club and its players have all loomed so large in cricket history that it would be foolish to minimize their importance. Yet in some respects the attention that we have been giving them is misleading, as it might tempt the unwary to forget that even at the height of its fame, the Hambledon Club was only one part, albeit a particularly glamorous one, of the cricket scene. In the next chapter we shall encounter other clubs, and other famous players who were sponsored by the great noblemen who often came to Hambledon. But we should always remember that below the highly skilled, professional level of the Hambledon Club and its opponents, there were still countless other village sides, revealed to us only fitfully and occasionally. That the game still retained traces of its peasant origins is evident in such things

1. *An Exact Representation of the Game of Cricket, c.* 1743, by Louis-Phillipe Boitard

2. Admission ticket to the Artillery Ground, for the Kent v. Slindon ('England') match, 18 June 1744. The 2s. 6d. price is a later addition by a dealer

3. *Cricket in Marylebone Fields*, *c*. 1748, by Francis Hayman

4. *Cricket at Kenfield Hall, Kent, c.* 1760.

5. *Edward 'Lumpy' Stevens*, *c*. 1783, by Almond

6. (*right*) *John Frederick Sackville, 3rd Duke of Dorset*, 1769,
by Sir Joshua Reynolds

7. *The Countess of Derby and friends playing cricket*, 1779, by 'T. H.'

8. 'The Gentlemen's Club' (forerunner of the MCC) playing in
White Conduit Fields, 1784, by [Robert Dighton?]

9. Sketches of cricketers from the notebook of George Shepheard, *c.* 1790.
Harris, Walker and Beldham were all Hambledon players

10. *Cricket at Moulsey Hurst, c.* 1790

11. The Bat and Ball Inn, Broadhalfpenny Down, as it was in 1879, by G. P. Gale

as the local variations in the rules that we occasionally encounter. In parts of Kent, for example, half-notches were recorded even in matches between quite well-known teams. When Canterbury played Bridge and Bourne in 1763, there was 'only half a notch difference' on the first innings.[52]

Cricket was a central feature of many celebrations in which the identity of a community was expressed. For a time in the 1780s, right on Hambledon's doorstep, the 'independent freeholders of the Forest of Bere' held annual feasts at which both cricket and horse-racing were among the 'usual diversions' on offer. As was always the custom on such occasions, the foresters were given plenty to eat and drink. In 1783 a newspaper reporting the affair thought it necessary to insist that it had all been 'remarkably respectable', and that 'the utmost harmony and conviviality reigned throughout the whole company'.[53]

There was plenty of other cricket in Hampshire. A Houghton blacksmith lost his watch at a match on Stockbridge Down in 1768, and a few years later there was a game near Ringwood in which a combined team from several local villages took on 'the noted players from Milford'. John Thorp, the Preston Candover farmer, reports a couple of matches involving his village in 1779, in one of which, he gleefully noted, 'Preston beat Basing twice in one day'. Portsea, a side that had played against Slindon in 1740, still had a team in 1781, as did Portsmouth, Gosport and Titchfield; the two last-named played each other for a guinea a man on Titchfield Common. When Gosport played Portsmouth, however, the stakes were much higher: fifty guineas a side. As always, spectators were lured to these games by the promise of good refreshments 'a cold collation, and exceeding good liquors . . . at a booth on the ground'.[54]

Cricket at Hambledon was played by men who were deeply rooted in the village and the communities which surrounded it. It received the enthusiastic support of the thousands who ringed the boundary at Broadhalfpenny and drank The Hut dry on match days. It expressed emotions – inspired by local patriotism and perhaps even by class feeling when their plebeian heroes were matched with grandees such as the Duke of Dorset – of which they were probably only dimly aware. In this we have at least a partial answer to the question posed earlier in this chapter: why Hambledon? There were plenty of other teams which did not generate the enthusiasm needed to make them into symbols of local identity. But Hambledon was the kind of place – a large parish with scattered settlements spanning the forest country and the Downs, and without the immediate attentions of a resident squire – which in earlier times had tended to encourage the growth of bat-and-ball games like cricket and stoolball. It was also a place that valued the independence forged in many a forgotten skirmish in the poaching wars. These are all undoubtedly contributing explanations for the strength of cricket there, though when all is said, some of Hambledon's success can only be attributed to luck. Having once built up a successful side Hambledon attracted players, and spectators, from all over the region. Success breeds success. The process becomes a cumulative one.

But the stirring events on the Down were also possible because Hambledon's real backers – and any eighteenth-century enterprise on this scale had to have them – were not remote aristocrats like the Duke of Dorset. They were Hampshire gentlemen who shared the local loyalties of their inferiors. Hambledon succeeded because it was a *Club*, supported by the patronage and the financial resources of the Hampshire gentry. There were plenty of other village teams in the eighteenth century, but none was backed by an organization as effective and influential as the Hambledon Cricket Club. To the Club and its membership we must now turn.

6

Hambledon: the Club and the Patrons

> Assist, all ye Muses, and join to rehearse
> An old English sport, never praised yet in verse.

So begins the song written in 1771 by the Revd Reynell Cotton in honour of the Hambledon Club. His verses, replete with classical allusions, tell of a mythical cricket match and praise the plebeian heroes who played in those epic struggles on Broadhalfpenny Down. 'What were Castor and Pollux to Nyren and Small?' Cotton exuberantly demands. A later stanza extols the rest of this great team:

> Buck, Curry, and Hogsflesh, and Barber and Brett,
> Whose swiftness in bowling was ne'er equalled yet;
> I almost forgot, they deserve a large bumper,
> Little George [Leer] the long-stop, and Tom Sueter, the stumper.

Eventually, inevitably (for we are in the eighteenth century) the song moves on from the players to their wealthy backers:

> Then fill up your glass, he's the best that drinks most.
> Here's the Hambledon Club, who refuses the toast!
> Let's join in the praise of the bat and the wicket,
> And sing in full chorus the patrons of cricket.[1]

Perhaps the most striking thing about the song is Cotton's generous praise for the ordinary players, who are clearly seen as the foundation of Hambledon's fame. Although due recognition is given to cricket's patrons, they are never actually named, not even such well-known cricketing noblemen as the Duke of Dorset and the Earl of Tankerville. Cotton's lines celebrate not individual great men, but the *Club*, the Hampshire and Sussex gentry who collectively underwrote Hambledon cricket, and the local men who played it.

*

Eighteenth-century clubs had many purposes, but a central one was always to enhance the social life of their members. There were thousands of clubs, in town and country: musical clubs, literary and philosophical clubs, book clubs (often linked to lending libraries), clubs which provided various forms of insurance for their members – friendly societies, in other words. Some clubs had no other purpose beyond sociability, such as the one that Thomas Marchant belonged to at Hurstpierpoint in the 1720s. It met on Tuesdays or Thursdays at the Swan Inn, and brought together some of the wealthier inhabitants for drinking and friendly conversation. Squire Campion turned up for at least one meeting in 1727. Sometimes business was done: on one occasion 'all the parish officers were there', Marchant tells us, and they made some decisions about a local charity. But business was not really the object of the exercise.[2]

Cricket clubs too were formed for the benefit of members who paid annual subscriptions to maintain them. The club might play competitive matches against other clubs, or it might not: there might only be weekly pick-up games in which the members played against each other, sometimes with paid professionals mixed in to improve the standard of play. Hambledon clearly originated as this kind of club. A similar one was founded at Coxheath, the ancient ground near Maidstone, in 1787. The organizers wanted the best players to come, so they promised always 'to choose as equal a match as possible'. Every week two teams, made up of club members and visiting professionals, would be selected to play each other. The professionals were not yet full-time cricketers depending solely on the game for their income; like many of those who had played at the Artillery Ground in earlier years, they also worked at other crafts or trades. But when they played cricket they were paid for it, which makes it appropriate to call them professionals.

The Coxheath Club promised to pay five shillings to each professional on the winning side, 2s.6d. to the losers; they would also get their expenses for horse hire, plus 1s.6d. for food and drink. Dinner would be laid on: two shillings for members, three shillings for non-members. The subscribers (at two guineas annually) included the three great patrons of Kent cricket – the Duke of Dorset, Sir Horace Mann and Mr Stephen Amherst. In August 1789 the members dined with Sir Horace at the Star Inn on the heath, but the club did not flourish, apparently because Coxheath was too bleak and remote to be attractive. It may also have faced competition from the nearby Penenden Heath Club, founded in 1785.[3]

An earlier club in Kent was the one at Bridge Hill, which in 1751 was meeting for practice every Wednesday afternoon. Bridge Hill was close to Bishopsbourne, where major matches were regularly played by the Bourne Club after Sir Horace Mann came to live there in 1765. By the late 1780s genteel cricket clubs were proliferating. In Suffolk the Sudbury 'Cricket Society' was holding weekly 'exercises' in 1787, and a year later it was reported that in the Isle of Wight 'a weekly cricket-match is settled among the gentlemen of this island'. Coxheath's experience shows that cricket clubs were often short-lived, ephemeral affairs. Sometimes there were efforts to revive those that had fallen by the wayside. In 1769 'the *late* Knightsbridge Cricket Society' announced that it would hold a meeting at the Bell in Hampton, to be followed by a game on Moulsey Hurst. They hoped that each member would bring a new recruit, but the prospects for collecting back-subscriptions were not very good, as the 'Club book' had been lost.[4]

We know from the previous chapter that cricket was being played at Hambledon by 1756, and almost certainly for some years before that date. Exactly when the Hambledon *Club* was formed, however, is still a mystery. Years later, Beldham recalled overhearing a remark made by the Revd Charles Powlett after Farnham had beaten Hambledon in 1780: 'Here have I been thirty years raising our club, and are we to be beaten by a mere parish?' This would date the Club from around 1750, though historians have been understandably cautious about relying too much on Beldham's memory. What we do know is that there was a successful Hambledon team, good enough to play Dartford, in 1756, and that when it played in London in 1764 it was known as 'Squire Land's Club'. Powlett's arrival may have led to a more formal organization. He became curate of Itchen Abbas, near Winchester, in 1763, but he was in the neighbourhood before that, having been elected a freeman of Winchester by 1756. In 1760 he was living at Chilland, just outside the city. It will also be recalled that Richard Nyren took over the Broadhalfpenny Hut in 1762. So the early 1760s appears to be the most likely period for the Club's foundation. It certainly existed by 1768, when one of the members umpired the match between the Harting women and those of Rogate.[5]

But although there may have been some sort of Club by this time, we have to wait until the next decade before we can find out much about it. On Saturday 16 November 1771, a general meeting of 'the subscribers to the Broadhalfpenny Club' was held at the George Inn in Hambledon, 'to appoint stewards, and settle the plan for the ensuing year'. It is clear from this that the Club, like clubs everywhere, was being run by its subscribers: *members*, almost invariably local gentlemen or people with some claims to gentility. In 1772 there were about twenty-five of them, a number which rose to over fifty in the following twenty years. New members were elected by ballot, and we search the lists of them in vain for any of the plebeian (and paid) players who represented the Club with such distinction. A few of the gentlemen occasionally turned out alongside paid players in the big matches against outside opposition, and others must have done so in the weekly practices on Broadhalfpenny Down. Gentlemen (amateurs) and Players (professionals): already we have the distinction that was to be embedded in English cricket for almost two centuries.[6]

General meetings of the members, such as the one in November 1771, were held at the George every autumn, with dinner always served at three o'clock. The Club's earliest minute book begins only in June 1772, and on the 30th of that month the first recorded weekly meeting was held at the Hut. (It was clearly not the first actual meeting, though, as several new members were elected who had been nominated at earlier ones.) By now Hambledon's role as a social, as well as a cricket, club was certainly established. At this same 30 June meeting the purchase of a 'wine cistern' was ordered – and given the thirst for wine which subsequent meetings reveal it is unlikely that the Club can have been functioning for very long without one.[7]

For sociability and good fellowship the provision of abundant wine was essential. The Club's minutes are full of it. In 1773 the members decided to pay for William Barber's wine licence: he had recently taken over the Broadhalfpenny Hut from Nyren. Wine was indispensable to the conduct of meetings: members who did not obey the president's order to keep quiet paid their fines in claret, a dozen bottles for each offence. Large quantities were bought from Gauntlett's of Winchester: a hogshead of port, 'fit to drink immediately', for example. In 1784, three dozen bottles of claret were ordered for the annual dinner at the George, a decent ration for the twenty members who turned up. Gauntlett's wine was not always up to standard – the Club once had to send back a consignment, it 'not being approved'. But the firm usually seems to have supplied drinkable stuff, and in 1785 Mr Gauntlett himself was elected to membership.

All this well-oiled conviviality had its inevitable consequences. In 1774 the Club tried to induce greater sobriety by announcing that only two toasts (to the King and the Club's president) would be permitted after dinners, but a few years later they gave up and allowed a few others. These included a puzzling one to 'The Queen's Mother', who was dead, and an obscene one to 'Madge', this being an eighteenth-century slang term for a woman's vagina.[8] We can easily picture the boisterous, noisy clubroom at the end of a meeting, probably resembling something out of Hogarth or Rowlandson. Like the players, the members were great singers. They must have given many a raucous rendition of the 'Cricket Song'. They were so proud of Cotton's verses that in 1790 they had them framed and glazed and hung up in the 'Club Room', and got a hundred extra copies printed. A smoky clubroom, too, for while the drinking was impressive, the members also consumed quantities of tobacco, both for smoking and for chewing: later half a dozen 'spitting troughs' were ordered.

Sociability may have been central to the Club's existence, but the promotion of cricket was equally important. Money was collected to be competed for in important matches – a purse of fifty guineas 'given by the Gentlemen of the Hambledon Club' when 'England' played 'Hampshire' at Broadhalfpenny in 1777, for example. The Club occasionally put out a team composed of gentlemen only – in 1771, playing as the Gentlemen of Hampshire, they were twice heavily beaten by their Sussex counterparts.[9]

Most of the members seem to have been content with watching or occasionally taking part in the Tuesday practices. They decided how much players should be paid, and made other regulations about the weekly sessions; batsmen were to retire if they made 30 (15 in a second innings), for example. The players had to be at Broadhalfpenny by noon, 'and the sides made at that time', but the starting-time was soon brought forward to eleven o'clock, with a 3d. fine for latecomers. After 1787 the fine was increased to 6d., to be used to buy punch for the virtuously punctual. We know from John Nyren how potent that punch could be: it was punch 'that would make a cat speak!' They bought a bell to give warning when play was about to start, and they did their best to see that the playing area was decently maintained. Barber was instructed to 'take care that the Down is repaired' and later, after the Club moved from Broadhalfpenny to a ground nearer Hambledon village, Windmill Down, they had the ground reseeded in the autumn, and then 'rolled and beaten all the winter'. They made sure that the players were smartly turned out, buying eleven hats for them in 1781. But they did not forget the Club's other purpose, adding an additional black hat for the drinks waiter. In 1773 the treasurer was told to buy a conveyance, or 'machine', to transport the players to away matches; some members objected, no doubt thinking that the money would be better spent on wine.[10]

The Club also paid a good deal of attention to the comfort of members and their guests. They had a temporary 'lodge' built at Broadhalfpenny, which provided those attending matches with shelter from the wind and from undesirably close proximity to noisy lower-class spectators. After the move to Windmill Down, in 1783 they commissioned Tom Sueter, who was a builder as well as a wicket-keeper, to construct a brick clubhouse – it was still standing on the Down decades later. While the clubhouse was being built they used tents for temporary accommodation. They heard about an 'elegant mess-tent' belonging to the Dragoon Guards which was up for sale after the end of the American war and deputed a member to buy it in time for the Kent match in July 1783 – too late, alas, as it had already been sold.

Tents adorned the boundaries at both of Hambledon's grounds. In 1773 green baize was ordered, to cover the seats in 'the tent for the ladies'. The ladies attending would of course have been genteel guests of the members, not players' wives such as Mrs Small, who used to park herself on the grass under a green umbrella and shout encouragement to her beloved husband. Well-bred ladies came frequently to Hambledon matches: these were social as well as sporting occasions. When Hambledon played at Kilmiston Down, a few miles to the north of Broadhalfpenny, the advertisement for Barber's refreshment tents assured the ladies that they would be 'as much at their ease as if they were in their own dressing room'. At another home game on Stoke Down, Nyren confessed that he could not provide the ladies with such fancy foods as aspic and blancmange, but promised that for those with good appetites there would be 'a quantity of beef, ham, chickens, tarts, etc.'. The comfort of female guests was attended to in other ways: in 1784 the Club decided to build 'a *dulce lenimen* [toilet] for the ladies'. It is not clear how they had managed until then.

Such, in brief, were some of the activities of the Hambledon Cricket Club. Who exactly were the members? They were, as we might expect, a fair cross-section of the gentry of the region. This does not mean that all of them were from ancient families, deeply rooted in the countryside. Claire Tomalin's biography of Jane Austen tells us a lot about the social world in which the novelist's family moved: it was largely made up of recent arrivals in Hampshire, people 'who aspired to live by the values of the gentry without owning land or inherited wealth'. They were, Tomalin points out, a fluid, unstable group, 'some floating in on new money, others floating out on their failure to keep hold of old'.[11] The Austens lived in the north of the county and their circle of acquaintances overlaps surprisingly little with the membership of the Hambledon Club, but in social terms it was probably not very different.

Whatever their origins, most of the Hambledon members tried to fashion themselves into passable versions of gentility. One who did not was the 'nabob' Richard Barwell, who had made a fortune in India, and like so many of his type came home to use it to advance himself in society. In 1781 he acquired Stansted Park, near Chichester, and bought a seat in Parliament. William Hickey gives a vivid portrait of how a newcomer who did not understand the conventions of English rural life could quickly become unpopular. Barwell, he says, at once made himself

obnoxious to persons of all ranks, shutting up gates and paths through his parks that had . . . always been open to the public, preventing the poor from supplying themselves with water from a spring they had long been used to frequent . . . Men, women, and children hissed and hooted at him as he passed, with all his oriental state, through the villages.

Barwell also affronted polite society by not turning up for a dinner that had been arranged in his honour by the Corporation of Chichester. He was promptly sent to Coventry: 'not a single gentlemen visited or took the least notice of him'.[12]

Hickey may have exaggerated the social ostracism that Barwell encountered, for he was in fact elected to membership in the Hambledon Club in 1782. But most of his fellow members would certainly have better performed the neighbourly and paternalist roles assigned to them by custom. They were, though, rather a mixed bag. Some of them came from the village itself. Edward Hale was the son of a local surgeon and farmer who had done well enough to build a fine house behind the George Inn. The son played for the parish team in 1784 but only became a member of the Club five years later. He was a keen sportsman, keeping a pack of harriers. Other Hambledon residents among the members included John Richards, the Club's treasurer for many years, and Captain Erasmus Gower, whose distinguished naval career earned him promotion to admiral and a knighthood.[13]

At the other end of the scale were the aristocrats. Among the active members were Lord Dunkellin and the Hon. John Thomas DeBurgh, the two sons of the Earl of Clanricarde, who lived at Belmont near Warnford. The younger brother played occasionally without much distinction, but was elected president of the Club in 1784. John Baker observed Dunkellin at Hambledon's match against Kent at Guildford in 1772, along with the Earl of Tankerville and Viscount Palmerston, father of the Victorian statesman.[14] The two latter were both Hambledon members, and we shall encounter Tankerville, a great patron of cricket, again. Other aristocratic members included Robert Henley, second Earl of Northington, who was president in 1778, and his successor, Henry Bilson Legge, who became Lord Stawell in 1780. A few years later Stawell employed Beldham to lay out a cricket pitch at Holt Pound Green, near Farnham. He was a keen cricketer, playing alongside Beldham for a combined Alton–Odiham team in 1784. He was as addicted to fox-hunting as to cricket, and went out with several local hunts, including the Kilmiston.

Far more numerous than the peers and their relatives were the county gentry. They included several men of that familiar eighteenth-century type, the fox-hunting squire. The most notable was Thomas Ridge of Kilmiston, master of the hunt there for many years. He was a more active cricketer than most of the members, turning out for Hambledon several times between 1769 and 1775, once making a respectable 24 against 'England' at Broadhalfpenny. He was a friend of Reynell Cotton, and Powlett also thought highly of him. Ridge, Powlett wrote in one of his hunting songs, was 'a man without guile', one who 'in plain English style, French manners and foppery defies' – in other words a model of the patriotic, honest country squire.

Another of the type was Bysshe Shelley, the poet's grandfather, who lived for a time at Hambledon. At least one of his children was baptized at the village church, and his second wife was buried there in 1781. He was selfish and acquisitive, and his famous grandson thought him 'a bad man . . . a curse upon society'. He was keen on horse-racing, but he also enjoyed cricket, and played for Hambledon on at least one occasion. John Baker encountered him at a match in Horsham in 1772, at which his brother, John Shelley (another Hambledon member) was one of the umpires.[15] More active in the Club was Henry Bonham of Petersfield, who was regularly elected to the important office of steward (responsible for the wines!) and was also secretary for many years before he handed the job on to his brother Thomas. The Bonhams owned property at East Meon as well as at Petersfield – enough to qualify Henry to be a Deputy-Lieutenant of Hampshire and to be one of the nominees for the office of High Sheriff in 1785. Thomas, who kept a pack of harriers, remained a faithful member of the Club almost to the end of his long life.

Wherever the eighteenth-century gentry congregated we are likely to find the clergy. There were several parsons among the Hambledon members: John Ballard of Portsea, John Dampier of West Meon, Jonathan Rashleigh of Wickham, for example. Then there was the Revd Reynell Cotton. He had been rector of St Lawrence, Winchester, since 1742, and around 1760 opened a school there. In 1751 he married Susan Baddeley at Hambledon, and at least one of their children was baptized in the village church, so Cotton had been connected with Hambledon for at least twenty years before he wrote the 'Cricket Song'. As they bawled it out in the Hambledon clubroom the more literate of the members would no doubt have appreciated the classical references: 'great Pindar' bragging of ancient heroes; Castor and Pollux (greatly outshone, of course, by Nyren and Small); the Greek Pentathlon; Ajax fighting Hector 'in sight of all Troy' as if engaged in some Attic cricket match. Among Cotton's friends were Ridge and Henry Bonham, and he was elected president in 1773; his son played for the club occasionally at about that time. Reynell Cotton was obviously one of the most active of the Hambledon members.[16]

Another sporting parson, however, was even more important, and some have regarded him as the real founder of the Club. We have encountered the Revd Charles Powlett several times in passing, but it is time to say something more about him. He was the eldest illegitimate son of Charles, third Duke of Bolton. In 1728, we may remember, Bolton had fallen hopelessly in love with the actress Lavinia Fenton when he saw her as Polly Peacham in *The Beggar's Opera*. His wife would not cooperate so there was no divorce, and Bolton was only able to marry Lavinia in 1752, after the Duchess had died. Bolton himself died only two years later without legitimate heirs, so the title went in succession to his younger brother Harry and two of his sons.[17]

Charles Powlett may have been illegitimate, but he grew up on the fringes of a family of immense wealth and power. During much of his lifetime the Dukes of Bolton dominated Hampshire politics. Charles went to Westminster, the most famous cricketing school in the country, at about the same time as another future backer of the Club, Philip Dehany of Kempshott Park. Sometimes known as 'Squire' Powlett (he owned the manor of Itchen Abbas), he shared in the usual pastimes of young gentlemen of his type – hunting, horse-racing, a spot of cock-fighting. In 1755 he took his MA from Cambridge, and was ordained soon afterwards. Itchen Abbas was one of several Hampshire parishes in the pocket of the Duke of Bolton, and in 1763 Powlett was installed as curate. We may well wonder how much time he spent there. He was a notable pluralist, holding several other livings (one as far away as Devonshire), and in 1782 he was appointed chaplain to the sixth Duke. By 1764 he was one of the county JPs, and evidently a pretty active one; on one occasion, it will be recalled, he helped Aburrow and Sueter get off when they were charged with poaching. His passion for cricket kept him well occupied, too. He was often at meetings of the Hambledon Club, and gambled heavily at matches – the famous occasion when he and Dehany lost after hedging their bets is unlikely to have been an isolated one. In 1774 he was one of the London committee which revised the Laws of Cricket. Yet we should perhaps not be too cynical about him. In 1765 the rector of Itchen Abbas reported that Powlett was indeed resident in the parish, and often took the services during the incumbent's own frequent absences.[18]

Charles Powlett's leading role at Hambledon inevitably prompts a question: was the Club an agency of the Bolton interest, much as the Charlton Hunt had been for the Duke of Richmond in Sussex years before? For until 1769 the Dukes of Bolton were the unchallenged leaders of Hampshire society. The one that most concerns us is Charles Powlett's cousin, the sixth Duke, who held the title from 1765 until his death in 1794. Before becoming a peer he held most of the local offices that were customary in his family: between 1751 and 1765 he sat in the Commons for three different Hampshire boroughs. But he was also a naval officer – promoted Admiral of the Blue in 1770 – and often absent from the county.[19]

Bolton's great house at Hackwood, near Basingstoke, was nevertheless always one of the chief social centres of the region. In June 1769 the Duke and Duchess put on a great masked ball for the local upper crust. Beds for 200 guests were booked in Basingstoke, and the roads leading to Hackwood were jammed with carriages. It rained, naturally, so the 'grand illumination and supper in the woods' had to be cancelled, but there was still a glittering gathering in the house. The Duchess played a Persian princess, Lady Waldegrave and Lady Mary Hay came as 'eastern sultanas', Lady Stanhope as a French 'nosegay girl', and Mrs Garrick was in Venetian carnival costume. The men were not outdone. The Duke of Manchester, a newspaper reported, was 'richly habited in the old English dress'; Thomas DeBurgh came as a character from *The Mourning Bride*, and an unnamed guards officer as the Devil. After midnight they all unmasked for a great supper, and the dancing went on until long past dawn.[20]

The Boltons' ascendancy in Hampshire was threatened soon after this spectacular event by the political ambitions of a rival duke. The Brydges family were originally from Gloucestershire, but in 1751 Henry Brydges, second Duke of Chandos, inherited an estate at Avington, near Winchester. He was extravagant and unreliable, but he soon got himself made High Steward of Winchester: no doubt the corporation welcomed someone to balance the hitherto all-powerful Powletts. Chandos was not much of a politician, and if the *Salisbury Journal* is to be believed he had no interest in courting popularity among his inferiors. On a narrow road, one day in August 1751, his carriage encountered a waggon, the plebeian driver of which decided that he had as much right to the king's highway as anyone else. Angry words were exchanged, and the Duke's coachman was set on by the waggoner and his friends. Chandos got out and flailed at them with his cane, but the locals, the newspaper reported, 'used his Grace in a very rude manner'. Faced with prosecution, however, they prudently submitted and apologized.[21]

At first Chandos seems to have accepted Bolton's primacy with a reasonably good grace. His son, the Marquess of Caernarvon, was elected to the Commons for Winchester in 1754, and may have been behind the election of Sir Simeon Stuart for the county in 1761. Like Chandos and Caernarvon, Stuart was a ministerial supporter, and the *Hampshire Chronicle* later noted that it was in this election that the 'baleful influence' of George III's favourite, Lord Bute, was first felt in Hampshire. But in reports of the major events of the Winchester social season – the races, the balls, the music festival – the Duke and Duchess of Bolton were always listed first among the quality, and Bolton continued to provide his annual venison feast for the city's dignitaries.[22] In 1769 all this changed. Chandos and his friends became more visible at

Winchester's great social events, giving lavish public breakfasts during race week. The outward harmony at the music festival had scarcely faded when, in late September, the Chandos group, helped by an 'independent club of freemen', elected their own man as mayor. Among those involved in the coup were several supporters of the radical John Wilkes, who had recently earned national fame by his stand for freedom of election in the tumultuous contests in Middlesex. Caernarvon was not really a very convincing recruit for the cause of liberty, for he had supported Wilkes's opponents in Middlesex, but as usual in eighteenth-century politics ideology had less to do with the matter than aristocratic factionalism, and the issue at Winchester was the citizens' resentment of Bolton domination rather than their enthusiasm for British freedom. When Chandos's newly elected freemen were sent congratulatory letters by the London Wilkesites they returned them unopened.[23]

Bolton, hitherto an opponent of Wilkes, now had perforce to support him, and in 1770 was one of a group of peers who signed a protest against Wilkes's exclusion from Parliament. During the following decade Hampshire's political alignments became closer to national ones, with Caernarvon (who succeeded his father as third Duke of Chandos in 1771) supporting the North ministry's war policies towards the Americans, and the Bolton interest opposing them. At a meeting in Winchester in November 1775, Chandos promoted a loyal address in favour of the government which condemned 'the spirit of delusion and sedition' allegedly animating its opponents. A rival meeting a few weeks later, chaired by Jervoise Clarke Jervoise of Idsworth Park, called for reconciliation and 'lenient measures' towards the colonies. In December Clarke Jervoise's friends formed the Hampshire County Club, established, it proclaimed, 'for the support of public liberty'. Its first president was the Duke of Bolton.[24]

The lines were now clearly drawn. Throughout the 1770s the rival dukes were rarely seen at the same social events. Chandos and his son now dominated Winchester. They routinely headed the lists of people attending the races and the music festivals, usually followed by such allies as Sir Simeon Stuart and Clanricarde's two sons, Dunkellin and DeBurgh. Their ascendancy was triumphantly displayed during the 1772 race week, when the third Duke gave a great public breakfast and afterwards attended the prize day at the College. In the following year Chandos himself was mayor and ostentatiously continued his programme of entertainment and charitable giving. Aristocratic proprieties were not quite forgotten: in 1777 Chandos was elected president of the Hambledon Club, and Bolton occasionally entered a horse at Winchester Races. Otherwise, though, Bolton was virtually invisible in the city.[25]

Chandos could control Winchester, but he did not control Hampshire. In November 1779 Stuart, the court-supporting MP, died and there had to be a by-election. The candidates were Sir Richard Worsley, a government supporter backed by Chandos, and Clarke Jervoise, who was both an oppositionist and a Bolton man. All over England the political situation was becoming increasingly heated as gentry opinion turned against Lord North and the American war. But Hampshire, normally so loyal a government constituency because of the large number of obedient voters from the Gosport and Portsmouth dockyards, was not expected to cause North much trouble.[26]

Unusually for an eighteenth-century election, however, this one was fought over policies and principles. Jervoise and the Bolton faction stood for peace with the Americans and an end to the corrupt use of place, patronage and outright bribery to maintain a parliamentary majority – for which North's government was increasingly blamed. But the Duke of Chandos also figured in the campaign. As one pro-Jervoise song put it:

> What tho' the great Duke has extended his skill,
> and issued his mandates to bridle our will?
> Let his wretched dependents his dictates obey,
> Clarke Jervoise and Liberty carry the day.

Chandos and Worsley responded with some old-fashioned 'Church and King' Tory rhetoric, and accused the Boltons of being 'abettors of rebels beyond the Atlantic'. It was to no avail: Clarke Jervoise was elected by over 600 votes.[27]

In the victory celebrations that followed, the gentry who had managed the election were soon reminded that they were not the only people demanding a political voice. On 3 January 1780 the new MP was chaired in triumph through the streets of Winchester. Suddenly the procession was met by another made up of local weavers marching behind their patron saint, 'Bishop Blaize'. The weavers' band played 'God Save the King', and it was all very loyal and congratulatory. 'Bishop Blaize' then addressed the crowd from the Market Cross, making the expected complaints about the cloth industry's problems – brought on, of course, by 'the obstinacy and misconduct of the present ministry' – and demanding the election of 'a free and independent Parliament'. Jervoise's procession then proceeded to the County Hall, where a petition for reform, modelled on one recently adopted in Yorkshire, was enthusiastically approved. The opposition's triumph was complete when, shortly afterwards, the Duke of Chandos resigned his position as Lord-Lieutenant of Hampshire.[28]

The election did not end the political uproar. In 1780 an organized campaign against North was launched, which produced petitions from numerous counties, including Yorkshire and Hampshire. There was also a meeting in London of delegates from several county reform associations, again including Hampshire.[29] The agitation continued after the fall of the North government. On 27 April 1782 the anniversary of the battle of Culloden, always a favourite Whig celebration, was observed by the Hampshire Club with special enthusiasm because of the overthrow of 'the late profligate administration'. Toast followed Whig toast: to the King; to what the Club described as the recent 'second revolution' ('a kingdom saved and no king extirpated'); to 'the Whig interest throughout the world'; to the Duke of Bolton and other Whig leaders, and to the two county MPs. But the enthusiasm quickly waned when national politics resumed their normal course and the reformist Rockingham and Shelburne ministries were succeeded by the cynical alliance between North and Fox. By 1783 the reform campaign was losing momentum. The Winchester citizens joined in one more national petitioning campaign, but their main purpose was to break the grip of the local oligarchy over the corporation. At Petersfield the Bonhams were unable to gain support for a reform petition. The mayor told its Yorkshire authors that local opinion was 'very apprehensive that you and your association will do much injury to Old England'.[30]

All this political excitement was an inescapable background to the more convivial activities of the Hambledon Cricket Club. It was impossible in the 1770s not to be affected by the discontents provoked by the American war. High taxes, militia burdens, fears of a French invasion, disputes over policy towards America and over the North government's alleged authoritarianism and corruption: all these combined to destroy the easy harmony that had prevailed at mid-century. The gentry had been politicized. So had their inferiors. Forty-four Hambledon freeholders voted in the 1779 by-election, every one of them for Jervoise.[31]

The Hambledon Club, as we have seen, was run by the local gentry, and there must have been much political debate at their meetings. Several members – the Duke of Bolton's friends, needless to say – were prominent in the campaign. When in 1775 Chandos moved the loyal address supporting North's policies towards America, it was Powlett's friend Dehany who most loudly opposed it. At a subsequent meeting Dehany moved a rival address, which he himself had drafted, calling for conciliation. When the Hampshire County Club was formed that December with Bolton as its president, Dehany was one of the two stewards elected. He was also a promoter of the 1780 petition, while the meeting at which it was adopted was chaired by John Richards of Hambledon. Henry Bonham supported Dehany's petition in 1775, and four years later he and his brother worked hard for Jervoise, using their family's influence in the Petersfield area. Dehany was present at the dinner which kicked off the election campaign and was denounced in a Worsleyite ballad as one of the leading 'liberty men'. Jervoise, Dehany, Richards and Charles Powlett all joined the fairly radical Society for Constitutional Information, and through the Hampshire Club (of which Powlett was steward in 1785) continued to support the reform programme until it dwindled into insignificance a few years later. Chandos's supporters were clearly a minority in the Cricket Club, though the Duke himself nominally remained a member for several more years.[32]

But politics was only one part of the cultural world of the Hambledon Club's members. They met at hunting parties and race meetings – always with their attendant social whirl of balls and assemblies – and at great gatherings such as the Winchester Music Festival, held every September. Handel's oratorios always dominated the programmes, though in 1760 the offerings also included Purcell's 'grand Te Deum, as improved by Dr Boyce'. At another 1760 concert Signor Giardini played violin solos, and Miss Spencer from London sang three songs, all to great applause. The leaders of Hampshire's social set were always conspicuous among the audience – which was particularly 'splendid and crowded' in 1765, it was felt – though only in 1769, just as the political storm was about to break, were the Dukes of Bolton and Chandos *both* present. Performers from London and Bath were widely advertised. In 1772 top billing went to the celebrated Linley sisters, who performed with 'taste and propriety', while their father Thomas Linley conducted the orchestra. In the following year the relentless round of Handel oratorios was interrupted by Signora Grassi from the London Opera who, it was announced, would sing 'favourite Italian songs' during the programme.[33]

After 1769 Winchester was run by the Chandos crowd. Southampton was more eclectic, though it at least provided the Duke of Bolton with somewhere to go when he was on shore. The town lacked Bath's brilliance, and its attempts to promote sea bathing eventually foundered through the absence of a cooperative tide, but it was developing a reputation as a lesser centre of leisure and fashion. In 1772 a visitor observed that 'pleasure seems to be the goddess of this place', with splendid, uncrowded Assemblies, an 'elegant little theatre', and plenty of beautiful women. Ten years earlier the diarist John Baker had sampled the Southampton season. Back in 1775, he was playing a lot of whist and going to numerous plays, including *As You Like It* and Sheridan's *The Rivals*. The town was quite successful in attracting royalty. In 1765 the King's brother, the Duke of Gloucester, was there; his theatrical tastes were clearly in the direction of broad comedy, as he insisted on command performances of both *The Jovial Crew* and *The Mayor of Garret*. A new Southampton theatre opened in 1766, and Gloucester was one of its patrons. It was a thriving enterprise, able to hire one of the stars from Bath's Theatre Royal for the 1773 season; among the offerings was Oliver Goldsmith's new play, *She Stoops to Conquer*.[34]

In that same year an array of royal and other dukes descended on the town: Gloucester, Cumberland (another of George III's brothers), Bolton, Dorset, and the radical third Duke of Richmond. Dorset, whose arrival was reported on 7 August, had been playing cricket for 'England' against Hambledon at Broadhalfpenny a day or two earlier. He was not alone in wanting to enjoy the cricket as well as Southampton's social round: a ball originally arranged for 26 August was postponed, it was announced, 'on account of the great cricket match at Broadhalfpenny, between Surrey and Hampshire'. Other sporting events in the neighbourhood occasionally lured people away from Southampton, among them Lyndhurst Races, which were attended by Gloucester, Bolton and Richmond.[35]

There may have been some in Southampton who did not welcome the famous visitors, in spite of the money they were bringing into the town. On 15 September there was a masked ball at the newly built leisure centre, the Polygon – tickets one guinea, which included tea, coffee and lemonade. During the festivities someone outside threw a stone, 'with great violence', smashing a window and narrowly missing the Duchess of Gloucester. But the agreeable diversions generally passed peacefully.

One Wednesday morning in August of 1773 you could have had breakfast at Martin's Assembly Rooms, with a concert following at noon featuring little Ann Storace, a child 'not eight years old'. The audience was disappointingly small, but she made enough of an impression to be awarded a couple of benefit concerts a few weeks later, 'by desire of several ladies of distinction'. Who could have guessed that in 1786 Ann Storace was to earn eternal fame as Mozart's first Susannah in *The Marriage of Figaro*?[36]

Other coastal towns were less successful than Southampton. Portsmouth had plenty of visitors because of the vast naval presence. Thomas Marchant was there in 1727, touring the dockyards and going over the *Royal William* – 'a very fine sight, as I think'. A few years later, John Whaley reflected that 'every Englishman's heart must be warmed' at the sight of the fleet and the dockyards. He was less impressed by the performances at the local theatre, however. Even when a successor, the Spring Gardens Theatre, opened in 1782 its chief attractions were tightrope acts and pantomime, not the higher quality plays being given at Southampton. The owners' anxious assurances that the theatre was patronized by 'very genteel company', and that no 'expression that could hurt the most delicate ear has been heard from any part of the house', suggest that seafaring audiences had a reputation for rowdiness. The town made some effort to advertise itself as a place for sea-bathing, but never attained the popularity of Weymouth once George III had made the Dorset resort so fashionable. Still, Portsmouth had its less-glamorous balls and assemblies, as indeed did virtually every other town of any size.[37]

One striking feature of polite culture common to all these places is a lively musical life. Many provincial towns had their own music clubs. The well-known festivals at Salisbury and Winchester naturally drew the biggest crowds, but even much smaller places found it worthwhile to publicize their concerts, as well as their balls and assemblies. Vocal and instrumental soloists from Bath performed at Devizes Town Hall in May 1764, Blandford put on a concert conducted by Mr Coombes, the organist at Wimborne, during the town's race week in 1767, and there were subscription concerts at Lymington and Poole, in the latter case being held at a pub appropriately called 'The French Horn and Trumpet'. Fareham had an annual music festival, while at the Crown at Ringwood in 1768 the programme included works by Handel and Purcell. With Arne and Boyce also among the favourites, the preference for English composers is clear. 'The compositions of our English masters,' a visitor to the Three Choirs Festival reflected, 'are not inferior to those of any other nation.'[38]

The urban season, except at some of the spas and in seaside places such as Southampton, was concentrated in the autumn and winter. However, Caroline Powys thought that the popularity of Bath and other spas was sapping the vitality of social life in lesser towns. In 1771 she noted that the 'race-assembly' at Reading was not as brilliant as in earlier years: Bath was luring away 'those young people who otherwise would be ambitious of shining at these annual balls'. But the gentry could still create their own amusements. After Christmas 1776 there was a 'gala week' in various country houses near Henley-on-Thames, featuring a band made up of 'the best hands from Italy', plays put on by professionals from London as well as local amateurs, and the usual glittering suppers and dances. The Henley townspeople and the tenants of local land-owners were graciously allowed in to watch the dress rehearsal of one of the plays, and even a heavy snowstorm did not affect the enthusiasm: visitors were paying up to sixteen guineas a night for beds in the Henley inns. There were good pickings, too, for the local highwaymen, who relieved several of the guests of their jewellery. The presence of the tenants at the dress rehearsal should remind us that old traditions of deference were not quite dead. Caroline Powys was at the tenants' feast at Fawley Court in January 1789. 'The young people,' she reported, 'danced with the tenants six or eight dances, then we all came up to cards and supper.' Both the gentlemen and the farmers entertained the company with 'clever songs' and 'droll toasts'. Among them were such impeccable, but at this date possibly significant sentiments as: 'Peace and Plenty'; 'May the rich be charitable and the poor happy'; 'May all great men be honest and all honest men great'. Two months later, she says, 'we had the farmers, their wives, etc., to dinner' to celebrate George III's recovery from mental illness.[39]

So paternalism survived in other aspects of life besides cricket. We have often observed how the game brought together patrician and plebeian both on and off the field – in the great crowds at the Artillery Ground paying their twopences to watch Lord John Sackville playing with and against the top professionals, in John Nyren's 'high feasting' at Broadhalfpenny, and on many other occasions. Any great assembly could of course bring people of different ranks together. When the crowds were streaming away after the King had reviewed the Royal Regiment of Artillery at Blackheath in 1772, a newspaper reported, 'at one view were to be seen Ambassadors, Dukes, Lords, gentlemen, beggars, chimney-sweepers, and thieves'.[40]

But class lines seem to have been unusually blurred at cricket matches, where an ordinary person could rub shoulders with a lord. In 1776 Richard Hayes, a yeoman from Cobham, went to Sevenoaks to watch Hambledon play Kent, and got close enough to hear the Duke of Dorset moan that if he missed even a single ball he was certain to be out (Lamborn might have disagreed). 'Cricket's the game for the low and the great', a song proclaimed in that very year, just as it had been in de Saussure's time. The social mixing was not confined to the great matches. When Horsham played Reigate in 1773, John Baker tells us, Lord Irwin, who had a strong political interest in the former borough, 'got out of the coach and stood with the crowd'. Gentlemen's families had no objection to playing cricket with their servants. In 1763 Baker's two sons had a game with their father's valet, and some years later the valet played in a game at Broadbridge Common with a few of the diarist's gentry friends. Baker took obvious pride in the performances of his coachman, William Wisdom, who played for Horsham and must have been a pretty good batsman. On one occasion he was 'catched out' before Baker arrived, but against Dorking in 1772 'our William' made 56, including 'four strokes of six each'.[41]

We must surely by now be sceptical about assertions that eighteenth-century cricket was totally dominated by the aristocracy. Around 1850 James Pycroft wrote nostalgically of the great days 'when the Earls of Thanet and of Darnley brought their own tenantry to Lord's or Dartford Brent, armed with the native willow wood of Kent'. This kind of feudal relationship, if it ever existed, was certainly uncommon by the years of Hambledon's pre-eminence. Still, we also know that both the nobility and the gentry were vital to the organization of the game, and that matches were arranged to suit their convenience. In 1779 John Farley, who held the concession for the refreshment booths at Bishopsbourne, was curtly informed that next Tuesday's match was off. It would 'not be convenient to the Duke of Dorset, Lord Tankerville, or any of the Hampshire or Surrey gentlemen' to be there, he was told; they had decided to play the match at Moulsey Hurst instead.[42]

We may wonder whether the Earls of Thanet and Darnley really could deliver their tenants, but there is no denying that they and people like them gave a lot of support and encouragement to the game. Lord George Kerr, son of the Marquis of Lothian, lived at Farnham, and years later Billy Beldham remembered how he would 'provide bread and cheese and beer for as many as would come out and practise on a summer evening'. Lord Stawell, who employed Beldham to lay out the pitch at Holt Pound Green, was also a Hambledon member, and had been president of the Club in 1779, before he succeeded to the barony.[43]

A more celebrated patron was Charles Bennett, fifth Earl of Tankerville. At Mount Felix, his great house near Walton-on-Thames, he employed a veritable team of cricketers. The famous 'Lumpy' Stevens was his gardener – 'a bit of a smuggler' in his youth, it was said, but now the most feared bowler of the day. So accurate was Lumpy that Tankerville once won £100 on a wager that he could land the ball on a feather placed on the pitch. Joseph Miller was the Earl's gamekeeper, William Bedster his butler, and other leading professionals – Shock White, John Frame, John Wood, for example – were also at one time or another in his employment. Tankerville was the leading sponsor of Surrey matches in the 1770s, but he also sometimes played for or against Hambledon (the nobs were not particular about which side they were on, as long as it made for an even match that was worth betting on). He was not a particularly formidable player, but he naturally received the special treatment appropriate to his rank. When 'England' played Hambledon at the Artillery Ground in 1777, it was reported, 'a tent was erected for Lord Tankerville, in which he dined'. He may have needed the privacy: he had just retired hurt after being hit on the shin. After 1780 he gave up sponsoring Surrey and took a post in government: perhaps he was troubled by the criticisms levelled at him a few years earlier for enjoying 'low and inferior company' on the cricket field.[44]

As in Surrey, cricket in Kent in the 1770s depended heavily on the involvement of upper-class patrons. 'Mr Louch's Club' at Chatham and 'Squire Farrar's Club' in the Isle of Thanet were both important local sides. But there were bigger men than these behind Kent cricket: Sir Horace Mann at Bishopsbourne and the third Duke of Dorset at Knole. Sir Horace's father was a clothier who got a nice contract to supply army uniforms, and was thus able to leave Horace an inheritance of over £100,000, as well as an estate at Linton, near Maidstone. His uncle (and namesake) was Horace Walpole's friend, the British agent at Florence; the wonderful Walpole correspondence gives us a lot of information about the younger Horace's interests and character. Walpole greatly liked Linton, telling his friend in Florence that 'the house is fine and stands like the citadel of Kent; the whole county is its garden'. In 1765, however, when he was twenty-one, Mann moved to Bishopsbourne, laid out a cricket ground and quickly made it *the* centre of cricket in East Kent. The Bourne Club, of which Mann was the moving spirit, and for whom he sometimes played, was soon involved in matches against other Kent teams such as Chatham and Dover, and the Bishopsbourne 'Paddock' became the site of major county games – Surrey played Kent there, for example, in 1773.[45]

Bishopsbourne Paddock had more elaborate accommodation than most cricket grounds of the period. At first spectators had to go to the nearby Bridge Hill House for their refreshments, but by 1767 there were the usual booths on the ground selling food and drink, including one for gentlemen 'in a tent pitched for that purpose, separate from all the other booths'. Until 1780 John Farley held the concession; after that date several publicans from Bridge and Canterbury were allowed to set up booths, though they in turn had to compete with rivals who operated just outside the Paddock. When Hambledon played 'England' there in August 1772 a grandstand was built to accommodate the huge crowd that was expected; a few years later tickets for it cost a shilling. But there was no admission charge for the rest of the ground, and it is clear that most of the spectators (20,000 were said to have been there on the first day of the 1772 match) were ordinary Kentish folk. A poem celebrating Surrey's victory in 1773 describes the Bishopsbourne crowd as follows:

> From Marsh and Weald their hay forks left,
> To Bourne the rustics hied,
> From Romney, Cranbrook, Tenterden,
> And Durent's verdant side.

Pleased as he was by Surrey's win, the author nevertheless deplored the temptation given to labourers to neglect their work, and hoped that such 'idle games / In harvest time may cease'.[46]

Like Tankerville at Mount Felix, Sir Horace collected cricketers. James Aylward was his most famous catch. Aylward never produced the form at Bishopsbourne that he had shown at Broadhalfpenny, but he did well enough for Mann to retain him in spite of his incompetence as a bailiff. By 1786 he was keeping a pub at Bridge, setting up his booth at the Paddock for Kent matches. Another of Mann's players was his huntsman, John Ring. Beldham recalls Ring's coming in to bat in a single-wicket match when Mann's side appeared to be losing. Sir Horace promised him £10 a year for life if they won and he was not out at the end; Ring was out for 57 when only two runs were needed, which Aylward painstakingly obtained. Ring had virtually won the match singlehanded, but Beldham does not tell us whether Mann kept his part of the bargain – the man, after all, had been out. Silver Billy vividly describes Sir Horace walking agitatedly around the boundary during Ring's innings, 'cutting about with his stick, and cheering every run', as if 'his whole fortune . . . was staked on the game'. Perhaps it was, for as Beldham knew, Mann 'always did bet some hundreds'.[47]

Sometimes more than hundreds. Mann's gambling was getting him into trouble as early as 1767, when his uncle worried about his 'thoughtless behaviour' in 'dissipating the fortune which his father had gained with so much industry'. Matters were no better six years later, when reports in the London newspapers convinced his uncle that young Horace was 'ruining himself at cricket'. Even the nephew admitted that his cricket was an 'idle pursuit', but he was unable to stay away from it. Cricket led not only to gambling, but also to extravagant entertaining. Sir Horace was a sociable person, who loved, it was said, to have 'all the world about him'. There was obvious rivalry between Mann and Dorset, expressed both on the cricket field and in the magnificent balls and suppers that accompanied their matches. When Hambledon played at Sevenoaks early in July 1782, the Duke gave a great ball and supper at Knole on the second evening of the match; when Hambledon played 'England' at Bishopsbourne three weeks later Mann responded with an equally elaborate entertainment. There was another expensive party in 1786 during a match between Kent and the White Conduit Club. The ball, a Kentish newspaper reported, attracted 'the most brilliant company that has been assembled in this part of the county for many years': Dorset, the Earls of Winchilsea and Thanet, and virtually all the 'principal families' of East Kent. After a lavish supper, they danced until six in the morning. The paper commended Sir Horace's generous hospitality, which, it said, 'ranks him with the first characters in the kingdom'. No doubt the tribute pleased Sir Horace, but his attempts to keep up with the Duke of Dorset eventually bankrupted him.[48]

It was a mistake to try to compete with a duke in eighteenth-century England. John Frederick Sackville, third Duke of Dorset when his uncle died in 1769, has already loomed large in these pages. He was the son of the Lord John who had been good enough to play in important matches at the Artillery Ground in the 1740s. This cricketing pedigree was strengthened by his education at Westminster School, the greatest stronghold of cricket among the public schools of the period – it will be recalled that he was the organizer of the match against the Old Etonians in 1768 which William Hickey's hangover almost caused the Westminsters to lose. Dorset was fond of other sports – tennis, billiards and fives, for example – but cricket was his passion. A later writer conceded that he was 'a most admirable cricket player', though he could find nothing more to say of him as he was 'not in possession of any brains'.[49]

Dorset may not have been bookish, but he lived stylishly and elegantly, in as well as out of doors. 'The grace of courts', Horace Walpole described him, while Georgiana, the famous Duchess of Devonshire, thought him 'the most dangerous of men', combining good looks with 'a simplicity and persuasion in his manner' that swept countless women off their feet. A succession of mistresses included the Italian dancer Gianetta Baccelli, Nancy Parsons (formerly kept by the Duke of Grafton) and most scandalously, because she, too, was an aristocrat, Elizabeth, Countess of Derby. Her cuckolded husband was so enraged that he got an anonymous author to publish a lampoon attacking the Duke for his frivolity. It made no difference. 'What is human life but a game of cricket? – beauty the bat and man the ball,' Dorset mused. With his help the Countess organized ladies' cricket at the Derbys' great house near Epsom (see Plate 7). Only in 1790, when he was forty-five, did Dorset marry and settle down, an event which also coincided with the virtual end of his patronage of cricket.[50]

Until then the game occupied a great deal of the Duke's time and energy. When he was in France in the 1780s he still came home during the summers to watch and promote it. He was not a bad player himself, a decent bowler and as a batsman something of a hitter. He was certainly better than any of the other noblemen who played at Hambledon. If he was made to look a fool by Lamborn's off-breaks, so were many other good batsmen. He spent lavishly on the game: he was said to have laid out over £1,000 a year on it, quite apart from the money that he lost on gambling and 'consequential entertainment'. The figure is certainly an exaggeration, but even a lesser amount would have been an extravagance, for although he inherited an impressive title and a great house his revenues for a long time were not commensurate with his ambitions. Visiting Knole as a sightseer in 1771, Caroline Powys went through the great rooms, 'with concern that this young Duke cannot refit the furniture of each'. Still, Dorset had recently bought a lot of pictures when he was abroad, adding to what Mrs Powys thought was already 'the finest, and no doubt the largest collection in England'. In 1780 Horace Walpole found the house gloomy, and complained of its 'silence and solitude'. The place may have been so silent because the Duke was away playing cricket at the time; Walpole was shown the pictures by an ill-tempered housekeeper in slippers who wondered why anyone should be interested in 'such old frights as covered the walls'. Dorset actually spent a good deal on renovations at Knole, and collected huge quantities of silver. He also bought paintings from Sir Joshua Reynolds, whose prices were certainly not low, and he was the patron of a lesser-known artist, Ozias Humphrey. The death of a kinsman in 1785 relieved what remained of the Duke's financial worries.[51]

Great men of this type had enough landed capital to be able to borrow huge sums, of course. The Duke's hospitality was legendary in spite of his financial difficulties, and much of it was connected with cricket. The great ball at Knole during the Hambledon match in July 1782 was one of many such extravagances. The Sackville papers are full of payments for large-scale entertainments, many of them cricket-related, others probably for one or other of those brilliant *fêtes-champêtres* that were becoming fashionable among the nobility at this time. 'Fruit and cream at the cricketing', 'fish at the cricketing', 'two large mahogany tea trays for the cricketing company', regular confectioners' bills (ranging in amounts from £71 to £141) for the great balls at Knole – these are all items that appear in the accounts. On 29 August 1769, the year in which the supposedly penurious Dorset succeeded to the dukedom, he spent lavishly on an entertainment at the house. There were musicians, fifty bottles of claret, fifteen of champagne, and other wines for a total of £33.16s.11d., which washed down sixty stone of beef, mutton and veal, plus fish, poultry and confectionery worth over £36. The whole affair cost Dorset just over £137, almost three times the £50 he had given to the poor of Sevenoaks during the previous Christmas season. This last item was not an isolated example of paternalism, for the Duke did make occasional Twelfth Night gifts to the local poor: 1,000lb of beef, the same amount of bread, and fifty cords of wood, for example, during the bad winter of 1772–3. But his spendings at Almack's and White's, at the Tennis Court and the Opera, far exceeded the cost of his philanthropy.[52]

Dorset, like Tankerville and Mann, had an impressive stable of professionals. For several years his head gardener was John Minshull, who earned undying fame when, playing for the Duke's team against Wrotham in 1769, he scored the first century ever recorded. At twenty guineas a year, he conscientiously supervised the garden staff, but unfortunately he was, Nyren tells us, 'as conceited as a wagtail'. The Duke was not one to allow inferiors to get above their stations, and in 1772 Minshull got the sack. Other Knole employees were more careful. William Bowra came from a Sevenoaks family which had for years worked occasionally at the great house. He was by trade a locksmith, but he also kept the clocks running, and got extra pay for looking after the dogs; in 1784 he is described as a gamekeeper. Others who played for the Duke's team, or for Kent (and the two were largely synonymous), included William Pattenden, who was paid £9 a year as a shepherd, and a Sevenoaks draper, Robert Bartram, who regularly supplied the estate with livery cloth.[53]

Why did Dorset, or Tankerville and Mann for that matter, spend so much time and money on cricket? Unlike the Duke of Richmond in the 1740s, Dorset does not seem to have used the game to promote his political influence. As a Sackville he was Lord-Lieutenant of Kent almost by right, and after 1778 was also colonel of the West Kent militia. He had briefly been MP for Kent before inheriting the dukedom, but until 1783, when he became Ambassador to France, that was about the limit of his political ambition. He made little effort to use his cricket to create an image of the virtuous country nobleman. Indeed, his enemies could easily turn his addiction to the game against him. The Earl of Derby's hack writer likened Dorset's (and Tankerville's) behaviour during the American war to Nero fiddling while Rome burned. 'For God's sake,' the anonymous author urged them, 'fling away your bats, kick your mob-companions out of your house, and though you can do your bleeding country no service, cease to accumulate insult or misfortune by making it ridiculous.'[54]

Dorset was a playboy, more interested in gambling than in politics, and with no sense of the responsibilities that many members of the aristocracy were beginning to accept as required by their rank. But cricket and the extravagant entertaining that went with it did proclaim his dominant position in Kent society; his agenda does not seem to have gone much beyond that. There is no doubt that he took the game seriously, both on and off the field. He employed a scorer who wrote down far more details about his matches than the official ones, who still did it by notching their sticks. Among his papers is one headed 'His Grace's First Hands [i.e., Innings] against Wrotham', with another column headed 'His Grace's Second Hands'. This is a record of the team's scores, similar to the batting page of a modern scorebook, run-by-run for each batsman, in the two innings of the match in which Minshull made his famous 107. It is the first such record that we have for any match anywhere, and Dorset obviously hung on to it because of Minshull's historic innings. But he cannot have known beforehand that Minshull was going to make a century, which indicates that his scorer must have routinely kept such records. The scorer made other notations that show how seriously Dorset took the game. We know from the newspapers that Joseph Miller was run out for 2 in England's first innings against Hambledon at Guildford in 1777; Dorset's scorer informs us that it was 'Minshull's fault'. The Duke's aristocratic friends were not spared. When William Bowra was run out for 12 in the second innings it was 'Lord Tankerville's fault'. We also know from the newspapers that both Aylward and Barber were bowled by Lumpy Stevens for ducks in Hambledon's second innings: Dorset's scorer tells us that in each case it was 'first bowl'.[55]

We began this chapter with Reynell Cotton's 'Cricket Song'. After Kent had narrowly beaten Hambledon at Bishopsbourne in 1772 a local enthusiast produced a plagiarized version: the names of Mann and Dorset figured prominently in it. Having rather tersely acknowledged the performances of some of the Kent players, the Kent song continues:

> With heroes like these even Hampshire we'll drub,
> And bring down the pride of the Hambledon Club.
> The Duke, with Sir Horace, are men of true merit,
> And nobly support such brave fellows with spirit.

The next stanza toasts the same two great men. It will be remembered that while Cotton's song also praises 'the patrons of cricket', it does not name individuals, instead giving the credit for Hambledon's victories to the whole Club collectively: 'Here's the Hambledon Club, who refuses the toast!' The Kent song suggests, as does a good deal of other evidence, that cricket in that county depended more heavily on the great individual patrons than it did in Hampshire, where the gentry-run *Club* was the key to its success.[56] At the same time, though, the aristocrats – the Dorsets, the Tankervilles, the Manns – helped to keep the game anchored in its rural base. Although they occasionally sponsored matches at the Artillery Ground, most of their cricket was played either at Broadhalfpenny or on or near their estates: at Sevenoaks Vine, at Laleham Burway, Moulsey Hurst and Bishopsbourne. They were willing to accept the inconveniences of travel between these grounds because these were the places where the best cricket was played, though it naturally helped if there were great mansions and lavish entertainments near by – or, in Hambledon's case, the fashionable resort town of Southampton.

The noblemen spent plenty of time in London, yet they were always happy to get back to their estates. However popular the game had become in the capital, cricket was still a country pastime, an expression of a rural culture which the aristocracy had never completely abandoned. The game fitted comfortably into deep-rooted assumptions about the superior, manly virtue of the countryside, which even the frivolous Dorset had not quite shaken off. In London these were the years of the macaroni – the affected, foppish, Italianate young men who ostentatiously rejected the solid, traditional, English virtues of their parents, and proclaimed their contempt for convention by their defiantly effeminate styles of dress, manners and speech. Dorset might be idle and irresponsible, but even his critics could not accuse him of being a macaroni. Indeed, a newspaper in 1782 complimented him on being one of the few noblemen to unite 'the elegancies of modern luxury with the more manly sports of the old English times'.[57]

Lower down the social scale, provincial prejudices against London were always freely expressed. It was in the capital, declared Canterbury lawyer and cricket-lover John Burnby, that 'vile effeminacy reigns'; there can be no doubt that he was thinking of the macaroni.[58] Even more than the famous victories over 'All England', what made Hambledon cricket so important was its role as a symbol of country virtue. But the rural game at the professional level represented by Hambledon and the other teams we have been describing was always precarious, dependent on the loyalty of the great aristocrats. After the mid-1780s both patricians and plebeians were unable to resist the lure of the capital.

7

The MCC and the Decline
of Hambledon

Towards the end of the 1781 season the Hambledon Club decided to abandon Broadhalfpenny. The great matches would be moved from the windswept hilltop to a field nearer the village, Windmill Down. Some of the Broadhalfpenny turf was transplanted there, and in the following August Hambledon played (and lost) their first match on the new ground. Several reasons for the change have been suggested. John Nyren felt that Windmill was simply a better ground – 'one of the finest places for playing on I ever saw'. Broadhalfpenny was common land with other uses – the village sheep pasture, the site of fairs and other traditional gatherings, all very bad for the outfield. Some of the members may have disliked the raucous, boisterous crowds that gathered there. Windmill, on the other hand, was under the Club's control, rented from Farmer Garrett at ten guineas a year. In 1783 the members consulted Tom Sueter about putting up a permanent clubhouse, and although for a while longer they had to rely on tents for accommodation, eventually one was built. There were, then, good arguments for the move. But there was another and more compelling one: the great men wanted it. The Duke of Dorset and other gentlemen, Nyren tells us, 'complained of the bleakness of the old place'; no doubt they preferred to be close to the more comfortable George Inn instead of the draughty, plebeian Hut.[1]

The move from Broadhalfpenny to Windmill Down was to a better-appointed and more convenient cricket ground, but it was also heavily symbolic. Cricket at Broadhalfpenny had belonged to the community; at Windmill Down it belonged to the Club. Nyren may have thought the new ground a better place for the big matches, but it is significant that it was on Broadhalfpenny that those days of high feasting that he so wonderfully evokes took place. No doubt many of the local population attended games at Windmill Down just as they had done those on the old common, and there is no sign in the Club's accounts that there was any admission charge. Yet it was Broadhalfpenny, not Windmill, that was the public space, heavily fraught with tradition, a space on which the region's communal sports and rituals had for centuries taken place. Something important was undermined when the move was made: the Hambledon team's role as an expression of community identity. And it occurred at the behest of the Duke of Dorset.

The move confirms that by the 1780s the gulf between patricians and plebeians was becoming more pronounced than ever, in cricket as in everything else. It had always existed, of course, but slightly less so in cricket than in other cultural relationships. Like the Duke of Richmond before them, Dorset and his friend Tankerville had wanted to play with and against the best professionals of the day, in the country, on their estates, or at such great public grounds as Broadhalfpenny. The lordly patrons thus ensured that cricket would remain the focus of the kind of intense local loyalties for which Hambledon was famous. The abandonment of Broadhalfpenny Down is the first sign that this was about to change. The local gentry, at least at Hambledon, were still loyal to their neighbourhood, and even the Duke, though he put his own convenience ahead of local custom, wanted to keep the rural game intact. But the next generation of the great aristocratic patrons had other ideas about cricket's future, and began the process of concentrating the professional game in London – a development that drained much of the lifeblood out of the sport in the rural southeast for years to come.

Two very different styles of patronage are represented by the Duke of Dorset and the next in the succession of the great cricketing aristocrats, George Finch, ninth Earl of Winchilsea. It is easy, as we have seen, to dismiss Dorset as a philandering wastrel. He still enjoyed 'associating with the inferior orders of the people' when he was ambassador in Paris; under the ambassadorial roof, a critic complained, 'fiddlers and buffoons, whores and parasites, sharpers and knaves were always welcome'. The Duke spent most of his time at billiards and hazard, 'unless when he relaxed from the fatigues of gaming in the arms of beauty'. One of the beauties, it was said, was the Queen of France; Dorset was rumoured to have had an affair with Marie Antoinette, and to have left her a cricket bat as a memento. His embassy ended in farce when he tried to arrange a cricket match to win over an increasingly anti-British Parisian populace during that chaotic first summer of the French Revolution. Some years earlier Dorset had organized a game in the Champs Elysées, and now in 1789 he wrote to his friend Tankerville asking him to bring over a team. The Earl duly assembled quite a respectable XI from his old Chertsey players – Lumpy Stevens, Bedster, Yalden and others – a bit long in the tooth by now, but still able to give a good enough account of themselves before a crowd of gaping Frenchmen. They got to Dover early in August, but luckily, before they could embark for Calais, they encountered Dorset scurrying ignominiously the other way. The cause was hopeless, he had decided, as the châteaux of the nobility went up in flames.[2]

We may think of Dorset as an irresponsible clown, yet a few things can be said in his favour. He had always been a patron of the rural game, and as long as he was in charge it continued to thrive at Sevenoaks and Hambledon and the other famous country grounds. We can picture him riding down to Hampshire, as we know from his accounts that he did, in the summer of 1780. He left London on 26 July, changed horses first at Kingston and then at Ripley, and spent the night at Godalming; on the next day he rode by way of Liphook and Petersfield to Portsmouth. On 5 August he made the return journey, apparently in a day. Then, after a short spell in London, he set off for another week in Hampshire. The Hambledon Club's records for 1780 are unfortunately imperfect, so we do not know which matches Dorset attended or played in, but cricket must surely have been one of the motives for these Hampshire visits. He had stayed at Southampton during an earlier match at Broadhalfpenny; Portsmouth would have been equally convenient. Later in August the Duke was off to Bishopsbourne, and his accounts record payments for other trips to Sir Horace Mann's ground a year later, for turnpike charges, for laundry, and for 'fruit on the road'.[3]

The Earl of Winchilsea was a more serious person than the Duke of Dorset and was just as devoted to cricket. Yet in the end his influence on the game outside London was far more detrimental than Dorset's had ever been. It was he, more than any of the other patrons, who destroyed Hambledon, and he did so in the interest of aristocratic convenience. Whether in the counties or in the capital the matches he promoted were much more dominated by the nobility than they had been in Dorset's time. His family, the Finches, came originally from Kent, but by the time he succeeded as the ninth Earl in 1769 they had moved their main seat to Burley-on-the-Hill in Rutland. There Winchilsea showed himself to be an autocratic landowner, but one more attentive to his tenants' needs than Dorset. He promoted the granting of small allotments so that otherwise landless labourers could grow their own vegetables, supported local friendly societies and parish work-houses for poor children – a typically paternalist proposal, even if it was a mixed blessing for the children and their families. The agricultural writer, Arthur Young, praised both his benevolence and his 'respectable moral character'. The contrast with the frivolous Dorset also extended to his public life. Winchilsea was a conscientious JP in Rutland, and between 1776 and 1780 he served in the American war, raising his own regiment at a personal cost, it was said, of £20,000.[4]

Like many other great men of his time, Winchilsea was an enthusiastic sportsman. He often won, or lost, up to £200 in an evening at White's or Boodle's; on one splendid night he walked off with £840. He also bet regularly on cricket, though less heavily than on the cards. Many of his cricket papers were later destroyed in a fire, but they survive for the years 1788–99, and show fairly substantial winnings and losses. In 1790 he took eleven guineas off Lord Darnley in several small bets on cricket, and in 1792 he won a total of £218 at various matches (including £73.10s. in one at Burley), while losing only about a third of that amount. Winchilsea was nothing like as good a player as Dorset. In one series of matches against Kent in 1789 he scored only 17 in eight completed innings. He did (let us be fair) make an occasional fifty, once in partnership with the famous Tom Walker. But Winchilsea's clear preference was to play his cricket with other London aristocrats, and his election as president in 1786 proved to be a disaster for the Hambledon Club.[5]

Before we explore in more detail the consequences of Winchilsea's election we need to look at the state of cricket at Hambledon in the 1780s. In the early years of the decade, apart from the replacement of Broadhalfpenny by Windmill Down, outwardly nothing much had changed. The great matches continued at Hambledon, Bishopsbourne and Sevenoaks Vine just as they had done ten years earlier. There were important technical innovations – the straight bat (needed to cope with the greater bounce now achieved by bowlers), the addition of a third stump to the original two – but they did not alter the fundamental character of the game. The greatest innovation in the 1774 edition of the Laws was the creation of a new mode of dismissal, leg before wicket, to discourage batsmen from defending their wicket with their legs, as some were now doing. However, hardly anyone was given out in this way before the end of the century. More obvious were the changes caused simply by the passage of time. The great players of Hambledon's early days inevitably grew old and retired, or became less effective as age dimmed their eyes and slowed their reflexes. Even the perennial John Small was no longer the dominant batsman he had been in the old days, though he was still good enough to score 40 and 24 against 'England' at Bishopsbourne in 1787, at the age of fifty.[6]

As Brett retired and Small and Richard Nyren declined, a new generation of Hambledon players came to the fore. Brett's successor as the most formidable strike bowler in the land was David Harris of Odiham, a potter by trade. A silver watch presented to him after a match on Windmill Down in 1783 can still be seen in the museum at Lord's; it is inscribed to 'David Harris, King of Bowlers'. Harris was a solid, genial man, with strict moral principles that sprang from his nonconformist religious upbringing, John Nyren thought. He took the game very seriously, and his bowling skills were honed on regular practice, summer and winter. He created an indoor pitch in a barn, and he was not the only one to do so: another professional later recalled that 'many a Hampshire barn' resounded 'with bats and balls as well as threshing'. Harris's devotion to the game was famous. He went on playing long after he was crippled by gout, and was allowed to have a chair on the field in which he rested between deliveries.[7]

Several of the new players were from places in Surrey near the Hampshire border, and were given travel expenses by the Club to attend practice sessions. The Walker brothers – Harry and Tom – came of a farming family from near Hindhead, and like Harris used a barn for winter practice. Their bony frames, clumsy hobnailed boots and broad accents proclaimed their deep roots in the Surrey countryside. 'Never,' Nyren says, 'came two such unadulterated rustics into a civilized community.' Tom was the more famous. Known as 'Old Everlasting' because of his tenacious defensive batting – in a single-wicket match he once took over five hours to make 26 – he was completely bereft of style or elegance, but had perfect concentration and determination, whatever the state of the game. George Shepheard's sketch vividly captures his skinny angularity as he stands at the wicket between deliveries (see Plate 9). Walker's manner of speech was both rustic and laconic: 'I doant care what ee zays,' is Nyren's attempt to reproduce it on hearing Tom complaining about an exasperated amateur.[8]

Another group of the new players came from the hop-country around Farnham. Four of them – the Wells and Beldham brothers – were recruited in 1785. They formed something like an extended family, for John Wells married the Beldhams' sister. William Beldham often boasted of the strength of cricket in the Surrey villages. Hambledon could beat 'England', he told James Pycroft, 'but our three parishes around Farnham beat Hambledon'. Beldham was not alone in this opinion, for in 1786 the *Reading Mercury* declared that the Farnham XI had attained 'the greatest perfection in this noble and manly game'. The Farnham players got excellent coaching from a gingerbread baker named Harry Hall: he taught Billy Beldham how to bat, and as John Wells was also a baker he may very well have taught him too. The four Farnham men had to ride twenty-seven miles each way when they played at Hambledon, and they usually did it on the day of the match – they thought about building a cart, but a tax was put on such vehicles so they abandoned the idea.[9]

William Beldham, better known as 'Silver Billy', was born at Wrecclesham, near Farnham, in 1766. He was certainly in the Farnham team by 1782, and in that year he and John Wells also played for Odiham against a Berkshire XI. More than fifty years later he told James Pycroft the story of his rise to fame and fortune. He could recall every detail of that early spring day in 1785 when he first realized that he was destined to be something more than just a village player. He was working in the fields at Farnham when he looked up and saw his employer, Farmer Hilton, walking across the meadow towards him in the company of a well-dressed gentleman. Now, Billy immediately decided, 'this is something about cricket'. In the previous summer, at the age of eighteen, he had batted against Hambledon (he says at Broadhalfpenny, but it must have been Windmill Down) and made 43 against an attack that included the formidable David Harris. He never forgot that innings, savouring it over and over again in his memory. 'No one ever could manage David before,' he told Pycroft. The Earl of Winchilsea, who had already spotted Beldham playing with the other young men at Farnham, saw the match at Hambledon, and the next year made sure that he was given his chance. There was a lengthy discussion – Beldham had to get time off to play – but at last the farmer agreed, and it was settled that in June Billy would go up to London to play for Hampshire (Hambledon, in other words) against 'England' at the new cricket ground in White Conduit Fields. 'For three months,' he told Pycroft, 'I did nothing but think about that match.' It was the first step on the path that was to make 'Silver Billy' the greatest professional batsman of his day.[10]

*

Beldham's destination for that match – White Conduit Fields – reflects the take-over of major cricket by London aristocrats that was well under way by the time his playing days began. Even though the Earl of Winchilsea was interested in Hambledon cricket he did not become a member of the Club until September 1786, when he was elected president; by this time he also had property near Moulsey Hurst and was sponsoring Surrey matches. Winchilsea may have been president of Hambledon, but he was also a member of the White Conduit Club, and it soon became clear that this was where his real loyalties lay. The White Conduit was an offshoot of a famous aristocratic club which had for many years met at the Star and Garter in Pall Mall. This is where the Jockey Club – the body which controlled horseracing – had been founded in the early 1750s, and it was the Star and Garter Club which had issued both the 1744 Laws of Cricket and the 1774 revisions. In 1778 members of this club – 'the noblemen and gentlemen of the Grand Cricket Club', as a newspaper described them – were collecting money to reward players for distinguished performances in important matches. By that time, and possibly much earlier, some of them were regularly playing cricket together. They found a convenient ground at White Conduit House in Islington, where one of the many small London pleasure gardens had an adjoining cricket field. In 1766 its owner, Robert Bartholemew, was advertising 'bats and balls for cricket and a convenient field to play in'. White Conduit Fields now became the venue for big matches in London (it will be remembered that after 1777 no more were staged at the Artillery Ground), and the Club also began to play away matches – against Kent at Sevenoaks in 1785, for example. Three years later the Star and Garter/White Conduit Club became the Marylebone Cricket Club, the famous MCC, the club which claimed supreme authority over cricket for almost two centuries.[11]

Cricket historians have often noted the dearth of major matches involving Hambledon at about this time. In 1777 the Club had played at least seven first-class matches. There was a temporary decline in the next few years, presumably reflecting the impact of the American war, but then in 1782 the number rose again to six, and it was only in 1784, when a mere couple of major Hambledon matches are recorded, that the decline becomes obvious. This does not mean that the Club had become moribund, for the members still turned up at the Tuesday practices to play cricket or drink, and there were occasional games against local sides. In 1782, for example, Hambledon played a combined

Alresford–Odiham team, and 'Hambledon Parish' played Petworth two years later. In 1785 there were several matches against Farnham, and it will be recalled that it was in that year that the Beldhams and the Wells brothers were recruited. But although the Club survived, and village matches were still common throughout Hampshire and the southeastern counties, there is no escaping the conclusion that something was happening to rural cricket. What was happening, of course, was that the great patrons such as Winchilsea were transferring the focus of their activities to London.[12]

The White Conduit Club's teams were originally drawn almost entirely from the gentry and aristocracy: Winchilsea and Col. Charles Lennox (nephew of the third Duke of Richmond) and their friends. But around 1786 the Club began raiding Hambledon, strengthening its team by including many of the Hampshire and Surrey professionals. In June of that year they (or the Star and Garter Club, which was virtually identical) played a match against a combined Kent and Surrey team in White Conduit Fields. As usual, among the White Conduit players we find the names of Winchilsea, Lennox and suchlike notables. But we also find several of the plebeian Hambledon men – the elder Small, Noah Mann, Tom Walker and others. Later that summer White Conduit played Kent at Bishopsbourne in a match that attracted one of those glittering assemblies of the great and the fashionable that Sir Horace Mann so loved to entertain. Once again the White Conduit team included six of the Hambledon stars: Tom Walker and Tom Taylor both made centuries (Walker made 95 not out in his other innings), ensuring that Kent were heavily beaten. The Earl of Winchilsea, candour requires us to record, contributed only 8 runs to the victory in his two innings. In the same season Winchilsea also played twice for Hambledon, scoring 6 and 5 on the first occasion, 6 and 0 on the second. A year later he did somewhat better (12 and 20) in a match at Bishopsbourne, but his role in Hambledon cricket, important as it was, owed little to his batting skills.[13]

Between 1787 and 1789 Hambledon contrived to play about four matches each season as a separate entity. But increasingly their players were being lured away to play for other teams. For London triumphalists these years are among the most glorious in the history of the game, as they witnessed the establishment of the MCC and the opening of the first Lord's ground. Some of the White Conduit aristocrats were uncomfortable with the public situation of the club's ground at Islington, and preferred to play in more private surroundings. So in 1787 Winchilsea and Lennox provided financial backing for one of the club's professionals, Thomas Lord, to lay out a ground near what became Dorset Square. It was the first of three locations for Lord's Ground: only in 1814 did he move to the present site off St John's Wood Road. Like George Smith at the Artillery Ground, Lord did well out of selling refreshments at the tavern adjacent to the cricket field, and the cricketing contacts he made were also helpful in promoting his subsequent wine business.[14]

The MCC and Lord's: we are in the new age of cricket, dominated from London as the game had never previously been, even in the heyday of the Artillery Ground in the 1740s. The first match at Lord's, between Middlesex and Essex, took place on 31 May and 1 June 1787, and a few weeks later an 'England' XI comprehensively defeated the White Conduit Club there by 239 runs. In what was to become common practice, the Hambledon players were divided between the two teams: Beldham played for 'England', Harris and the two Walker brothers for the Club. This shuffling of players between teams went far beyond the old custom of adding one or two 'given men' to equalize the two sides, and it affected matches in rural as well as London settings. On 17 July 1787 the Hambledon Club's minutes read: 'No meeting. A match at A. Smith's Esq. No gentlemen on [Windmill] Down'. The match in question was played over thirty miles away at the other end of the county, between XIs raised by the Earl of Winchilsea and Thomas Assheton Smith of Tidworth. Six Hambledon men played for Winchilsea, six for Smith: old John Small and his son played against each other. In another striking example of the shuffling of players to suit the patrons' convenience, a match between Hambledon and an 'England' XIII at Lord's in 1789 was interrupted so that sixteen of the players could go to Coxheath to play in an East Kent vs. West Kent game.[15]

The pattern is clear. By the 1790s, Beldham told James Pycroft, 'the play was nearly all professional'. He meant, of course, the serious play; even some of the gentry, he thought, 'made a profession of it' by betting on their own or others' performances. Lord Frederick Beauclerk, the best amateur batsman of the day, said that he made roughly six hundred guineas a year out of the game. The MCC, of course, existed for the benefit of the amateurs, and their teams often contained only two or three professionals, but these were usually the key players. When the Club beat Kent at Lord's in 1791, for example, the side included Winchilsea, Beauclerk, Assheton Smith and other men of quality; Beldham and William Fennex were the only professionals, but they were also the only MCC players to score over 50. In the same summer Beldham and another Hambledon player, Richard Purchase, were the only two professionals in an MCC side that was beaten by Middlesex. Hambledon tried in vain to stop its players being drained away to London. On 30 September 1788 the Club ordered 'that the players who are paid for practising on Windmill Down are hereby forbidden to engage themselves to play in any county or other great matches' except with the stewards' permission. This might perhaps have been effective had they not provided an exception for teams raised by the Duke of Dorset, Sir Horace Mann, or any other Club member – by Winchilsea, in other words.[16]

As the 1790s wore on the dominance of the new MCC establishment grew ever stronger. Teams raised by Winchilsea, the Earl of Darnley, Assheton Smith and other great men provided the gentry with their fun and the professionals with their money. Most of the major matches were played at Lord's, but there were still some in the country at such traditional sites as Sevenoaks Vine, or at Winchilsea's Burley Park. Assheton Smith put out a team on Perriam Downs against Sir Horace Mann in 1790, and there were occasional matches on Windmill Down, where Winchilsea's XI played the Earl of Darnley's in that same year. The power of the MCC over rural cricket was made dramatically clear in July 1791, when there was a dispute over a catch during a game at Windmill between Hampshire and 'England'. The umpire was hopelessly bemused. 'I really think the ball hit the ground, but I cannot be positive,' he told the Hambledon committee. The dispute was promptly decided by the MCC members present. They included Charles Powlett and one of the Bonhams, but more importantly Winchilsea, Lennox and Assheton Smith. In the few games that they played under Club auspices in 1791 the Hambledon players were more smartly turned out than ever: they wore 'sky-blue coats with black velvet collars, and the letters CC (Cricketing Club) engraved on their buttons'. All very pretty, but the days when Richard Nyren, Small, and Brett could legislate the width of the bat, as they did after the Shock White affair, were long gone.[17]

So too were the days when Hambledon could inspire the passionate local loyalty of which John Nyren later spoke so eloquently. Teams described as 'Hampshire' played occasional matches and usually included some of the Hambledon stars, though when they played Surrey the Beldham, Walker and Wells brothers were likely to be playing for the latter county – of which they were, of course, natives. As always, the teams in these matches are often given different names in different sources: Hambledon players might be playing for sides variously described as Winchilsea's XI, Hampshire or 'England'. When 'Hampshire' played the Brighton Club at Windmill Down in 1792 the team was headed by Winchilsea and included three other gentlemen, only one of whom (Edward Hale) had Hambledon, or even identifiably Hampshire, connections. Four of the ordinary players were from Hambledon, but of these only Richard Veck had been a member of the team during its days of greatness. Although games continued sporadically at Windmill Down, and the weekly Club meetings were still held there, increasing numbers of the big matches in Hampshire were now played at Stoke Down, ten miles or so to the north. When Hampshire met MCC there in 1797, several of the familiar Hambledon men were in the team: the two John Smalls among them. But there is no sign that the local inhabitants responded with anything like their old enthusiasm. And by the end of the century Hampshire teams were looking less and less like Hambledon ones.[18]

What we have been describing might from one point of view be regarded as the decline of Hambledon, or even of rural cricket more generally. From another point of view, however, it might be described as a further stage in the growth of the professional game. If men such as Billy Beldham and the Walkers were going to make a living out of cricket, they had to be detached from the villages in which they had grown up and had begun their careers. Farnham, says Beldham's chronicler, James Pycroft, 'found London the best market for its cricket, as for its hops': Beldham himself is an obvious example. So is John Small the younger, of Petersfield. He was a decent player, though nothing like the batsman his father had been, yet by the mid-1790s he had become something like a full-time summer professional. In 1794, for example, he was playing on at least thirty-two days – and probably more, for the records we have are obviously incomplete – between 9 June and 19 September, for teams described as 'England', E. Morant's XI, R. Leigh's XI, David Harris's XI, Hampshire, and Kent and Hampshire combined. These matches took place at Lord's, Dartford Brent, Stoke Down, and Oldfield in Berkshire. Small played only rarely, if at all, on Windmill Down that year.[19]

Not that Beldham, Small and their like were particularly well paid: in comparison with the vast wealth of their aristocratic employers they were not. Beldham could remember getting five guineas for a win, three for a defeat, in the 1780s; twenty years later this had increased to six guineas for a win and four for a defeat. Still, even though the players would have had to pay their own expenses out of it, this was good money compared with what other young men of their social class were making. Five guineas for three days' work in the 1780s was five times what a London artisan, and more than twenty times what an agricultural labourer, would have earned in the same time. Good money, indeed – but still a pittance in the scale of the winnings the gentry and aristocracy could make from their wagers. By 1800 the London game was being seriously corrupted by professional gamblers. There had been plenty of betting in the old Hambledon matches, yet we rarely hear allegations of bribery and corruption in those days. This does not mean that it never happened, but the earlier absence of complaints about declining moral standards compared with their frequency after 1800 must surely have some significance.[20]

The bookies soon found out how to reach the players. When they were in London the cricketers usually congregated at a pub in Oxford Street called The Green Man and Still. Naïve newcomers were easy to spot. 'There was no mistaking the Kent boys,' Beldham recalled, 'when they came staring in to the Green Man. A few of us had grown used to London, but Kent and Hampshire men had but to speak, or even show themselves, and you need not ask them which side they were on.' Accustomed to their modest ten shillings or so a week on the farm, they were easy prey for the bookies, even with their match pay of five or six guineas. Beldham could remember it all as if it were yesterday. Quietly drinking in the Green Man, the innocent player would be approached by a 'sharp gentleman' who would buy him a drink and play on his resentments against the great men who promoted the matches. The knowledge that Beauclerk made far more from his cricket than the ordinary professional inevitably aroused suspicions that he, and other aristocrats, sometimes 'sold' matches to protect their wagers. Beldham professed not to believe this, and recounted an experience which he felt proved his case. Travelling down to Kent with an unnamed nobleman (Beauclerk, perhaps?), Beldham was intrigued by his companion's confession that he would lose £100 if their side won the match. 'Well, my Lord,' Silver Billy replied (trying him out, he says), 'you and I could order that.' The peer did not reply, and when the game reached a critical stage he and Beldham were batting together. But instead of intentionally losing, they got their heads down and won the match, even though every run was 'a guinea out of his Lordship's pocket'.[21]

'Matches were bought, and matches were sold,' Beldham told Pycroft, but he blamed a minority of the players, not the patrons, for the corruption: 'not a few of the great players earned money to their own disgrace'. Silver Billy naturally claimed that he himself was almost completely blameless, admitting only to helping sell a match at Nottingham – but only to recoup the £10 he had been cheated out of by the same players in a previous match. He resolutely refused, he tells us, the many offers of much bigger money that he received. 'You may make a fortune if you will listen to me,' the bookie Joe Bland once told him, 'so much for the match with Surrey, and so much more for the Kent match.' Beldham would have none of it. But the old man's memories, vividly captured for us by Pycroft, are full of stories of the corruption that was almost unavoidable when poor men were exposed to the temptation of money so easily earned. In a match on Penenden Heath in Kent in 1807, Beldham and Lord Frederick were breezing along in a partnership of 61, needing only another 30 to win. Then they got out, and 'six of the best men in England' were out for a mere eleven runs. It might have been entirely innocent – inexplicable collapses are part of cricket's charm – but Silver Billy's suspicions were confirmed ten years later, when one of the culprits admitted that the rest of the team had been bribed. Corruption affected matches of all kinds, but it was most likely to occur in single-wicket contests when there were only three or four men on each team. In one such game at Lord's a player on each side had been bought, and eventually one of them had to bowl at the other. 'For seven balls together,' Beldham recalled, 'one would not bowl straight, and the other would not hit,' while the other players, who could see what was going on, could scarcely suppress their laughter.[22]

So there was a darker side to cricket that we should always remember when we read about the glories of the MCC's ascendancy. Young Beldham's journey from Farnham to London was also the first step on a path that led inexorably downwards from rural innocence into the maelstrom of gambling and corruption that was soon to engulf cricket. The bookies congregated for the big matches at Lord's as eagerly as they did for the racing at Epsom or Ascot. Pycroft lists some of them for us: 'Jim and Joe Bland, of turf notoriety, Dick Whitlom of Covent Garden, Simpson, a gaming-house keeper' and others. The corruption was not confined to cricket: in prize-fighting things got so bad by the early 1820s that the sport was virtually ruined. Eventually, of course, it all came out. Beldham told of a quarrel between two professionals at Lord's in which each loudly accused the other of taking bribes to lose matches, and in 1817 William Lambert – next to Beldham the best batsman of the day – was banned from ever playing again at Lord's. Eventually, at some time in the 1820s, the MCC recognized that the corruption was killing the game – as well as costing 'gentlemen who meant honestly', as Beldham describes them, large sums of money. The bookmakers were expelled from Lord's, and only in the later twentieth century, another age devoted to the worship of mammon, were they allowed to return.[23]

Needless to say, this did not mean the end of betting on cricket. The great Kent player Fuller Pilch recalled a single-wicket contest in 1838 between Alfred Mynn and a Yorkshireman named Dearman, in which 'a deal of money' was lost: Frederick Gale, who was also there, says that the actual stake was only £100, but obviously much more money than this would have been wagered by the bystanders. The betting, Pilch insisted, was always on a much smaller scale than at racecourses, although 'the farmers did like their sovereign or five pounds on Kent'. Pilch would wager a sovereign at the start of his innings, in return for being paid a shilling a run: 'and a good thing I made of it sometimes'. No one minded the small stakes put up at most single-wicket contests – for five shillings a man, or a boiled leg of mutton – and they undoubtedly continued. But the matches for larger sums were virtually over. When a bookmaker tried to revive them in the 1860s there was so much opposition in the sporting press that it came to nothing.[24]

It is easy to blame great noblemen such as Winchilsea for the withering of rural cricket in the southeast. There is no doubt that members of the aristocracy and the wealthier gentry class increasingly preferred the polite pleasures of London and Bath to the old world of rural sociability and hospitality, and that this process helped to separate them from the traditional country pastimes. But there were other reasons for cricket's decline. Earlier in the eighteenth century even quite humble labourers could find the leisure to watch or play cricket and other rural sports. There is no single date at which this began to change, but in the course of the century a combination of circumstances transformed the face of the English countryside and the lives of its inhabitants. Few historians now subscribe to the picture of doom and gloom which used to characterize the agrarian history of the period: the story of deprivation and pauperization that was supposed to have followed the vast enclosures of open fields and common lands during the century after 1750. Yet there is no doubt that a massive transformation was under way in these years, from a rural economy defined in terms of custom and subsistence to one defined by market relations and written law. In any such transformation there are bound to be losers as well as winners. The losers were, inevitably, the poorest and most vulnerable members of the rural population.[25]

Everyone knows Oliver Goldsmith's lament for the passing of the old order in 'The Deserted Village'. Sentimentalized they may have been, yet Goldsmith's lines still capture something of the flavour of the age that was passing – or indeed in many places had already passed. We should remember that the conditions which had produced the relative prosperity of the earlier years of the century – a stable population and high agricultural productivity leading to low food prices – did not disappear overnight when demographic pressure returned after 1750. But by the time Goldsmith wrote 'The Deserted Village' in 1770, what he described in the poem was already recognizable. The poet's memories of a community 'where health and plenty cheered the labouring swain' led him to a celebration of the village sports, which must surely have included cricket:

> How often have I blessed the coming day,
> When toil remitting lent its turn to play,
> And all the village train, from labour free,
> Led up their sports beneath the spreading tree,
> While many a pastime circled in the shade,
> The young contending as the old surveyed.

But Goldsmith was commemorating something more than a village society destroyed by avaricious enclosure, by individual ruthlessness and greed. He was celebrating a lost way of life, one in which community and cooperation had been more important than profit and market relations. Like William Cobbett and John Nyren fifty years later, Goldsmith saw the pernicious consequences of a system in which 'one only master grasps the whole domain', while the rest of the population were demoted to the status of landless labourers or driven into cities or the colonies. Who can forget his eloquent repudiation of the new market economy?

Ill fares the land, to hastening ills a prey,
Where wealth accumulates, and men decay;
Princes and lords may flourish, or may fade;
A breath can make them, as a breath has made;
But a bold peasantry, their country's pride,
When once destroyed, can never be supplied.

Goldsmith's pessimism is of course greatly exaggerated and over-drawn. Among other things, the years after 1770 were the very ones in which rural cricket reached its zenith at Hambledon, and in which those great throngs which Nyren described flocked to Broadhalfpenny. George Crabbe answered Goldsmith with a more realistic (and angry) picture of the typical village of his time, asking what had happened to the lads

who, daily labour done,
With rural games played down the setting sun;
Who struck with matchless force the bounding ball,
Or made the ponderous quoit obliquely fall?

They were, it seems, drinking themselves insensible, or had turned to smuggling for a living.[26]

Yet Goldsmith was not the only writer to be aware of the changing rural scene. The growth of population was inexorably driving food prices up and keeping wages down: in 1772 the newspapers were full of complaints of 'the exorbitant price of provisions'. Some, like Goldsmith, put the blame on enclosing and engrossing (the practice of combining several small farms into one), which had led to the destruction of many independent farmers. A traveller visiting Swaffham in Norfolk around 1770 found 'the houses tumbling into ruins, and the common fields all enclosed'. A merchant from King's Lynn, he was told, had bought up about twenty farms in the region and converted them into seven larger ones. The economy of scale certainly made for efficiency and greater profit in the market place; but it also threw many small farmers off their land, adding to the swelling ranks of the landless. While some of these joined the age-old migration into London, or the newer one into the industrial towns of the Midlands and the North, the majority did not, and the expanding pool of surplus labour inevitably fed the cycle of declining wages and pauperization. A letter to the *Hampshire Chronicle* in 1772, ostensibly from a labourer and written in a bogus local dialect, complained that at six shillings a week wages were insufficient to feed a family, even when the parish paid the rent. As late as the 1780s, Gilbert White was still optimistic about the condition of the poor at Selborne. There were plenty of them, he admitted, but many lived 'comfortably in good stone or brick cottages, which are glazed, and have chambers above stairs'; the villagers, he claimed, enjoyed 'a good share of health and longevity'. But whatever was happening at Selborne, this happy scene was vanishing in many other places.[27]

In these depressing circumstances, great men such as Winchilsea and even Dorset tried to fulfil their charitable obligations. In 1789 the Knole accounts record the distribution of over 300 loaves of bread to the poor of Sevenoaks and a couple of neighbouring villages, and there were probably similar handouts in the following decade. But the 1789 bounty was spread out between Midsummer and Christmas, so it is unlikely to have done much to relieve the widespread suffering. The war with France, and the consequent high taxes, made it harder for the gentry to dip into their pockets to alleviate the situation. Clarke Jervoise, the victor of the famous 1779 election, ran up ten years' arrears in his annual subscription to the Hampshire Club – the political club – before submitting his resignation early in 1796. A few months earlier, at the annual meeting of the Hambledon Cricket Club at the George Inn, it was agreed that 'on account of the high price of provisions' the sum paid to Richard Nyren for the dinners should be doubled, to two shillings.[28]

Continuing population growth and a run of terrible harvests in the mid-1790s drove grain prices ever upwards. Food riots at Newhaven in Sussex in early 1795 were brutally suppressed, and soldiers who had joined the rioters were executed. Paul Langford speaks of this as a 'disastrous year', one of the worst in a terrible decade. Things had not improved by 1800. In January of that year Elizabeth Chute, the wife of a Hampshire MP, was fearing the worst: 'The poor man cannot purchase those comforts he ought to have: beer, bacon, cheese. Can one wonder that discontents lurk in their bosoms?' In Sussex later in the year a letter to the Hambledon member, Henry Shelley, blamed the high prices on corn factors from Kent, who were taking over 100 cartloads a week out of the county from Lewes market alone. Using the old language of the 'moral economy', the writer called them 'engrossers . . . monopolizers', men 'growing rich on the misfortunes of the times'. Local opinion held that for every sack of grain consumed locally, eighteen or twenty were sent out of Sussex, although 'the fear of insurrection or popular odium', it was said, prevented much exporting by sea.[29]

It is not surprising in these circumstances that there was a noticeable decline in the amount of rural cricket. Until the later 1780s the game was holding up reasonably well. Pubs were still organizing matches: in 1784 an Oxfordshire landlord sponsored one, with a dozen pairs of gloves for the winners. Three years later there was a game near Bagshot between two teams of craftsmen: the 'woollen aprons' against the 'leather aprons'. The Baptist John Burgess watched several matches at Ditchling in Sussex during the summer of 1788, and in the same year he went to Brighton to see the celebrations in honour of the Duke of York's birthday. Among the 'many diversions' that he observed were 'cricketing, stoolball, football, dancing, fireworks, etc.'.[30] But when the war with France broke out in 1793 the local gentry who might have sponsored matches were less able to afford to do so as taxes (and the poor rate) rose, and in any case many of them were busy with the militia or other war-related activities. Many of the lesser folk were too preoccupied with keeping body and soul together to have much time for cricket.

A few of the more determined patrons did still manage to promote the local game: in 1792, for example, young Lord Barrymore played for a combined Wargrave and Twyford side against Wokingham, and in the following year Thomas Assheton Smith raised an Andover XI to play against Newbury. Cricket continued in some of the larger Hampshire towns such as Portsmouth, Southampton and Winchester, who in 1800 played home and away matches against the much smaller Micheldever. There was also still a fair amount of local cricket in Kent and Sussex: at Hawkhurst and Steyning, for example. In 1794 visitors to the house of William Frankland at Findon left five shillings to be split among the workmen. They all got their share, the steward recorded, 'except Dick and Thorp, who were at cricket'. In Kent, the Bridge Hill Club survived, and there were still a few great matches at Bishopsbourne as long as Sir Horace was there. In 1794 the Gentlemen of East Kent played the Isle of Thanet at Mann's other ground, Dandelion Paddock near Margate. And there were many lesser games, such as the one at Tenterden in 1790 when the local team played a combined team from Brenchley and several other parishes, for five shillings a man. There were matches at Dover throughout the war, including one in 1807 against the officers of the Surrey Militia.[31]

Everywhere the decencies of rank and class were more strictly observed than ever. When Ipswich played Needham and Stowmarket in 1792 two marquees were provided for refreshments: one for ladies and gentlemen, the other 'for the spectators in general'. Some thought it improper for local teams to rejoice too openly after beating more aristocratic sides. Bray, near Maidenhead, had been a great centre of cricket ever since Waymark's time. Once in the 1790s they beat a visiting MCC XI and had the church bells rung to celebrate the victory. This so enraged the MCC gentlemen that they refused to stay for the elaborate dinner that was to have followed the game. Local patriotism was all very well, but it had to be appropriately expressed. We may recall Beldham's comment on the 'pride and honour in the parishes' from which the professionals came, as local people followed their performances in London.[32]

But when all is said, rural cricket was certainly declining after about 1785. Pycroft encountered two old players – one from Kent, one from Essex – who recollected that when they were schoolboys in that decade cricket was 'more of a village game' than it became later. 'There was a cricket bat behind the door, or else up in the bacon rack, in every cottage,' and the game was played 'in every school and village green'. Some village grounds were abandoned, including one very famous one. This was at Farnham, where Beldham and the Wells brothers had learned their cricket. Farnham Castle belonged to the Bishop of Winchester, and for many years easy-going bishops had tolerated the use of the park by the local inhabitants. But in 1781 an improving bishop arrived, by name Brownlow North, half-brother of Lord North the Prime Minister. A visitor to Farnham describes what happened:

A cricket ground had so long been suffered [in the park] that the people conceived that they now had a right to it . . . Such a scene of riot and disorder, with stands for selling liquor, just under the castle windows . . . The bishop took the gentlest methods he could to remove the nuisance; and at last, though not without some difficulty, got it effected.

It was a classic confrontation between an autocratic landlord (in this case a bishop) and a local community which mistakenly believed it had use-rights over a piece of land long devoted to recreation – a collision between the old world and the new.[33]

*

Hambledon were never turfed out of Windmill Down, but there is no mistaking the malaise that beset the Club as the 1790s wore on. There was a steady decline in membership, with those resigning regularly exceeding new recruits. In 1791 fifty-two members are listed in the accounts, but almost a dozen – including Beldham's patron, Lord Stawell – resigned during the year, and another dozen failed to pay their subscriptions (though some of them did so later). Only two new members were elected. By 1795 attendance at the weekly meetings at Windmill Down was so poor that it was decided to hold them every fortnight instead. By then the nominal membership had fallen to forty-three, but only sixteen of these are noted as having paid their subscriptions. The impact of the war in these years is evident in the occasional laconic observation in the accounts, 'gone to sea'.[34]

Yet somehow the Club managed to limp along. The professionals were paid, as they had always been, for the weekly scratch games. Some of the gentlemen also took part in these, others came to watch, and no doubt they all drank a lot of wine and gambled. That the consumption of wine still played a large part in the proceedings is clear from the Club's accounts, which record that in 1793 they paid Gauntlett's of Winchester £36.19s.6d. for wine. Given the Club's reputation for drinking it is surprising that there often seems to have been a surplus, and this must reflect the poor attendance at meetings; Richard Nyren regularly bought bottles of both port and sherry from the Club. They employed a local man named Peter Husted as their waiter, and he also helped out with rolling Windmill Down. Nyren still provided teas and dinners for the ladies at big matches on the Down – at a cost of £7.17s. for the match between the Earl of Winchilsea's and Leigh's XIs in 1795. As in happier days, Nyren had carefully advertised this match in the local newspapers. Besides the Club-sponsored cold dinner for the ladies, 'all sorts of liquors and cold provisions' would be sold at his booth. And he appealed to his old customers: 'the finest players in England' would be taking part in the match, so, he concluded pathetically, 'his old friends, he trusts, will not forsake him'.[35]

But although the sociable aspect of the meetings was as important as ever, Hambledon was still a cricket club. Payments to the players totalled almost £50 a year in the early 1790s, but fell to £33.5s. in 1796, when there were only eight meetings, compared with the sixteen that had been held in the earlier years of weekly practices. For matches against attractive opposition there sometimes were extra charges: in 1791 a tent had to be hired at a cost of 12s.6d. Money was also regularly spent on advertising matches and printing notices about future meetings. Windmill Down was carefully tended. To supplement Peter Husted's efforts, in 1792 a team of horses was hired to roll the Down, and two bushels of grass seed were sown. Bats and balls were bought from the elder John Small, at a total cost of £3.7s. in 1793, for example. Tom Sueter kept the clubhouse in good repair, and two local men, Charles and Thomas Clay – both of whom played for Hambledon for many years – were paid for bricklaying and whitewashing. Husted also picked up a bit of money for doing odd jobs such as cleaning the chimney and shooting the birds which nested in the roof.[36]

The weekly practices may have continued, but the big games in Hampshire were now played at Stoke Down rather than at Hambledon. In the 1790s Windmill Down was mainly used for local matches, though a few 'Hampshire' matches, in which Hambledon players were prominent in the county side, still took place there. A Hambledon parish team was narrowly beaten on the Down in 1791 by West Sussex, who were strengthened (if that is the right word) by the inclusion of the Earl of Winchilsea. Sueter and the younger Small played for Hambledon, but the rest of the team was made up of lesser local men: Edward Hale, one of the Clays, John Goldsmith, two Fosters, a couple of the numerous Stewart clan. In 1792 a team described as 'Hampshire (so called)' – the qualification presumably being made necessary by the inclusion of Winchilsea, the Hon. Edward Bligh (the Earl of Darnley's brother), and other players with no known Hampshire qualification – beat the Brighton Club at Windmill, just after the conclusion of a Hampshire–Surrey match on the Down. A year later it was announced that a game between Hambledon and XXII of Hertfordshire and Essex would be played on Broadhalfpenny. This may have been an error for Windmill Down, though it is worth noting that in 1791 a traveller in Hampshire reported having 'crossed the famous cricket ground called Broadhalfpenny', observing that 'the inhabitants of this town have long been famous cricketers, and a club here is not afraid to challenge all England'. He used the present tense, but it may be that he was not told about Hambledon's recent decline. If so, it suggests that the local people with whom he spoke retained their pride in the team's past achievements, while still associating them with 'their' own common. But by the end of the century the old ground had reverted to its accustomed role of sheep pasture. 'There is a good flock of South Down sheep kept here,' another visitor to Hambledon noted, 'and fed on Broadhalfpenny Down.'[37]

From 1794 onwards only Henry Bonham and two members who lived in Hambledon – John Richards and Henry Coles – attended Club meetings with any regularity. Members understandably stayed away when the weather was bad, but on 30 June Nyren recorded that it was 'a fine day but no gentlemen'. Charles Powlett was still one of the stewards, but rarely seems to have attended meetings. He put his name to the announcement of the annual meeting at the George in October 1795, but did not attend it; Bonham, Richards and Coles were the only ones who did. Attendance picked up a bit in 1796, with several meetings attracting five or six members and sometimes a fair number of guests. But the old enthusiasm was gone.[38]

The last weekly meeting of the Hambledon Club in 1796 is the most mysterious one in the entire history of the organization. In the clubhouse one late August day sat the faithful trio of Henry Bonham, Coles and Richards, along with a full dozen of non-members – far more guests than had attended for many years. Outside on the Down the familiar, comforting rituals of a cricket match were being performed: a combined XI from Hambledon, Petersfield and East Meon was playing, and beating, Portsmouth. At least two members of the home team would have been immediately recognizable: the two John Smalls, father and son. The twelve guests being entertained in the clubhouse included Edward Hale of Hambledon, who had allowed his membership to lapse a few years earlier but still turned up occasionally, and a number of others who cannot be confidently identified – the usual mixture of parsons, army officers and local gentlemen that would have graced many a Hambledon match in the old days. But among these otherwise obscure guests, the minute book lists one far more famous name: 'Mr Thomas Paine, author of The Rights of Man'.[39]

If the entry is accurate – and it might, after all, have been some huge, to us unfathomable, joke – there is real puzzle here. The great radical was living in France at this time, taking refuge from an almost certain sentence of death in England for high treason. The previous year, 1795, had been the high-water mark of revolutionary Jacobinism in Britain. To be sure, not all of the discontent was inspired by popular sympathy for the French Revolution. With the price of bread reaching unprecedented heights there were widespread food riots, some of them – as we have seen happened at Newhaven – receiving the open encouragement of the soldiers who were supposed to be suppressing them. At Speenhamland near Newbury the Berkshire magistrates desperately adopted a policy of subsidizing agricultural wages out of the poor rate, inaugurating a system that was to contribute to the growing pauperization of English rural labourers during the next thirty-five years. But besides the economic distress there was also serious political unrest. The London Corresponding Society's demands for democratic reform (automatically assumed by the authorities to be French-inspired) provoked the government into a series of repressive measures which in the end cowed or imprisoned the radical leaders.[40]

Hampshire was relatively quiet in 1796, although even in that political backwater three men were charged with sedition and subsequently convicted at Winchester Assizes. The authorities were obsessed with the danger of French-inspired subversion, yet here, apparently, is the foremost radical of them all, Tom Paine, who had himself been a member of the French National Assembly, sticking his head into the noose by secretly returning to England. And this too not far from Winchester, where he had been burnt in effigy only a few years earlier. The crowd on that occasion had been whipped up by members of John Reeves's Tory Association for the Preservation of Liberty and Property, with the help of the Corporation, so we should not necessarily regard it as a genuine expression of local opinion. Indeed, after the mob had been plied with liquor, it was reported, 'some few did cry out Tom Paine for ever – Tom Paine for ever'. But again, this does not mean that the great republican was popular throughout the Hampshire countryside, especially among the gentry.[41]

Paine's recent biographer notes that he spent most of the summer of 1796 recuperating from illness at the home of the American consul, Fulmer Skipwith, at Versailles. On 13 August he wrote to a French official asking for safe passage for a friend, the banker Sir Robert Smyth, but there then follows a period of a few weeks in which there is no record of his movements. So it is theoretically possible that Paine might have been at Windmill Down on 29 August. Hambledon was not far from the south coast, and it would not have been too difficult for him to slip across the Channel on a dark night. But why? Why should so prominent a fugitive have been willing to risk his neck in this way? And why should anyone have wanted to bring him to Hambledon?[42]

We can surely dismiss the thought that Paine came just to watch the cricket. He would have been familiar with the game from his days as an exciseman at Lewes more than twenty years earlier, and he was certainly no stranger to mixing sport with politics. As a member of the Bowling Green Society at Lewes he would often join the other members in animated political discussion – and of radical politics at that – after their games had finished. But there is no evidence that he had any real interest in cricket, and even if he had, the local match that was going on on that late summer day was not of sufficient importance to attract spectators from afar. It has been suggested that the Hambledon Club had by this time become a seditious organization, a cover for anti-government plotting. Now it is true that before the war both Richards and the Bonhams had been prominent in the opposition to Lord North's ministry, active in the 1779 election, and eventually members of the mildly radical Society for Constitutional Information. But there is no sign of their carrying this (by the standards of the 1790s) tepid radicalism into the sort of seditious activity that Paine's presence at the Club meeting would imply. In the absence of evidence that would enable us to identify as conspirators some of the others present at that 1796 meeting we can only admit defeat and accept that the entry remains a tantalizing mystery.[43]

This is the last record that we have of a meeting of the Hambledon Club for another dozen years – until 2 May 1808, to be precise. Nobody turned up for the annual meeting in September 1796, and there is no record of any officers being elected for the following year. It may well be that the Club became virtually moribund for a few years. But as we shall see in the next chapter, it certainly functioned after 1808, and it also sponsored matches on Windmill Down in 1800 and 1804. So the common assumption that the Club folded up during the 1790s is wrong. The date usually given for its collapse, 1791, is based on John Nyren's mistaken recollection of his father having left Hambledon then to live in London. It may be that Richard left the village for a time, for there was a party in his honour at The Bat and Ball on 4 September of that year. But he still lived in Hambledon until 1796, every year collecting the members' subscriptions and buying the surplus bottles of port and sherry from the Club. He died in April 1797, and that event may have been one cause of the temporary interruption of the Club's activities. But cricket in Hambledon, as in many other villages, was overwhelmed by a combination of more universal forces: the war against revolutionary France, a series of bad harvests, and the increasing poverty of England's rural population. To which we might perhaps add the metropolitan preferences of the ninth Earl of Winchilsea.[44]

8

The Hambledon Club's Last Years

By the 1820s an idealized picture of village cricket is beginning to enter the literature, always a sign that something is amiss. One example is the charming account of the prelude to a local match in Mary Russell Mitford's *Our Village*. The place about which Mitford wrote with such affection, Three Mile Cross, is in Berkshire, but only a few miles from the Hampshire border, and when she wrote her best-seller she was obviously thinking as much of her native county as of the one into which she had recently moved. She had been born in 1789 at Alresford, where cricket was an accustomed part of the rural scene. Her cricket match, like the rest of her village, is suffused with an improbably romantic glow of tranquillity and harmony. Anyone who has played village cricket knows that it is not, and never has been, that idyllic. Still, some of the things Mitford says about early nineteenth-century rural cricket ring true.[1]

The match Mitford describes is not, she says, 'a pretty fête in a gentleman's park, where one club of cricketing dandies encounter another such club': a social ritual that was 'exceedingly elegant and exceedingly dull'. Instead it is 'a real solid old-fashioned match between neighbouring parishes, where each attacks the other for honour and a supper, glory and half-a-crown a man'. Not for her the over-dressed Regency dandies; her players are healthy country lads, 'accustomed to the flail or the hammer' and 'so much lissomer – to use a Hampshire phrase' than the gentry. There were limits, she says, to the deference which rural folk accorded to their betters. In another essay Mitford describes the gentry turning up at a match at the appointed hour, only to be kept waiting by the plebeian players. 'Your country cricketer, the peasant, the mere rustic,' she reflects, 'does love, on these occasions, to keep his betters waiting, if only to display his power.' Such subversion of social hierarchy was rarely possible; but as we have seen at Hambledon, it could occasionally happen on the cricket field.[2]

Besides the social contrasts, something else is worth noting about Mitford's match. It is that it was unusual to play against another village: local players were generally perfectly content to play among themselves. This was the normal situation in village cricket, and even at Hambledon it was uncommon – after 1790, at any rate – to play more than one or two matches in a season against outside opposition. Yet when they were played they aroused a strong sense of community involvement, which Mitford may have idealized, but surely did not invent. 'To be one of a numerous body,' she reflects, 'to be authorized to say *we*, to have a rightful interest in triumph or defeat, is gratifying at once to social feeling and to personal pride.' There is nothing, she decides, more inspiring than 'the genuine and hearty sympathy of belonging to a parish, breathing the same air, looking on the same trees, listening to the same nightingales!' Apart from the nightingales, she might have been speaking of Nyren's Hambledon, Newland's Slindon or Tom Marchant's Hurst-pierpoint.

As in many such exercises in literary nostalgia, Mitford was celebrating a vanished past. Yet for a brief moment after Napoleon's defeat the good old days did seem to have returned. After the earlier hard years in which food prices had escalated, bountiful harvests in 1813 and 1814 brought improvement to many parts of rural England. Low prices were good for consumers – the landless labourers, the townspeople, the rural craftsmen, in other words the overwhelming majority of the population – even if the producers, the farmers, complained about them. Some thought the farm labourers spoiled and overpaid. A report on Hampshire agriculture in 1813 claimed that they did so well that they were now rejecting the usual long hours, and could be seen leaving work in the middle of the afternoon. The lure of higher wages in the Portsmouth dockyard, the author noted, as well as the familiar attractions of the lawless neighbouring forests, meant that there was a shortage of good, docile, hard-working farm hands.[3]

People grumbled, but for everyone there was relief that the war was over, as well as pride in British victories. In the summer of 1814, when Napoleon first fled from Paris, there were joyful peace celebrations across the land, none more enthusiastic than in rural Hampshire. At West Meon, the *Hampshire Chronicle* reported, a band played, 400 poor people were given a free dinner and 'plentifully regaled with good old English beer', and Lady Gage gave money to the needy. After singing

'God Save the King' they all went home delighted with the hospitality they had received. At Avington the Marquess of Buckingham gave a free dinner to nearly a thousand poor people from the adjoining parishes, while Mr Richard Norris of Basing Park was equally charitable to the poor of Froxfield and Privett. Besides the band, the Froxfield festivities included fireworks and such rustic fun as 'a jingling match, jumping in sacks, driving wheelbarrows blindfold, etc.' – very like the contests at village revels that Miss Mitford describes.[4]

Celebrations in which both patricians and plebeians participated – the one providing, the other consuming the beer – had become more elaborate and determinedly patriotic during the war years than ever before. The year 1815 was naturally another festive one. There was a maypole at Cheriton on May Day, and further celebrations for the King's birthday a month later. When the news of Waterloo reached Hampshire there was more noisy revelling. Lord Buckingham paid for another huge entertainment at Avington: over 700 people enjoyed 'an excellent old English dinner, consisting of roast beef and plum pudding', washed down by seven hogsheads of beer. There was the usual dancing, in which the Marchioness, Lord Temple, and other top people joined. The day ended with yet another firework display.[5]

These agreeable examples of genteel hospitality did not, alas, mean that the old days of imagined harmony had been restored. Hampshire, like other cereal-growing counties, was in the throes of the brutal economic transformation which plunged the labouring population into ever deepening misery once the brief period of wartime prosperity ended; these years have been described as the climax of the farm labourers' 'long and doomed struggle against poverty and degradation'.[6] But at a superficial level it did look as if merry England was not quite dead. Besides the special festivities of 1815, there were many traditional occasions on which the gentry could convince themselves that they still had the interests of the whole community at heart. As late as 1826, when poverty and gloom were stalking the villages, Sir Henry Tichbourne entertained 300 labourers and other poor people to a splendid dinner of roast beef and beer, an occasion, the *Hampshire Chronicle* dutifully reported, 'of the most gratifying gaiety and old English hospitality'. In the following year the absentee squire of Longparish, Peter Hawker, noted that his steward had entertained close to 300 people at the 'harvest home' after the haymaking. A local band led the dancing, and a great dinner was the climax of what Hawker complacently called an 'unrivalled rustic fête'. In 1828 'our grand *fête champêtre*', he reported, was still one of the high points of the village calendar.[7]

After 1815 May Day celebrations were quickly resumed in many of the Hampshire villages; the newspapers always describe the dancing as being 'kept up with much spirit'. But the festivities were becoming more restrained and respectable than in former times. A report from Alresford in 1820 unmistakably points to the quality of the participants. The Maying, we are told, provided an impressive display 'of beauty and fashion': the common folk were being excluded. And virtually everywhere there was the mandatory patriotic conclusion, with the dancers proudly singing 'God Save the King'.[8]

At a more plebeian level, the old rural sports also made something of a comeback. Bull-baiting and cock-fighting were in decline, but we still encounter them occasionally. The Crown at Bishop's Waltham had a particularly fine cock-pit; a main there in 1824 was said to have attracted many 'sporting characters' from Winchester and other nearby towns. Cudgel-playing had survived at village feasts throughout the war, and occasionally in more formal settings: there was a match between Wiltshire and Somerset during Salisbury Races in 1808. These two counties were the real heartland of the sport, and their champions dominated contests in Hampshire; appealing to local competitors, the announcement of a singlestick contest at Easton in 1814 stressed that no Somerset or Wiltshire men would be allowed to take part. At Fareham a year later the local gentry organized the affair, offering prizes as high as £40. But at the last minute the Wiltshire contingent pulled out, 'having from year to year suffered such defeats from the Somerset men'. A smaller purse was hastily made up and won by two of the Somerset visitors, with another being fought for by the less-skilled Hampshire lads. At the end of a great war there could be no argument about the promoters' claim that 'this manly practice' encouraged 'the accustomed and natural hardihood of Englishmen'. The spectators at cudgel matches, an account of one in London observed, came mainly from 'that class from which are drawn our soldiers and sailors', who would naturally draw the appropriate moral.[9]

Rural cricket also recovered after 1815. The war had seriously interrupted it in many places. John Mockett, of St Peter's in the Isle of Thanet, recalled that as late as the mid-1820s the young men of his parish were 'much in want of some pastime' now that military training no longer occupied their leisure time. He decided that 'the manly game of cricket' was the solution, so he formed a club and let them play in his pasture. They were emulated by neighbouring villages, and by 1835 the old Thanet club had been resurrected. In other parts of Kent cricket seems to have continued during the war years with less interruption than in Thanet. There was even a single-wicket match in 1813 on Goodwin Sands, which ended with the players drinking the King's health, 'three times three', before the tide came in. Many Kent villages traditionally had cricket on fair days. In July 1830, just before the region was engulfed in rioting, Rainham beat Gillingham by 60 runs on the Downs during Meopham Fair.[10]

Sussex was another county where cricket often took place at fairs. On Whit Monday 1818, it was announced, there would be cricket, 'with every other amusement the field will afford', at Firle Fair, with prizes for the winning team and a ball at the Ram Inn in the evening. In the same year there was a match during Broadoak Fair, on the famous Dicker ground. A country fête at the Broyle, near Chichester, attracted an 'immense concourse' of people in 1825. Besides the usual jingling matches, sack races, and blindfolded wheelbarrow races, there was a cricket match between two pick-up sides. Trying to have it both ways, a newspaper reported that it all ended with 'much hilarity', but also complete order and decorum. Meanwhile, well-known village teams such as Henfield and Slindon were still functioning, as no doubt were many that have left us no record. Crowds were beginning to drift back: when Chichester played Slindon in 1823 the Broyle, it was said, was 'thronged to excess'. At the top of the Sussex cricketing hierarchy was the Brighton Club, who played on a ground that had been laid out by the Prince of Wales in 1791. It was renovated by the promoter James Ireland in 1823, after some years of disuse, and was soon drawing big crowds. Brighton's best-known player was the bowler George Brown, so fast that he sometimes placed eight fielders behind the wicket. Not always successfully: one of his deliveries once eluded them all and killed a dog roaming outside the boundary. Another famous Sussex professional was William Lambert, soon to be the scapegoat for the betting scandals at Lord's.[11]

In Hampshire there was also a partial recovery after the wartime decline. A club survived at Winchester, which in 1807 played Southampton on Twyford Down. It was still going strong in 1825, but a few years later it seems to have become completely moribund, in spite of there being plenty of good players in the city. There was also a fair amount of wartime cricket between militia teams. When the war ended the game quickly revived, and in 1815 there were matches all over the Hampshire downlands. Alresford played Holybourne home and away, as did Droxford and Fareham, Meonstoke defeated East Meon, while not far away Privett played Newton Valence in Richard Norris's park at Basing. In the following year Southampton played the Isle of Wight in a three-day match. The Winchester newspaper identifies the players in many of these games as 'gentlemen', but we should remember not to take this description too literally.[12]

County cricket followed much the same pattern. Teams operating under the name 'Hampshire' played several times at Lord's between 1803 and 1807; as in the previous decade they were largely composed of gentlemen, once again with an infusion of some of the now ageing Hambledon professionals. When cricket resumed after Waterloo there appears to have been some real enthusiasm in Hampshire, and within a few years it was not totally absurd to claim that the county had recovered its old pre-eminence. In 1823 over 3,000 spectators were said to have watched Hampshire play MCC in Sir John Cope's park at Bramshill. Strangers travelling through Hampshire, a visiting sportsman noted, were amazed 'to see all classes quitting their several occupations to be present at a cricket match'. Spectators were reappearing at club matches, too. When Emsworth (who now included the fearsome George Brown) played Winchester in 1820, the crowd was bigger than had been seen on Emsworth Common for twenty-five years. Bramshill was at this time the main centre of Hampshire county cricket, and well-known players could often be seen there: on one occasion in 1824 Cope's XI included the great Lord's amateur, the London banker William Ward. A new generation of professionals was also emerging – Beagleys from Alton, Lillywhites from Havant and Chichester – but the county teams were nevertheless dominated by the gentry.[13]

Professionals such as Brown and Lambert were occasionally to be seen in these country matches, but not as often as in London. In the capital they dominated the game on the playing field, as the nobility and gentry dominated its organization. Miss Mitford had no time for the metropolitan game, the 'set match at Lord's Ground for money, hard money, between a certain number of gentlemen and players ... people who make a trade of that noble sport, and degrade it into an affair of bettings, and hedgings, and cheatings'. Yet the game was still popular in the capital, and not simply with the betting fraternity. 'Tom Lord's flag was the well known telegraph that brought him in from three to four thousand sixpences', Pycroft says. With its high fence to keep out gatecrashers, Lord's generated more reliable profits than the old Artillery Ground – £500 from one early match, it was said. If you could forget the bookies and the rumours of sharp practice, Lord's was indeed the pinnacle of the game. Professionals such as Beldham and Fennex played alongside such outstanding amateurs as Lord Frederick Beauclerk and the hard-hitting E. H. Budd. Beauclerk, son of the Duke of St Albans, and thus descended from Charles II and Nell Gwynn, was a fine batsman, but also selfish, ill-tempered and possibly corrupt. He was President of the MCC in 1826, but fortunately for the Club's reputation his influence soon waned in favour of the better-mannered and less suspect William Ward. Ward was a good player as well as a rich man and a more appealing leader; in 1820 he made 278 in a single innings for MCC against Norfolk.[14]

However memorable the cricket, money was never far from the surface. It was fair enough that Tom Lord should make a decent living from his sixpenny admissions. But he wanted more, and in 1825 was proposing to use the ground for property development; it was rescued by Ward, who bought out the lease for £5,000. Meanwhile, the reign of the gamblers continued. There were those who suspected Beauclerk of cheating to achieve his six hundred guineas a year. And the bookies were still doing their corrupting work. In 1817 William Lambert scored two centuries for Sussex in a match at Lord's – the first time this had ever been done. It was later in that same year that he was banned from Lord's for cheating.[15]

The gulf between the amateurs and the professionals in these matches was real enough, but we should not exaggerate it. Professionals such as Beldham might ride to matches in the coaches of well-bred amateurs, and men who were separated by a very wide social gulf could still enjoy amicable relations on the field of play. A young gentleman named Frederick Reynolds was subjected to a form of good-natured sledging by the professionals in a match at Stoke Down in 1795. Reynolds, who was not much of a player, had gone to the game as a spectator and was pressed into service when somebody did not turn up. He was understandably scared stiff when he had to go in to face the formidable David Harris, and his terrors, he tells us, were 'much increased by the mock pity and sympathy of Hammond, Beldham, and others round the wicket'. Through sheer luck he managed to get three runs off Harris, and some of the gentry present then took up a collection for him – a parody of the custom by which professionals who had done well were rewarded. The fluidity of class relations made it possible for real friendships to exist across the social divide. John Nyren and the younger John Small had grown up together at Broadhalfpenny, and remained close friends to the end of their lives – Nyren speaks of Small with wonderfully warm affection. Yet Small played cricket as a professional, Nyren as an amateur; they were on opposite sides in the first Gentlemen vs. Players match.[16]

One famous rural club was among those which held out against the domination of the game by the London aristocracy. Historians have often supposed that the Hambledon Club collapsed in the 1790s, or, if they knew that it existed after that date, that it had become nothing more than a village team. But the truth is that the Hambledon Club which survived until 1825 was in many respects little different from the old club which had flourished down to the 1790s. To be sure, Hambledon no longer took on 'England', Kent and Surrey, in those great matches on Windmill Down. But as we have seen, these major games had virtually disappeared by the early 1790s, when the leading professionals were carted off to London by the Earl of Winchilsea. The central purpose of the Hambledon Club had always been the entertainment of the members, through weekly meetings in which sociability was encouraged by the consumption of ample food and drink, and where cricket was played by a minority of the members (in the company of paid professionals) and watched, and wagered on, by the others. The Hambledon Club had always been an asssociation of gentry. After the Napoleonic wars it still was.

A good deal can be learned about the Club's later years from its recently discovered account book, covering the years 1808–25. But the absence of any surviving records between 1796 and 1808 does not mean that the Club had ceased to exist during those years. There may have been a short hiatus after 1796, but when the accounts resume in 1808 they have all the marks of being part of a series, not the first record of a new or refounded club. Local newspapers contain occasional reports of Hambledon matches during the otherwise unrecorded years. In 1800 Hambledon played East Meon and Meonstoke at Windmill Down, and two years later they twice defeated Emsworth, home and away. In September 1804 two club members, Thomas Bonham and Charles Clavering, made a match at Windmill for fifty guineas a side, in which the local players were split between the two teams. The newspaper which announced this also reported that on the following day 'the anniversary of the Hambledon Club' would be celebrated by a dinner at the New Inn. And in August 1807 Hambledon narrowly defeated Winchester in a match that extended over two days.[17]

Hambledon continued to play a few matches against outside opposition, but never more than one or two a season, and in some years not even that. In July 1808 they twice played Froxfield; in 1809 another match against Froxfield was postponed 'on account of the badness of weather'. In the same year a match against a combined team from Fareham, Wickham and Bishop's Waltham, the account book crows, 'was won by Hambledon hollow'. In several of these matches both the Hambledon players and their opponents were paid by the Club; the Froxfield men were even paid five shillings for the 1809 rainout. These were indeed village matches: Froxfield was tiny, with a population of only 548 in 1821, less than a third of Hambledon's. The fixture may well have been arranged because two of the Froxfield players, Edward and John Carter, were often among those paid to take part in the weekly games on Windmill Down. The combined team beaten hollow in 1809 was of course drawn from a much bigger population, and Emsworth was probably an even stronger side. But for the most part the quality of Hambledon's opponents during this period does not look very impressive.[18]

Between 1812 and 1824, however, Hambledon played much stronger sides, and was indeed part of a network of the leading Hampshire and Sussex clubs. These included Winchester (opponents in both 1812 and 1821), Portsmouth, now otherwise known as the Portsea Club (played at least six times between 1814 and 1823), Havant (1816), and the Goodwood Club (once in 1823 and twice in 1824). Other teams in this network included Emsworth (now strengthened, as we have seen, by the fast bowling and hard hitting of Brown of Brighton) and Midhurst. In 1822 the last-named club was strong enough to consider challenging the MCC.[19] Several of Hambledon's matches took place over two days, and the Club spent a fair amount of money on them. The 1812 Winchester match, for example, cost them £32.17s.6d: £28.17s.6d. for the players (both teams were paid by Hambledon), and £4 for the umpires and scorers. These were respectable sums, though far less than the London professionals were earning. Even in the 1820s, when financial difficulties closed in, Hambledon's players were still given eight or ten shillings for an outside match.

We have the scores from a few of these games, but very little else. There was a huge row at one on Windmill Down in September 1814 which shows that partisan feeling was as strong as ever, and that even the gentlemen were sometimes unable to control it. Portsea were batting in their second innings, with the match finely poised. At this point a ball was hit into the refreshment booth, and there was a dispute over how many runs should be awarded for a 'booth ball'. During the argument the batsman wandered away from his wicket, the ball was thrown in, and he was apparently run out. The umpires were unwilling to make a decision, a newspaper reports, so there was an appeal to 'the gentlemen in the booth, who pronounced him not out'. Hambledon refused to accept this, and the dispute became so heated that play had to be suspended until the two teams met again on Southsea Common a week later, Portsea winning by two wickets. A match at Southsea which immediately followed was said to be the first two-day match in the Portsmouth area for thirty years, and Portsea's double victory over Hambledon also their first for thirty years. Once again it needs to be stressed that during this period Hambledon played occasional two-day matches, just as they had done in the old days. This does not sound much like a run-of-the-mill village club.[20]

Yet after 1808 the Club was a much slimmer affair than it had been in earlier days. In the 1790s annual receipts and expenditures always totalled well over £100; even in 1796, the last year for which we have accounts, the Club spent £131.10s.7d., though this includes payment of a long-overdue wine bill from Gauntlett's.[21] After 1808 they never spent, or received, anything like these sums. However, these later accounts contain nothing about the purchase of wine, and it may be that if we had the wine account the scale of operations would not seem very different from what it had been twenty years before.

Indeed, in one respect there was almost no difference at all, at least until after the year of Waterloo. The weekly practice games had been resumed – weekly, not fortnightly as in the straitened years of the 1790s – and they were on much the same scale as in earlier decades. Between 1791 and 1794 payments to players had totalled about £2.15s.6d. per meeting; in the years 1808–11 they were slightly below that figure, but in the next four years they averaged £3.9s.10d., well above the numbers for the 1790s. The accounts tell us something about how these games were organized. There were, naturally, two sides, with the winners paid more than the losers – three or four shillings for the winners, 2s.6d. or three shillings for the losers. Some of the youngsters were paid less – 1s.6d. or a shilling. The players were mainly local Hambledon men, but outside professionals, paid at a higher rate, were often brought in. Some of them would have been well known on Windmill Down. The younger John Small was often there before 1815, and one of the others also had a familiar Hambledon name: G. Leer, perhaps a son of the outstanding long-stop of the Club's great days. Two regular visitors were Edward and John Carter, both of Froxfield. And it is possible that the Brown who played in 1814 was 'Brown of Brighton', the famous fast bowler.[22]

Gentleman members also played in these matches, though at first not very many. In July 1808 there was a special 'gentlemen's match', but more usually the handful of the gentry who turned out were divided between the two sides. Sometimes half a dozen took part, sometimes only one or two, and often none at all – the Windmill Down cricket would be between two teams of paid local players. There were days with too few people for an eleven-a-side match, and others with an odd number of players; to even the teams up, one player would bat for both sides. On 1 June 1812, for example, each team had ten men, and William Garrett batted for both. Scores, alas, are never recorded, though in June 1823 a 'tie match' is noted.

After the end of the 1815 season there is a gap in the accounts, and they only resume in 1819. Something must have happened during the missing years. Whereas down to 1815 very few gentlemen played in the weekly matches, beginning in 1819 many more did. Only on the rarest occasions were there now as few as half a dozen gentlemen, and on many weeks ten or twelve. The 'Anniversary' was sometimes celebrated by an eleven-a-side match between the gentlemen and the paid players. In 1820 it was a two-day affair, and the gentlemen were strengthened by the inclusion of the great William Ward; the players, however, won an exciting, high-scoring game by three runs. On 26 June 1820 twelve gentlemen turned up, and a thirteen-a-side match was played, with each team having six of them, plus seven local players. Whatever may have been the cause of the change, the result was that the expenditure on players fell dramatically, from an average of £3.9s.10d. a week in 1812–

15, to less than half that amount between 1819 and 1825. Outside professionals still came occasionally and as usual were paid considerably more than the locals. Thomas Beagley, from Alton but with kinsfolk in Hambledon, was one of the leading batsmen of the 1820s, good enough to make centuries at Lord's. Another occasional player in 1813, and a more regular one in 1819, was a certain 'T. Lillywhite', perhaps a connection of the famous bowler William Lillywhite, who came from the Chichester neighbourhood. Beagley played in several matches against other clubs, but whereas before 1820 Hambledon teams in such matches were mainly made up of local paid players, after that date they were almost entirely limited to the gentlemen.[23]

So the Club in these years was still a serious cricketing organization. Besides the routine purchases of bats and balls (often from old John Small), there were annual payments for rolling and maintaining Windmill Down: in 1821 three hundred turves were bought, and somebody was paid six shillings, for 'three days' work laying turf'. Tom Sueter still kept the clubhouse in good repair, and every year seven shillings was spent on 'advertising the Anniversary'. Special punch was laid on for the players in these matches, and the occasion was not one at which the attendance of gentry members was required, as none of them were at the anniversary in either 1811 or 1812. Some other weekly meetings must also have entailed elaborate entertainment: on 31 July 1820 a man was paid two shillings 'to put the marquee up'.

If there was punch for the players there must have been wine for the gentry. Sociability was clearly still a principal purpose of the Club, even if meetings were sometimes poorly attended – but that had been true in the old days, too. There was the usual occasional rowdiness. An old member recalled that the clubhouse used to contain an ancient curved bat, hanging up 'over the dining room'. But after a dinner in 1819 a drunken member, 'by way of frolic', took it down and had a hit with it, in the course of which it completely disintegrated.[24] Members paid for their own dinners, but the landlord of the New Inn, John Stewart, was paid three shillings as compensation for each absent member if fewer than seven attended. Thus on 17 June 1822 only three members stayed to dinner, so the Club paid Stewart twelve shillings for the four absentees. A week later several gentleman turned up to play, but, Stewart noted, there was 'not one gentleman to dinner', so he collected the whole weekly allowance of one guinea. On 15 July the full complement of seven stayed for dinner, so Stewart got nothing extra from the Club.

This is precisely how Richard Nyren had been paid thirty years earlier, and like him Stewart also collected subscriptions and paid the players and the miscellaneous bills. In 1811 the annual subscription was only £1.11s.6d. – half what it had been in the old days – and Stewart collected this sum from at least nineteen members, two of whom also paid arrears from previous years. But there must have been more than nineteen members, as the Club's accounts for that year show expenditures at a level considerably above the recorded receipts. By 1825, however, the decline is unmistakable. The annual subscription was down to a guinea, and if Stewart's accounts are accurate he collected it from only nine members, several of whom also paid outstanding arrears. How the Club had managed to survive that long is a mystery. Either Stewart's accounts are seriously deficient, or a good many gentlemen were coming to play without having paid their subscriptions: very few of those who still played in the weekly practices are listed in the pathetic list of paid-up members.

Years later one of the members, Thomas Smith of Droxford, recalled that the Club 'was very well kept up until about the year 1825, when many members left the neighbourhood; the old clubhouse having fallen into decay, the Down also was shortly broken up'.[25] Smith was certainly right about the date, but he offers no explanation for the departure of so many members: it may be that they did not leave, but now had other preoccupations instead of cricket. To understand what happened we need to look at both the gentlemen and the players of the Hambledon Club between 1808 and 1825, and the circumstances of those times.

The gentlemen were not very different from the members of the Club in the old days. A few of them were indeed the same people. Old Thomas Bonham, for example, had been a stalwart Hambledon member ever since the 1770s, succeeding his brother as secretary in 1783. He was still attending post-match dinners in 1810, when he was almost ninety. By now he was living in Hambledon, and was buried there in 1815. Another old member was Edward Hale of Hambledon House, son of the village surgeon who had been an energetically innovating farmer earlier in the eighteenth century: one of two 'ingenious men' by whom the lands of the parish had been 'exceedingly improved', a report on Hambledon agriculture declared. The Hales were sporting types who had their own pack of hounds, and they were among the biggest landowners in the parish, farming over 450 acres in 1819, including Windmill Down. They had owned the Down at least since 1799, when Edward Hale was rated £4.8s.4d. on a property described as 'late Garrett's land'. Hale may have let the Club use the Down for nothing: there are no records of rental payments in these years, as there had been to Farmer Garrett. Hale was still playing in 1800, and was still a member in 1811.[26]

Even more prominent in the village was a new arrival, Col. Thomas Butler. He bought Bury Lodge – the old house where Charles II had been sheltered after Worcester – in 1800, then pulled it down and rebuilt it. He also married the daughter of a baronet, was appointed to the county bench, and was quickly established in Hampshire society. He owned over 300 acres in Hambledon, according to the 1819 rating. He was also a leader in village government, perhaps the most influential member of the parish vestry. Butler was another fox-hunting squire, the virtual founder of the Hambledon Hunt. Within a few years of his arrival the Hunt was a thriving concern, its importance to the neighbouring gentry evident in its annual subscription of ten guineas – a far cry from the pathetic guinea and a half of the cricket club. The Hunt always held a race meeting early in May on Soberton Down; in 1812 at least 2,000 spectators were said to have attended. After the racing there was dinner for the gentry at the New Inn, followed by a ball and supper at the George. In 1818 the dancing went on until five in the morning; as usual 'all the beauty and fashion of the neighbourhood' were there. But although the Hunt was his top priority, Butler was also a keen cricketer, playing in the Windmill Down matches – often with one or more of his sons – throughout the 1808–25 period. At one time he was also treasurer of the club. When Frederick Gale visited Bury Lodge around 1880 Butler's son showed him a screen in the dining-room, 'with the original scores of the Old Hambledon, commencing in 1777, printed on paper'. Butler was born in 1776, so the screen must have been started long before he could have had anything to do with it; the family was obviously devoted to the Club's traditions.[27]

Other Hambledon residents were still active. The vicar, Richard Richards; the village doctor, John Bulbeck; and substantial landowners such as John Foster, Henry Friend and John Goldsmith were all members. But just as in the old days, a good many others came from outside the village. There was the usual sprinkling of clergy from nearby parishes, one of them being Richards's friend, the Revd Brownlow Poulter, rector of Buriton. Some of the members were military or naval officers; the most distinguished was Admiral Sir Charles Hamilton, who lived near Midhurst but also owned property in Hambledon. There were, as we should expect, many members from other Hampshire gentry families: Edward Knight of Chawton, Thomas Smith of Droxford and Richard Norris of Basing Park and Froxfield were among the most regular.

Hambledon's paid players present a striking contrast. They were probably a fair cross-section of village society, but for the most part of its bottom rung. A few of the wealthier farmers were willing to take the three or four shillings on offer at the weekly games. John Jarman farmed 262 acres in the 1819 rating, but he was usually paid for playing. On one occasion in 1811 he is listed as 'Mr. Jarman', but he still accepted the three shillings for being on the winning side; he later played without pay in 1819, only to be paid again in 1825. He was a good enough cricketer to be recruited as a 'given man' for Portsmouth against Emsworth in 1817. William Garrett was a given man in the same match; it will be recalled that the Club had rented Windmill Down from one of that family in the 1780s. Poor-rate assessments show that several other players were reasonably prosperous: the butcher John Knight, the miller John Langtree, the maltster Richard Pink, and John Stewart, the cricket club factotum and landlord of the New Inn. But compared with the landowners like Hale and Butler, these were small men indeed, for whom the weekly payments must have been welcome.[28]

They must have been even more welcome to the rest of the players. Out of twenty-six players from the bottom rung whose occupations we can identify with reasonable certainty, there are twelve labourers, four bricklayers, three tailors, and a scattering of butchers, thatchers, carpenters and wheelwrights. It seems reasonable to suppose that if we knew the occupations of all the unidentifiable players in the accounts the proportion of labourers in the whole cricket-playing population would not be very different. In 1811 Arthur Young estimated the average weekly wage of a labourer as about 14s.4d., a level which had certainly not kept pace with the cost of bread during the hectic wartime inflation and which further declined during the post-war depression. By 1830 a Hampshire farmworker would have been lucky to earn 12s. a week at harvest time, and during most of the year a lot less. If playing cricket on

Monday afternoon cost him a day's wages (which even on Young's optimistic figures would have been only 2s.6d.) he was still better off than doing the usual back-breaking work in the fields. If the labourer was out of work and dependent on poor relief, the cricket earnings would have been even more important to him. For self-employed craftsmen like the tailors and bricklayers a day off might have been more costly, but only if they had enough regular work to keep them fully occupied for a six-day week. Again, the money from the cricket would be useful – and more fun to earn.[29]

Most of the players from the lower reaches of Hambledon society have left few traces. But we know a bit about the bricklayers Charles and Thomas Clay, at least one of whom played for the Club as far back as 1791. Both took part in the contentious match against Portsea in 1814, and played against the same team on a couple of later occasions. Just by being cricketers they could pick up an odd job here and there: Charles did bricklaying work on the clubhouse in 1791, and later his brother was paid for doing some whitewashing. But they were not well off. In 1819 Charles Clay was sharing a house with another cricketer, the thatcher Peter Husted: a shared house is usually an indicator of poverty. Husted, it will be recalled, had been the drinks waiter in the 1790s, also helping out by doing odd jobs for the Club. He and several of his sons played sporadically down to 1823.

Stewart's lists contain many other plebeian players, but they remain only names in an account book. What is striking about the accounts is that they show that the gentry members were still playing on Windmill Down with and against men from the very poorest level of the community. Sometimes, especially before 1815, there might be only one gentleman playing, among a score of local men. Masters played alongside servants: in 1811 'Mr Hamilton's man' several times played with or against his employer, and was paid the usual two or three shillings according to whether his team won or lost. A few weeks later 'Mr Ridge's man' also took part in games with his master. Even in the gloom of rural poverty cricket permitted some blurring of class lines.

Somehow the Club struggled on, but it could not last for ever. The last match played by the old Hambledon Club took place at Windmill Down on 24 and 25 August 1824. There is a certain poignancy about the fact that it was against the Goodwood Club, if we remember Goodwood's role in the development of cricket a hundred years earlier, in the days of the second Duke of Richmond. In 1823 Hambledon, with a team made up entirely of gentlemen, had beaten Goodwood easily. They played again at Goodwood, in front of the great house, on 18 August 1824; this time Goodwood won a comfortable victory, though we know none of the details. For the return match on Windmill Down the Club included two professionals: Beagley and a local man named Kelsey. The game had a splendidly rousing finish. At two o'clock on the second afternoon Goodwood appeared to be coasting to victory, but then Edward Knight turned the game on its head by a display of what the Winchester newspaper describes as 'very superior hitting'. Knight made an unbeaten 53 out of a total of 114, and Hambledon just scraped home by two wickets.[30]

It would have been an appropriately romantic ending for the Club, but history does not often provide romantic endings. Goodwood still expected to meet their 'friendly opponents' at Hambledon again in 1825,[31] but instead there was anti-climax. The new summer saw only a pathetic handful of weekly practices, with several blank dates, and often with only a few members and players in attendance. The last one took place on 1 August 1825, when seven gentlemen, headed by Col. Thomas Butler, and eight local men who were paid 2s.6d. each, played cricket together on Windmill Down. Stewart's notes for each of the remaining four weeks of the season sadly record 'no meeting', along with his claim for the full guinea allowance for uneaten dinners. Teams from Hambledon, composed entirely of gentlemen, played a handful of games during the next few years: two with Midhurst in 1829, two more against Newport, Isle of Wight, in 1833. It looks as if some of the old members could not bear to give up, for the teams included a good many who had played regularly before 1825. But although two of them took place on Windmill Down, these were not matches sponsored by the now defunct Club. An 1833 report clearly distinguishes between the Newport *Club* and their opponents, who were described only as eleven gentlemen of Hambledon. The days of the Hambledon Club, the club which had sponsored John Small, Tom Brett, David Harris and the rest of John Nyren's heroes, had ended.[32]

By now the gloom was fast closing in. In 1822 and 1826, the great Tory radical William Cobbett twice came to Hambledon. He describes these visits in *Rural Rides*, his vivid, angry description of the decaying farming country of southern England.[33] Cobbett's journeys of rediscovery provoked in him a cry of rage against the relentless proletarianization of the English peasantry; against the malign influence of London, the 'Great Wen', and the other towns which were draining the life-blood of the countryside he so much loved, by the parasitic burden of taxes and debt-payments; against the ruination of the ordinary townsmen and villagers by predatory corn-dealers and farmers, with their newfangled threshing-machines; and against the tithe-gathering clergy.

Cobbett's first visit was in November 1822. He came by way of Kilmiston, where that red-blooded, fox-hunting Hambledon member, Thomas Ridge, had once lived. Ridge was still remembered in the neighbourhood and was thought to have ruined himself by his extravagance; but, Cobbett characteristically observes, 'it was the Pitt-system [the income tax], and not the fox-hunting' which had destroyed him. Kilmiston had once been a healthy village, but it had now 'mouldered into two farms, and a few miserable tumble-down houses for the labourers'. The rest of the region was no better. 'The villages,' Cobbett says, 'are all in a state of decay. The farm-buildings dropping down, bit by bit. The produce is, by a few great farmers, dragged to a few spots, and all the rest is falling into decay.' When he got to Hambledon Cobbett stayed with his old friend, John Goldsmith of West End, a pillar of the community who had also been a member of the cricket club for many years. That such a man was a friend and admirer of William Cobbett is a striking indication that some of the village leaders sympathized with their poorer neighbours' plight. Hambledon was no exception to the general atmosphere of poverty and depression. From the size of the church, Cobbett concluded, the village must at one time have been much bigger, but now it had been ruined by the 'tax-eaters' and the diversion of wealth into seaport towns such as Portsmouth and Gosport, which ironically were now themselves falling into decay.[34]

Matters had not improved by the time of Cobbett's second visit. He again found his way to West End, and then had another look at the village. 'A village it *now* is,' Cobbett reflected, 'but it was formerly a considerable market-town, and it had three fairs in the year.' 'There is now not even the name of market left,' he complained, '. . . and the fairs amount to little more than a couple or three gingerbread-stalls, with dolls and whistles for children.' This was a bit unfair, for there had always been a toy-fair on Broadhalfpenny Down, and the first cricket meeting of the season used to coincide with it. By now the market-house had fallen down after years of neglect: the manor court had been complaining ever since 1755 that the Bishop ought to have it repaired. The whole village, Cobbett lamented, was 'a tumble-down rubbishy place'.[35]

Cobbett had no interest in cricket and makes no mention of Hambledon's fame, even though the collapse of the Club just before his second visit ought to have been grist to his mill. There are strong similarities between his underlying prejudices and those of John Nyren. They share the same hatred of London – Nyren describes the Thames as 'the infernal black stream (that type of Acheron!) which soddens the carcass of a Londoner' – and the same dislike of the modern centralizing state with its burdensome taxation. 'We had not sixty millions of interest to pay in those days,' Nyren observes in his account of the high feasting on Broadhalfpenny. They share the same contempt for foreigners, especially the French, a contempt evident in Nyren's dismissal of modern Frenchified punch in favour of the 'good, unsophisticated John Bull stuff' of his youth. They share the same idealization of an imagined peasant society, now corrupted by urbanization and the market economy, the same nostalgia for a vanished past, for a harmonious old England.

There was not much harmony in the 1820s. The gradual, centuries-long process in which the commons and open fields had been replaced by individual farms was now virtually complete. And the farmers were finding a more economical way to pay their labour force. Instead of the live-in 'servants-in-husbandry' of the old days, they now preferred to employ labourers who lived in their own cottages and received a weekly, or daily, wage for their work. This became even more advantageous to the farmer as labour became cheaper through the return of a quarter of a million men to civilian life after the wars, and through the inexorable increase of population. The arable-farming counties of southern and eastern England, in which the worst conditions prevailed, had an almost stable population of about 1.5 million in the fifty years before 1751. By 1801 that population had risen to 2 million, and by 1831 to 2.9 million, an increase of nearly fifty per cent in thirty years.[36]

It will be no surprise that in these circumstances there was a marked increase in rural unemployment, and that the wages of those still employed steadily declined. In some places they declined even more dramatically because of the 'Speenhamland' system – the policy adopted by the Berkshire magistrates in 1795 of not merely paying poor relief to the unemployed, but of subsidizing the wages of those employed to get them up to a subsistence level. It was a well-meant humanitarian decision, to deal with an emergency situation when famine threatened. But it became a recipe for demoralization and disaster, for if poor relief was so readily available why should the farmer pay a living wage, knowing that the parish would supplement the pittance he paid with regular relief? Not many Hampshire parishes practised the Speenhamland procedures, but in all of them there was a dramatic increase in the poor rate, the local tax from which relief payments were made. One solution was to provide work for the unemployed, usually at breaking stones to repair the roads, universally seen as a degrading activity. Another, familiar in our own times, was to cut welfare payments so as to force people to find jobs – if there were any.[37]

In the far-off days before 1750 the gentry had often tried to protect the poor from the vagaries of the market economy in times of dearth. After 1815 some of them still sympathized with the labourers' despairing demands for work at a living wage, but many others had abdicated their old paternalist roles. A good Hampshire example of the absent squire is Peter Hawker of Longparish, whose diary tells us something about the county during this bleak decade. Hawker had served in the Peninsular War and was still an officer in the militia, taking pride in turning 'lads from the plough' into something approximating effective soldiers. But he regarded the countrymen as a different breed, exempt from the physical discomforts of gentlemen like himself; in December 1820, he noted, the weather was so cold 'that even the labourers are nearly frost bitten'. A year later he expresses concern for poor people made homeless by floods, but does not seem to have done anything about it. However, after a bad fire at Longparish he complacently remarks that he 'had the pleasure of being somewhat useful to the poor sufferers, by starting a subscription'.[38]

This does not sound like much of a record for a supposedly paternalist squire. The fact is that Hawker was often away in London, or engaged in continental travel. He had a passion for music – one of his few attractive qualities – publishing a book on the musical education of children, perfecting a 'new invention for playing the scales of a pianoforte, by mechanical means', and regularly attending concerts during the London season. There were occasional musical evenings in Hampshire, too, but when he was at Longparish Hawker was totally obsessed with his shooting. His diary is largely a record of slaughtered wildlife, full of such exultant entries as, 'Two hundred and fourteen head of game in three days shooting!!!' So successful was he on one glorious day of

sport in September 1819 that he thought no one would believe him, so
he got the parson to certify in writing that his tally of dead birds was
accurate. His two passions – music and shooting – once nicely dovetail
in an admiring reference to his gunner, James Read, 'the Mozart of all
the wildfowl-men'.[39]

It was not unusual for gentlemen to be passionately devoted to country
sports. But shooting was different from fox-hunting or cricket in being
an essentially solitary pleasure, lacking the sociable nature of the other
pastimes. Occasionally Hawker went shooting with one or two friends,
but more often he went alone, accompanied only by his beloved dogs
and his servants. Even when he showed some awareness of the hardships
of those around him, Hawker worried most about their possible impact
on his shooting. After a spell of terrible weather at the end of 1821, he
hopes that 1822 will be better, 'not only for our sport, but for the
farmers and the poor, and reasons of more consequence'. In 1828 he
worries about the increasing number of arson attacks by unemployed
labourers. A fire near Longparish burned five ricks; there had been no
lightning, the usual cause of accidental fires, so, Hawker concluded,
it must have been set by 'some damnable incendiary'. The date was
5 November, Gunpowder Treason Day, now being celebrated with
bonfires of a sinister kind.[40]

Hambledon was not exempt from the problems of rural poverty and
overpopulation. When Henry Friend made out the census return in 1811
the parish contained 1,495 inhabitants. But in 1821 there were 1,886: a
startling increase of almost twenty-seven per cent in a single decade. The
housing problem inevitably worsened, with more families having to
share their cottages with others. And the increase in the number of
families 'chiefly engaged in agriculture' was significantly greater than of
families 'chiefly engaged in trade'; even more seriously there had been a
dramatic change in the ratio of males to females, a sure signal of an
increasing burden on the poor rate. In 1811 the numbers of males (747)
and females (748) were almost equal, but ten years later there were
1,001 males to 885 females. Hambledon was an 'open' village – one in
which the manor court was unable to prevent the settlement of outsiders
– and many of the newcomers were undoubtedly unemployed labourers
looking for work. But in Hambledon, as in most other places, there was
no work.[41]

The village was situated in what we already know to have been the most severely affected part of England: the arable-farming south and southeast. Even in 1815 paupers amounted to ten per cent of the population of Hampshire. Poor rates rose everywhere between 1815 and 1819, reaching over three per cent of the national income; in Hambledon the yield from the assessments rose from about £1,500 to £2,500 annually.[42] A new valuation of properties was undertaken in 1819, to spread the burden equitably. At the same time the village was maintaining a Poor House for the indigent and infirm: Edward Aburrow, the old cricketer, was in charge of it in 1809–10.

Hambledon, like everywhere else, desperately strove to bring its poor rates under control. To the extent that it did so, the price was inevitably paid by the labourers. In 1795 the Berkshire JPs had recommended that an adult male's weekly wage ought to provide him with three and a half 'gallon' loaves; in 1822 the Hampshire magistrates allowed only enough to buy *one* gallon loaf. Whether things were quite as bad as this in Hambledon is impossible to tell – the returns made by the parish to Parliament tell us only the total annual expenditures, not the amount of relief actually received by individuals. But the sums being distributed were certainly being sharply cut in the mid-1820s. Between 1819 and 1821 Hambledon's expenditure on the poor averaged £2,377 annually; by the years 1827–29 this had fallen to an average of £1,697 per annum. Is it fanciful to think that until 1825 the cricket club operated as a kind of welfare institution for a favoured few among the poor? This would explain the gentry members' apparent willingness to tolerate fairly large expenditures at the weekly matches down to 1815, even though few gentlemen attended, as well as the sharp drop in the number of players supported in the later period, when upper-class attitudes began to change because poor relief was getting out of hand.[43]

In 1824 Hambledon's elite decided that they needed a more efficient system of local government. Hitherto the parish had been run by a Vestry in which all ratepayers had, at least in theory, the right to participate. Obviously this made it difficult to cut relief payments or to undertake other unpopular measures which would adversely affect the neighbours and kinsfolk of many of the poorer vestrymen. So a new 'Select Vestry', consisting of a small number of the wealthier inhabitants, was created, though the larger 'Legal Vestry' also continued to function. The Select Vestry first met on 13 July 1824. The composition of the committee which established it clearly shows who was running the parish. The committee was headed by Col. Thomas Butler, and also included Cobbett's friend John Goldsmith and his son, two of the Jarmans, old Curry Aburrow and John Stewart of the New Inn (and the cricket club).[44]

The Select Vestry was already setting the Poor Rate by February 1825, and in March they announced a new, harsher policy, ordering that 'all children above seven years of age be sent to stonepicking' (for the highways). In 1827 they made an even more draconian decision by ordering that 'the children of paupers receiving monthly pay be ordered into the Poor House' – the more stringent welfare system was now being used to break up the families of the unemployed. The larger body, the 'Legal Vestry', however, retained more of the old paternalist inclinations, for in 1825 they considered setting up a school for pauper children. There is, however, no sign that one was ever established.

It is clear from the parish's sketchy Poor Law accounts that old cricketers often received special help when they fell on hard times. The Clays are a good example. On 21 July 1827 Charles Clay was given eight shillings, 'he having been out of imploy some time', while in the following year Thomas was twice allowed two pounds to help him with his arrears of rent. An undated list of paupers receiving 'Head Money', probably belonging to the early 1830s, has Charles listed among the 'sick and infirm', and receiving 12s.6d. a week. He was well enough in April 1830, though, for the Vestry to employ him to help repair the parish Poor House. Other cricketers who were helped include John Boyes, allowed five shillings for his daughter 'now in the Infirmary at Portsmouth', and Peter Husted, who was given £1 towards his rent. The 'Head Money' list also includes several names which are the same as those of cricketers, but it is impossible to be certain of the identification. The cricketers were not of course the only Hambledon people to be given special help: among the others was a labourer named George Gough of whom we shall have more to say. In 1827 he was given seven shillings, 'his wife being ill', as well as two payments of £1 towards his rent, and he too makes several appearances in the 'Head Money' list.[45]

After a succession of reasonably good harvests in the mid-1820s things took a turn for the worse. The average price of grain at Reading market rose from sixty-three shillings a quarter in the harvest year 1827–8 to seventy-three shillings in 1828–9. The 1829 harvest was a bit better, but in 1830, in spite of some early optimism – the *Hampshire Chronicle* reported that October had been 'exceedingly propitious to every description of field labour' – in the end grain prices rose nearly to their 1828–9 level. The Hambledon authorities were naturally worried about it. In March 1830 the Vestry had appointed a committee to 'ascertain the number of able-bodied labourers belonging to the parish, and the best means of regularly employing the same'. The committee reported that there were 200 unemployed men in the parish – ten per cent of the population, almost exactly the proportion of paupers in the county as a whole. They were wastefully being put to work on the highways, and to end this 'abuse' the committee proposed that occupiers of land should be required to employ them, each in proportion to his share of the total rateable value of the parish. But the Vestry could do nothing about this, it appeared, until Michaelmas. Michaelmas came and went, and early in October they were still debating 'the best means of employing the superabundant labourers of this parish'.[46]

The doomed, desperate explosion that Cobbett had predicted was now upon them. There had been serious trouble in Kent, in the shape of arson attacks on farmers, during the summer. On 28 August a gang of men smashed a threshing-machine near Canterbury, and during the next few days other threshing-machines were destroyed by the same party. New technology is always unpopular with the people whose labour it replaces, and threshing-machines deprived poor people of already scarce winter employment. Some farmers caved in and agreed to stop using them; those who did not became the targets of further attacks. Machine-breaking and arson continued and during October groups of labourers began assembling in Kent to demand higher wages. Their demands were nearly always conservative – a return to the imagined olden days of social justice and the 'moral economy' rather than any drastic political changes – but in a few places political radicals used more inflammatory language. At Langley they warned that if nothing was done they would 'bedew the country with blood'. Landlords, farmers and parsons began to receive threatening letters, signed by a mysterious 'Captain Swing'. Swing existed only as one of those mythic heroes who so often appeared in popular protests in preindustrial times – which did not make him any less menacing. By November much of Sussex as well as Kent was in a flame.

The violence soon spread into Hampshire.[47] In spite of reassuring reports about the harvest, propertied people in Basingstoke were worried that the 5 November celebrations would be used as a pretext for rioting.

Nearly 300 special constables were sworn in; they dispersed a group of men coming 'from the Common with weapons'. The day ended without even a bonfire, and the specials were rewarded with a supper at the Town Hall. A newspaper saw Basingstoke as a model for other Hampshire towns: 'the rabble can really do nothing when the advocates of lawful authority and good order are determined to keep the peace'. Basingstoke had escaped, but a few days later farmers near Portsmouth received anonymous warnings not to use threshing-machines, and barns and ricks were fired at Farnham and near Gosport. On the 17th the first destruction of machinery in the county was reported near Whitchurch; the next day several more threshing-machines were smashed near Havant. All over the county riotous assemblies of desperate men demanded higher wages. At Overton, a crowd of several hundred processed through the village chanting that they would no longer subsist on a diet of potatoes and bread. They returned the next day carrying flails and sticks, and were only pacified by the arrival of the famous radical leader 'Orator' Hunt, who somehow persuaded the farmers to promise an increase in wages.[48]

At Longparish the vicar received one of the familiar warnings: 'Take care of your things on the 23, for the vicarage shall come down this night – from Swing'. Another like it went to Richard Leach, steward to that great sportsman Peter Hawker. Before the riots, Leach had unsuccessfully tried to persuade the local farmers to make 'an increased allowance for the poor'. Hawker was in London when the storm broke. On the 20th he heard that there were '300 men surrounding the farmers at Longparish'. Two days later, more-reassuring news arrived, the farmers having belatedly agreed to Leach's proposals. But in spite of continuing 'dreadful accounts' from other parts of the county, Hawker did not go down to Longparish until 4 December, long after the trouble was over. It would have been highly inconvenient to have gone earlier – and the shooting would not have been very good.[49]

By 22 November there was rioting all over Hampshire: 300 labourers destroyed the workhouse at Selborne – Gilbert White's halcyon days of harmony were long forgotten – and another workhouse was pulled down at Headley. There were other riotous assemblies at Upham, Kimpton and Charles Powlett's old parish, Itchen Abbas, and a serious incident near Andover, where an iron foundry which made parts for threshing-machines was completely wrecked. At Avington the Duke (as he now was) of Buckingham organized a posse of 100 of his tenants and labourers to resist ungrateful rioters who had forgotten his hospitality in 1815. Led by the local parson, the better armed and disciplined force put the rioters to flight and handed over twenty-nine prisoners to the magistrates.[50]

Hambledon escaped the worst of the violence, but it was touch and go. People were subsequently indicted for rioting at several nearby villages, East Meon, Wickham and Bishop's Waltham, among them. On 23 November threshing-machines were broken at Droxford, only a few miles away, and on the same day the crisis reached Hambledon itself. The Vestry had shown their alarm a few days earlier, when they held a special meeting, with the vicar, Mr Richards, in the chair. They were still rather more concerned about the burden on the farmers than the condition of the poor, as they noted the ratepayers' dissatisfaction at paying the labourers employed on the parish roads. But they did recognize that real work had to be found for the unemployed. Yet another committee was charged with finding a way to have the surplus labourers 'more profitably employed in the service of the farmer, rather than wasted and frittered away' on maintaining the highways. On the 23rd an angry crowd gathered in the village street, demanding action.[51]

Their leader was a labourer named George Gough – 'General' Gough, the locals called him. Years later an elderly lady in the village remembered him as a kindly old man in a 'smock frock', who had comforted her as a little girl when she fell into a bed of nettles. But in 1830 Gough and his friends were in a less genial mood. They waited impatiently outside the George Inn. Inside, the Vestry committee anxiously discussed the situation, while rumblings from the street floated ominously through the inn windows. Eventually they agreed that labourers' wages should be increased to 10s.6d. a week, that farmers would be required to provide employment according to their share of the Poor Rate, that paupers' rents should be no more than a shilling a week, and that only the aged and infirm would in future be employed (nominally!) on the highways. They also promised to support a petition to Parliament 'to take off all taxes on the necessaries of life'. Col. Butler went to the window and addressed the crowd in what the local newspaper describes as a 'conciliatory and expressive manner'. He must have known how to talk to the common folk – those afternoons shared with the plebeian cricketers on Windmill Down gave him credibility, and no doubt enabled him to understand their plight. When he had finished relaying the

Vestry's decisions, the labourers gave him three rousing cheers and went home.[52]

And that, it seemed, was that. Troops were brought in to pacify the county, and the most notorious rioters arrested. Some were tried by a special commission at Winchester, others at the 1831 Lent Assizes. Over a hundred Hampshire men were convicted of capital crimes, though in the end only five were executed, the rest being either imprisoned or transported to Australia. A Fordingbridge man attributed his crimes to his laxity in observing the sabbath, and in particular to his having so often played cricket on that day. None of the victims was from Hambledon. The village had troubles enough, but the old lines of paternalism and deference had somehow managed to hold. Some of the credit for this must surely go to the cricket club, which had preserved the fragile cultural ties between people of different social classes that had so often withered away elsewhere. The Club's final disintegration in 1825, when the sickness of rural society overwhelmed it, still left a dwindling legacy of goodwill.[53]

It may be that we can read something of that legacy in a speech given at the trial of one group of Hampshire rioters. It was made by a barrister named John Poulter, a familiar figure at Winchester Assizes. He must have been giving his services for nothing, as the people he was defending were poor men, for whom the services of learned counsel would otherwise have been ludicrously remote. Poulter referred to the dreadful poverty and distress which had led his clients to demand higher wages. They were, he went on,

persons from which this country has derived great benefit. There had been a long war; and when their country wanted them, did they not answer the call? These persons, or their fathers, were a sample of that noble race who, in times of difficulty, fought their country's battles, and earned her renown to the remotest regions of the earth . . . Do not let us depress that noble spirit that has existed in our peasantry.

Poulter was almost certainly a Hambledon cricketer. His father, the Revd Edmund Poulter, rector of Meonstoke in 1794 and later a canon of Winchester, had certainly been a member of the club in the old days, and the barrister may well have been the 'Mr J. Poulter' who played fairly often on Windmill Down between 1810 and 1822. His clients were all found guilty and sentenced to various terms of imprisonment, but his eloquence is one more reminder that the Club may have played a significant role in softening the harsh realities of class conflict.[54]

Yet most of the propertied quickly put Swing behind them. The Hambledon Hunt had its annual Christmas meet on Broadhalfpenny on 27 December, and the Vestry went about its usual business of helping poor people with special needs. In March 1832 there were fourteen paupers in the Poor House, a year later twice that number. Among those who came and went were several former Windmill Down cricketers: George Husted, for example, son of the Club's old drinks waiter. Labourers' wages were still subsidized out of the rates: Husted was being paid three shillings a week by the parish after having 'entered into service' in July 1832. Thomas Butler was an honourable man, and there is no reason to doubt the sincerity of his dramatic speech from the inn window on that November day. But through no fault of his, the promises he made were bound to be empty ones. There was nothing the Hambledon Vestry could legally do for the poor unless it had statutory authority to do it, and with Parliament now dominated by Whig adherents of laissez-faire, no such legislative backing was likely to be forthcoming. Wages could be left to the impersonal force of the market.[55]

What was forthcoming, in 1834, was the infamous New Poor Law. Out-relief was ended and replaced by a system designed to make welfare less attractive to its recipients than *any* form of work. This was done by herding paupers into workhouses – 'Bastilles', their critics called them – which, supporters of the new system freely admitted, were deliberately made 'as like prisons as possible'. In the name of Benthamite, utilitarian efficiency, the workhouses would be controlled not by the local parish, whose Overseers might still retain some vestigial sympathy for paupers they knew, but by the more remote Poor Law Unions, groupings of several villages with a single common workhouse.[56]

Hambledon was within the Droxford Union, and in March 1835 the Vestry elected four representatives to its governing body, the Board of Guardians. Two of them, however, refused to serve, obviously because they could not accept the harsh authoritarianism of the new law. Their names were Edward Hale, grandson of the eighteenth-century doctor, and Cobbett's friend John Goldsmith. They and their forebears had long been pillars of the village community: churchwardens, overseers of the poor, members of the Vestry. Goldsmith had presided at the annual dinner of the Hambledon Friendly Society, held at the New Inn in July 1830. His 'kind attentions' to the needs of the ordinary members, an observer noted, were always 'eminently conspicuous'. Hale and Goldsmith were both also former members of the Hambledon Cricket Club. Their resignations are a fitting illustration of the connection between the collapse of the Club and the death of the old village community.[57]

Epilogue: Beyond Hambledon

While I was writing this book allegations about the bribing of international cricketers by gambling interests began to appear in the press. The first charges were made by Australian players against members of the Pakistan team, but the Australians, it later transpired, had themselves been approached by bookmakers. Shane Warne, one of the greatest spin bowlers of all time, recalled being in a Sri Lankan casino and having a run of bad luck at the roulette table. He was approached by an Indian bookmaker, who offered to cover his debts. No one has suggested that Warne agreed to throw a match in return for the £2,000 he was paid – all he was required to do, apparently, was to provide last-minute information on the state of the pitch and the likely impact of the weather on a particular game. But further charges have subsequently been levelled against the Pakistan XI, based on suspicions aroused by their abject performance against Australia in the final of the 1999 World Cup, and their earlier defeat at the hands of Bangladesh.

More recently still, the cricket world has been convulsed by the sacking of the South African captain, Hansie Cronje, for taking money from bookmakers. There have been suspicions, based partly on police reports, that the corruption in some of the national teams goes much deeper than the sale of inside information about the pitch or the likely composition of the team. At the time of writing we still do not know the full story, and perhaps we never shall. But we know enough to be sure that the integrity of international cricket is seriously at risk. As the distinguished West Indian commentator Tony Cozier asks: 'Can we again take anything we see on the cricket field at face value?'

Now I am in no position to know how far the infection has spread in the South African and other international teams, and have no opinion on the adequacy of the fines imposed on Warne and his colleague, Mark

Waugh, by the Australian Board of Control. But Shane Warne's story must surely remind any reader of this book of the one that Beldham told Pycroft about the approaches made by the bookies to far less well-paid London cricketers in the early 1800s. In Beldham's story the scene is an Oxford Street pub, the Green Man; in Warne's case it is a Colombo casino, but the essentials of the situation are the same. There are the same cricketers who want more money (not that the incomes of Beldham and Warne, even allowing for inflation, are remotely comparable), the same plausible gentlemen who introduce themselves as cricket fans and admirers, the same offers to help – even if in Warne's case the *quid pro quo* did not involve anything as serious as attempting to alter the result of a match.

Whatever the outcome of these miserable affairs, one thing is clear: that professional cricket is part of the global economy and thus subject, as never before, to the enticing lure of money. This is evident in other things besides the players' vulnerability to the blandishments of professional gamblers. Cricket is now awash – though less so than some other sports – with money derived from corporate sponsorships and television contracts. The interests of the sponsors and the television channels are naturally often preferred to those of the ordinary cricket lover in such matters as the hours of play, the days of the week on which matches are played, and the seating arrangements at grounds. The demands of television may even influence the playing conditions in a given match. This appears to have been the case at Old Trafford in the 1999 season, when the groundsman was unable to prepare a satisfactory pitch because camera angles required that big matches had to be played on one restricted area of the square. And while international players make far more money than they have ever done before, they are increasingly subject to conditions dictated by sponsors which distract them from what ought to be their first priority, concentrating on the game. This is not just a matter of wearing advertising logos on their clothing and equipment, demeaning though that may be. Players are also required to make personal appearances at the behest of the sponsors, and even to allow sponsors to lay down what they are allowed to drink in celebrations after a victory.[1]

Cricket is not, of course, the only sport under threat. Gambling interests have tried to undermine the integrity of English football, with the same sort of approaches to players as in cricket, and more recently the sabotaging of lighting systems to prevent the completion of matches that from the point of view of 'the knowing ones' were going the wrong way. In some other countries the corruption has of course been far more blatant than in Britain. And just as in cricket, the sponsors who pay the footballing piper all too often call the tune. Brazil, for example, has agreed to allow its sponsor, Nike, to arrange a large part of its fixture-list over a five-year period.

Other sports have not been spared the monetary onslaught. In recent years the news has been full of reports of under-the-table inducements to persuade members of the International Olympic Committee to award the Games to this or that city. We have seen the reputation of one of Europe's supreme sporting events, the Tour de France, undermined by a succession of drug-related scandals. In England, we have seen rugby clubs trying to buy their way to promotion by taking over teams from a higher division of the league, and justifying it as a straightforward commercial transaction. Speaking of his club's take-over bid for London Scottish, Bristol's Chief Executive declared quite simply: 'We would be buying a 100 per cent shareholding in a limited company.'[2] And we have been bombarded with news about the attempt of BSkyB television to buy the richest football club in the world, Manchester United. After this move was blocked by the Monopolies Commission, the club was soon the target of another approach, this time from a professional gambling syndicate. Nor is Manchester United the only football club to receive the attention of television companies; the purchase of a £22 million stake in Liverpool by Granada may be a sign of similar things to come. In the United States, full or part-ownership of sports teams by media conglomerates is so common as scarcely to excite comment.

These are only a few random examples of developments which, in England at any rate, have severely tested the loyalty of ordinary followers of the sports involved, cricket included. All too often, decisions made by a governing body are prompted by openly commercial reasons, often at the expense of the real traditions of the game: the football authorities' decision to allow Manchester United to withdraw from the 1999–2000 FA Cup so that the club could take part in a lucrative tournament in Brazil is a case in point. The defection of the previous season's winners completely devalues the Cup, putting the interests of Manchester's shareholders above those of the thousands of ordinary football supporters throughout the land who correctly read the message that even the most prestigious of competitions takes a back seat when money is involved.

Once again sport is trapped in the global economy. Yet, as a devotee of lowly Carlisle United pointed out in a despairing protest, 'for the majority of us, football is a *local* matter'.[3]

So it used to be with cricket. The later chapters of this book observed the undermining of cricket in the rural southeast as the game's aristocratic bosses transferred its centre of gravity to London, to Lord's and the MCC. There were of course other reasons for cricket's comparative decline in this region after 1800, among them the general immiserization of the labouring population and the collapse of rural morale in the face of the agricultural and social changes of the period. But the process of centralization was an important part of the story. One consequence of all this was the shift of the game's regional vitality to the industrial Midlands and the North, to Yorkshire, Lancashire, and Nottinghamshire, where by the later 1820s the game was spreading rapidly and attracting great crowds. The modern parallel with this is the shift of the game's centre of gravity to the countries of the Southern Hemisphere and the Indian sub-continent, after it was undermined in England by the short-sighted mismanagement of the Lord's establishment, as well as by social forces for which even they cannot be blamed. Cricket did not of course die out in southern England in the nineteenth century, and in Kent especially it continued to flourish in the era of great players such as Fuller Pilch and Alfred Mynn. But the rural game was now dominated by the aristocracy in ways that in most places reduced the dynamism and vitality that had been present in the great days of the Hambledon Club.

Professionals were still employed by the county clubs during this period, but their interests were, as always, subordinated to those of the gentry and aristocracy. In the 1840s they revolted and, in a display of entrepreneurship that Samuel Smiles, the author of *Self Help*, would have been proud of, formed the All-England XI. Their leader was the Nottingham professional William Clarke. Clarke's organizational skills were quickly translated into profits, which were shared between himself and the other players – though eventually a group of them split off to form a rival team, when they thought that Clarke was helping himself to too big a slice of the pie. The All-England XI was a touring team, with no local base. But it brought the spectacle of cricket played at the highest level of skill to places, particularly in the northern counties, previously denied it, and thus set an example for local players to emulate, raising the standard all round. The power of the XI was such that its matches were almost invariably played against odds, against XX of Sheffield, or XXII of Leicester, for example. Huge crowds flocked to see these games, and the XI's success reinforced the lesson taught by Hambledon in the previous century – that cricket's appeal was to a public much wider than the upper classes.

But there were some obvious problems that in the end led to the demise of the touring professional XIs. They were so strong that their matches were rarely really competitive, except when they played each other at Lord's, as they were eventually allowed to do. They also lacked any connection with the sort of regional consciousness that Hambledon had so spectacularly represented. So by the 1870s, when the arrival of the railway age made competition possible over a much wider area, the counties revived, and the players went back to their local teams. It is no accident that something resembling the County Championship emerged in cricket during that decade, just as at the same time the FA Cup provided a national competition in football. The counties were still under gentry or aristocratic control, but they reconnected big-time cricket to the local community. And during the same period cricket produced its dominating national personality in the person of the Gloucestershire doctor, W. G. Grace, whose skills were such that he regularly headed the national batting averages and brought crowds of spectators to watch wherever he played. 'W. G.' was ostensibly an amateur – during his years of greatness the annual match between the Gentlemen and the Players, hitherto often laughably one-sided in favour of the Players, was now nearly always won by the Gentlemen – but he made more money out of the game than any professional. He was an appropriate hero for the Victorian middle class to which he belonged.

This, essentially, was the compromise that made possible the great age of county cricket between 1870 and about 1970. What its beneficiaries comfortably perceived as a secure social order was reflected in the organization and composition of the county sides: middle-class, gentry or aristocratic leadership, but with plenty of popular participation by people of all classes both on the field and in the grandstands. Like the national government, teams had to be led by gentlemen who, it was believed, were the only people to possess the necessary qualities of leadership. At the same time the other gentlemen who had time to play in the regular round of three-day matches could be stiffened by the presence of lower-class professionals. Yorkshire, the most completely professional of the county teams, were captained around 1900 by Lord Hawke, a fierce disciplinarian, but also a fine batsman whose presence certainly did not weaken the side. There were class tensions, but they were generally submerged in the team spirit that took over on the field once the game was in progress. And the pride a club, particularly a successful one, could inspire in its locality sometimes transcended class in a way almost reminiscent of John Nyren's Hambledon. After Somerset, its team almost equally divided between professionals and amateurs, had sensationally defeated powerful Yorkshire at Leeds in 1901, they got off their train at Taunton at three o'clock in the morning and were greeted by a large and enthusiastic crowd accompanied by a band. The professional Len Braund and the amateur Lionel Palairet had played equally crucial parts in the victory.

After the Second World War the system began to unravel. For a decade or so the counties continued to command popular support, thanks to the appeal of such great characters as Denis Compton and Len Hutton. Traditional rivalries of the type expressed in the 'Roses' matches between Lancashire and Yorkshire still attracted massive crowds. But it was increasingly difficult to find amateurs of sufficient quality to make credible captains, and some of those who attempted to do the job were ludicrously ill-equipped for it. Other leisure-time activities provided much stronger competition for the attention of all but the hard core of cricket followers, while the increasing proliferation of international 'Test' cricket made the county game seem parochial and uninteresting.

We come, then, to our own days and to the domination of the game by its corporate sponsors. During this time, the almost endemic feebleness of England's national team has encouraged the demand, sedulously promoted by cricket's London-based media establishment, that the interests of the county game should be totally subordinated to those of the national team. The policy may generate large revenues from television, but it is also likely to lead to the interests of the ordinary cricket watcher in the provinces being contemptuously neglected. There has been less and less Saturday play, and often none at all on Bank Holidays. So the years of trashing county cricket by writers who themselves rarely attend matches outside of London or the other Test match grounds have proved to be self-fulfilling prophecies. The assumption that club and county cricket only exists in order to provide recruits for the national team is rarely questioned, and when it is, those responsible are usually dismissed as old fogeys out of touch with modern realities. Yet it does not seem to me that the primacy of international cricket is in fact so self-evident, or that it should justify undermining the game at the lower levels.

If there is one thing we ought to have learned from the whole sorry history of the twentieth century it must surely be the pernicious consequences of excessive nationalism. Of course it is good that people should retain honestly patriotic feelings, based on a sense of what is best in their country's culture and traditions. But nationalism is not the be-all and end-all of our lives. In a healthy society people will have a secure sense of *local* identity too – a sense of place and neighbourhood. One of the most unhappy developments of the past thirty years or so has been the weakening of that sense of identity, that pride in the place from which we come. Carried to extremes, it too can have undesirable effects, as the excesses of football hooliganism should remind us. But there has not been much of that in cricket, except very occasionally in the one-day, limited-overs variety. Local awareness has been undermined by the obliterating power of the mass media (that has been going on for much longer than thirty years, of course); by the impact of the local government reforms which began in the 1970s and have made people less and less certain about their regional roots; and by the ever-increasing centralization which has made counties and towns more subject than they have ever been to the authority of London and the rate-capping state.

Sport, as we have so often repeated, reflects the larger society, so it would be naïve to expect cricket to be exempt from the impact of changing social assumptions about the connection between the individual and the community. If it continues unchecked, the reduction of all relationships to monetary ones will in the end destroy the spirit of the cricket that has been played – admittedly with many ups and downs – ever since the days of Hambledon. The structure of cricket is still sufficiently different from that of many other sports for there to be some remaining defences against the worst features of the new order. Most counties are still *clubs*, with members devoted to the real interests of the game in their localities, rather than shareholders interested only in profits and dividends, but it would be rash to predict that this will continue for much longer. Lovers of cricket should take warning from American sports, in which owners of teams have no compunction about moving their activities to another city if they are unable to blackmail their current one into building them a new stadium at the taxpayers' expense.

*

It is easy to be pessimistic, and even paranoid, about cricket's future, especially in the country in which it originated. Former players regularly note how the game no longer seems to be as much fun as it used to be. This is not simply the nostalgia for the past that affects all of us as we get older. Anyone who has watched English cricket over the years now searches almost in vain for players who convey the sense of enjoyment that was so immediately recognizable in players of the calibre of Arthur Wellard and Denis Compton, of Fred Trueman and Colin Milburn, or in more recent times of David Gower, Ian Botham and Derek Randall. 'The trouble is,' another great player, Brian Close, has said, 'the game doesn't come first these days, the money comes first.' Stephen Chalke, in whose book I find this and many similar comments, wonders if, 'in the drive for profit and prosperity, we have started to forget why we created such a wonderful game'.[4]

Through all the disasters at the higher levels, cricket has survived in the localities because people want to play it for fun, not money. Even that may be threatened by the attitude of the game's present lords and masters, who hand down from London decrees about the composition of leagues, the length of matches and the number of overs that can be bowled in provincial club cricket, with apparently no interest in listening to what the ordinary players want. It is an outlook which the ninth Earl of Winchilsea would have approved of, but it is surely destructive of the grassroots vitality of what ought to be a democratic game, a game 'for the low and the great'. If cricket is to survive in any worthwhile form, we need to rediscover its value as it has been (and sometimes still is) played at Taunton, at Worcester, at Cheltenham and at Canterbury; but even more as it is played at Chew Magna, Milnrow, Pudsey St Lawrence – and Hambledon. It may help us to do this if we reflect on the way it was played, more than two centuries ago, on Broadhalfpenny Down.

Notes

Preface

1. John Nyren, 'The Cricketers of My Time', in *The Young Cricketer's Tutor*, ed. Charles Cowden Clarke (London: Effingham Wilson, 1833). In this book I have for the most part relied on F. S. Ashley-Cooper's later edition of the same work (London: Gay and Bird, 1902), though I have sometimes preferred Ashley Mote's more recent *John Nyren's The Cricketers of My Time: The Original Version* (London: Robson Books, 1998).

2. The original is in the MCC Library at Lord's. The letter bears the date 1739, and this has been accepted by most cricket historians. But the '3' has clearly been written over some other digit, which can only be a '7': the correct date is 1779.

1 Cricket and Culture: the Prehistory

1. Nyren, ed. Ashley-Cooper, pp. 95–7.

2. Both Nyren's intentions and the question of authorship are discussed by Ashley Mote in the introduction to his new edition of *The Cricketers of My Time*.

3. A good recent guide to all this is Peter Wynne-Thomas, *The History of Cricket: From the Weald to the World* (London: HMSO, 1997), p. 18.

4. The Guildford deposition has been often quoted, for example in Christopher Brookes, *English Cricket: The Game and its Players through the Ages* (London: Weidenfeld and Nicolson, 1978), p. 16.

5. Daniel Defoe, *A Tour through the Whole Island of Great Britain*, ed. Pat Rogers (Harmondsworth: Penguin Books, 1971), pp. 131–2, 165.

6. L. R. A. Grove, 'A Note on Early Kent Cricket', *Arch. Cant.*, LXIII (1950), 154. For the geography of the southeastern counties I rely primarily upon Defoe's *Tour*; Brian Short, 'The South-East: Kent, Surrey and Sussex', in Joan Thirsk (ed.), *Agrarian History of England and Wales*, vol. V, pt I (Cambridge: Cambridge University Press, 1984), chap. 9; and John Talbot White, *The*

South-East Down and Weald: Kent, Surrey and Sussex (London: Eyre Methuen, 1977).

7. W. S. Lewis *et al.* (eds.), *The Yale Edition of the Correspondence of Horace Walpole* (New Haven: Yale University Press, 1937–83) (hereafter, *Walpole Correspondence*), vol. XXXIII, p. 222. Esther Meynell, *Sussex* (London: Robert Hale, 1947), p. 225.

8. Gilbert White, *The Natural History of Selborne* (Oxford: Oxford University Press, 1937), pp. 20–21.

9. I have discussed the impact of similar regional contrasts in Wiltshire and Dorset in my *Revel, Riot, and Rebellion: Popular Politics and Culture in England, 1603–1660* (Oxford: Clarendon Press, 1985).

10. Peter Borsay, *The English Urban Renaissance: Culture and Society in the Provincial Town, 1660–1770* (Oxford: Clarendon Press, 1989).

11. V. J. B. Torr (ed.), 'A Tour through Kent in 1735', *Arch. Cant.*, XLIII (1931), 274–5.

12. I shall often be using the term culture, and it requires some explanation. The anthropologist Clifford Geertz has given us a useful working definition. The culture of a community – whether nation, region, or village – consists, he says, of the 'historically transmitted pattern of meanings' that its members share, and the verbal, visual and symbolic means by which those beliefs are expressed. As Geertz's own work shows, sports are among the most useful cultural forms that help us to understand the communities we are examining. See Geertz, *The Interpretation of Cultures* (New York: Basic Books, 1973), esp. p. 89.

13. For this paragraph and the pages that follow, see David Underdown, 'Regional Cultures? Local Variations in Popular Culture during the Early Modern Period', in Tim Harris (ed.), *Popular Culture in England, c.1500–1850* (London: Macmillan, 1995), pp. 37–42. The Prison Bars reference is from *Lloyd's Evening Post*, 19–21.9.1764.

14. There are various spellings which seem to refer to the same game, including 'stobball', 'stowball', 'staffball' and 'stopball'. See [John Goulstone], 'Stob-ball as a 17th Century Form of Cricket', *Sports History*, vol. 1 (1982), 19–21.

15. Grove, 'A Note on Early Kent Cricket', pp. 153–5. [K. S. Martin] (ed.), *Records of Maidstone* (Maidstone: W. Hobbs & Sons, 1926), p. 270. Dennis Brailsford, *British Sport: A Social History*, rev. edn (Cambridge: Lutterworth Press, 1997), pp. 44–6. See also Stephen Green, 'Some Cricket Records', *Archives*, vol. 18, no. 80 (October 1988), 187, 190; and Green, 'References to Cricket Pre-1700', *JCS*, vol. 10, no. 3 (autumn 1981), 54–6.

16. T. J. McCann and P. M. Wilkinson, 'The Cricket Match at Boxgrove in 1622', *SAC*, CX (1972), 118–22. T. J. McCann, 'Seventeenth Century Sussex Cricket: East Lavant, 1628', *JCS*, vol. 15, no. 2 (spring 1991), 54–6. *Sussex N&Q*, XII (1948–9), 42–3. R. F. Hunnisett, 'Early Sussex Cricket', *Sussex N&Q*, XVI (1963–7), 217–21, 319–20.

17. *Sussex N&Q*, XVI (1963–7), 31. George B. Buckley, *Fresh Light on 18th-*

Century Cricket: A Collection of 1000 New Cricket Notices from 1697 to 1800 A.D. (Birmingham: Cotterell, [1935]), p. 1.

18. BL, Add. MS 33188 (Pelham MSS), fol. 19. Rowland Bowen, *Cricket: A History of its Growth and Development throughout the World* (London: Eyre and Spottiswoode, 1970), p. 29, and Wynne-Thomas, *History of Cricket*, pp. 6–7, both stress the Wealden origins. I am indebted to Gerald Howat for the point about the implements. Aubrey is quoted in Christina Hole, *English Sports and Pastimes* (London: Batsford, 1949), p. 60.

19. Bowen, *Cricket*, pp. 28–9, 46. See also [Goulstone], 'Stob-ball as a 17th Century Form of Cricket'.

20. Filmer was from East Sutton, a few miles east of Coxheath. For evidence of the royalist sympathies of the other players, see [Martin], *Records of Maidstone*, pp. 118, 145, 158–63, and Edward Hasted, *History and Topographical Survey of the County of Kent* (Canterbury, 1778–99), vol. II, pp. 101, 418, 579. For the Cranbrook incident, see J. Goulstone, 'Some Cricket Grounds and Clubs in Kent', *Cantium*, vol. 2, no. 2 (April 1970), 34. For the gentry's involvement in popular sports, see Robert W. Malcolmson, *Popular Recreations in English Society 1700–1850* (Cambridge: Cambridge University Press, 1973), pp. 67–9.

21. John Marshall, *Sussex Cricket: A History* (London: Heinemann, 1959), pp. 2–3. Timothy J. McCann, 'Cricket and the Sussex County By-Election of 1741', *SAC*, CXIV (1976), 122.

22. Cesar de Saussure, *A Foreign view of England in the Reigns of George I and George II*, ed. M. Van Muyden (New York, 1902), p. 295.

23. James Pycroft, *The Cricket Field: Or, the History and the Science of Cricket* (Boston, Mass: Mayhew and Baker, 1859), p. 79.

24. Isaac Kramnick, *Bolingbroke and his Circle: The Politics of Nostalgia in the Age of Walpole* (Cambridge, Mass: Harvard University Press, 1968). For the Jacobite segment of the Tory gentry, see Paul Monod, *Jacobitism and the English People 1688–1788* (Cambridge: Cambridge University Press, 1989).

25. Underdown, *Revel, Riot, and Rebellion*, p. 64.

26. *SJ*, 6.9.1756; 4.10.1756; 9.5.1757; 30.5.1757; 13.6.1757.

27. Ibid., 9.5.1757; 13.5.1765; 11.8.1766–13.10.1766. For the notion of a traditional, just, economic order, see E. P. Thompson, *Customs in Common* (London: Merlin Press, 1991), chaps 4 and 5.

28. *SJ*, 3.10.1757.

2 'Good Old English Entertainments': Village Games in the Eighteenth Century

1. W. S. Blunt (ed.), 'Extracts from Mr John Baker's Horsham Diary', *SAC*, LII (1909), 69. R. W. Blencowe (ed.), 'Extracts from the Journal of Walter Gale', *SAC*, IX (1857), 188, 191. On rural conservatism, see Bob Bushaway, *By Rite:*

Custom, Ceremony and Community in England 1700–1880 (London: Junction Books, 1982), esp. chap. 1.

2. *SJ*, 23.5.1748; 27.7.1767. For the role of publicans, see Malcolmson, *Popular Recreations*, pp. 71–4. Thompson, *Customs in Common*, pp. 54–6, notes the JPs' ambivalent attitude to popular festivals.

3. For selections from the diary, see Edward Turner (ed.), 'The Marchant Diary', *SAC*, XXV (1873), 163–203. I have also used the microfilm of the original diary in Yale University Library (hereafter Marchant, MS Diary).

4. Malcolmson, *Popular Recreations*, p. 31. Ronald Hutton, *The Rise and Fall of Merry England: The Ritual Year 1400–1700* (Oxford and New York: Oxford University Press, 1994), p. 229. For the decline of churchales in the seventeenth century, see Underdown, *Revel, Riot, and Rebellion*.

5. *Gentleman's Magazine*, vol. 8 (1738), 465. 'Remaines of Gentilisme and Judaisme', in John Aubrey, *Three Prose Works*, ed. John Buchanan-Brown (Carbondale, Ill.: Southern Illinois University Press, 1972), p. 212. *Lloyd's Evening Post*, 12–15.8.1757. *SJ*, 6.7.1767.

6. Bushaway, *By Rite*, pp. 37, 40, 153. *VCH, Berks.*, II, 314–15. *SJ*, 25.6.1770. Malcolmson, *Popular Recreations*, p. 80. Underdown, *Revel, Riot and Rebellion*, p. 96.

7. Underdown, *Revel, Riot, and Rebellion*, p. 110. Richard Suggett, 'Festivals and Social Structure in Early Modern Wales', *Past and Present*, no. 152 (August 1996), 100–108.

8. *SJ*, 29.9.1755.

9. Ibid., 26.10.1742; 15.2.1748; 9.7.1750. For the change in the gender of skimmington targets, see E. P. Thompson, ' "Rough Music": Le Charivari Anglais', *Annales*, vol. 28 (1972), 294–5.

10. Defoe, *Tour*, p. 115. *SJ*, 24.10.1748; 31.10.1748. Marchant, MS Diary, 2.8.1721. HRO, Q9/2/3 (QS files, 1741). *HC*, 14.2.1774. *Portsmouth Gazette*, 10.2.1794. Bushaway, *By Rite*, p. 46.

11. Bushaway, *By Rite*, pp. 37, 39, 50, 64–74. Malcolmson, *Popular Recreations*, pp. 25–6. *HC*, 8.11.1773.

12. Paul Langford, *Public Life and the Propertied Englishman 1689–1798* (Oxford: Clarendon Press, 1991), p. 124. Bushaway, *By Rite*, pp. 74–8. There is a report of 29 May festivities in west-country towns in *SJ*, 2.6.1755. For popular Jacobitism, see Monod, *Jacobitism and the English People*, part III.

13. *Gentleman's Magazine*, vol. 8 (1738), 465.

14. Malcolmson, *Popular Recreations*, pp. 21, 31: *SJ*, 26.6.1739. Marchant, MS Diary, 6.6.1721. Earl of March, *A Duke and His Friends: The Life and Letters of the Second Duke of Richmond* (London: Hutchinson, 1911), vol. I, pp. 290–91. Dennis Brailsford, *Sport, Time, and Society: The British at Play* (London: Routledge, 1991), p. 64. *Kentish Weekly Post*, 18–21.8.1769. David Vaisey (ed.), *Diary of Thomas Turner 1754–1765* (Oxford: Oxford University Press, 1984), pp. 102, 104, 109, 150, 252.

15. Malcolmson, *Popular Recreations*, pp. 34–40, 82–4, 113, 116, 139–40. Bushaway, *By Rite*, pp. 38, 47, 252. On football in the southern downlands in the seventeenth century, see Underdown, *Revel, Riot, and Rebellion*, pp. 75–7.

16. *SJ*, 13.5.1751; 4.6.1764; 5.5.1766; 1.6.1767; 9.5.1768; 16.5.1768; 8.5.1769. For an explanation of singlestick, see Malcolmson, *Popular Recreations*, pp. 43–4.

17. *SJ*, 31.7.1738; 25.7.1757; 26.9.1757; 25.9.1760. According to a later definition, a broken head was one in which 'the blood runs an inch': *HC*, 23.5.1808. It is hard to see how this can have applied when padding was worn.

18. *DA*, 14.9.1744. Malcolmson, *Popular Recreations*, pp. 44, 57. *SJ*, 6.5.1748; 25.8.1755; 22.9.1755; 4.10.1756; 24.6.1765; 15.7.1765; 22.7.1765.

19. Ibid., 31.7.1738; 4.9.1739; 20.5.1740; 2.6.1766; 6.7.1767; 26.6.1769.

20. Ibid., 4.6.1764. Malcolmson, *Popular Recreations*, pp. 48–9, 119–22. Henry T. Waghorn, *The Dawn of Cricket* (London: MCC, 1906), p. 31. For this and the next paragraph, see Keith Thomas, *Man and the Natural World: Changing Attitudes in England 1500–1800* (Harmondsworth: Penguin, 1984), chap. 4, esp. pp. 158–60, 174–7.

21. Malcolmson, *Popular Recreations*, pp. 45–6, 66–8, 118–19, 122–5. John Hampden (ed.), *An Eighteenth-Century Journal: Being a Record of the Years 1774–1776* (London: Macmillan, 1940), p. 321. *HC*, 2.8.1773; 9.8.1773. Buckley, *18th-Century Cricket*, p. 37. *SJ*, 27.9.1756; 31.3.1760; 19.5.1760; 30.4.1764; 9.10.1769; 9.4.1770. John Sawyer, 'Some Extracts from the Journal and Correspondence of Mr John Burgess, of Ditchling, Sussex, 1785–1815', *SAC*, XL (1896), 139. *VCH, Berks.*, II, 296.

22. *SJ*, 6.2.1738; 3.7.1739. John R. Guy, 'From the Reformation to 1800', in L. S. Colchester (ed.), *Wells Cathedral: A History* (Shepton Mallet: Open Books, 1982), p. 172. Malcolmson, *Popular Recreations*, pp. 49–50, 122.

23. Brailsford, *Sport, Time, and Society*, p. 71. *SJ*, 29.1.1750; 6.5.1751; 13.5.1751; 3.6.1751. Vaisey, *Diary of Thomas Turner*, pp. 226, 250, 292.

24. Roger Longrigg, *History of Horse-Racing* (New York: Stein and Day, 1972), pp. 30, 39–40, 46–7. Borsay, *English Urban Renaissance*, pp. 181–95, 358–9, 366. *SJ*, 28.8.1739.

25. Wray Vamplew, *The Turf: A Social and Economic History of Horse Racing* (London: Allen Lane, 1976), pp. 18–21. Philip Yorke (ed.), *The Diary of John Baker* (London: Hutchinson, 1931), p. 217. Emily J. Climenson (ed.), *Passages from the Diaries of Mrs. Philip Lybbe Powys of Hardwick House, Oxon. A.D. 1756 to 1808* (London: Longmans Green, 1899), p. 133 (hereafter, *Powys Diaries*). Torr, 'Tour through Kent', 277.

26. *HC*, 5.10.1772. *Hampshire N&Q*, I (1883), 91. Brailsford, *Sport, Time, and Society*, p. 58.

27. Turner, 'The Marchant Diary', 183. Marchant, MS Diary, 3.9.1718; 8.3.1720; 17–18.5.1720; 15.8.1722; 11–12.8.1727; 9.8.1728. Vaisey, *Diary*

of Thomas Turner, pp. 12, 62, 108, 160, 209–10, 254, 278, 300–301. *SJ*, 5.7.1756; 3.9.1764; 26.8.1765. *HC*, 17.5.1773.

28. *SJ*, 10.4.1738; 10.7.1738; 24.7.1739; 2.9.1740. Turner, 'The Marchant Diary', 170, 175. Marchant, MS Diary, p. 111.

29. Borsay, *English Urban Renaissance*, p. 185.

30. *SJ*, 31.3.1755; 28.4.1766; 19.10.1767. Vaisey, *Diary of Thomas Turner*, p. 183.

31. *SJ*, 4.5.1742; 9.6.1755; 30.6.1755; 19.8.1771.

32. Buckley, *18th-Century Cricket*, p. 3. M. M. Verney (ed.), *Verney Letters of the Eighteenth Century from the MSS. at Claydon House* (London: Ernest Benn, 1930), vol. II, p. 189 (I am indebted to Leland Bellot for this reference). The 1743 pamphlet is quoted in Borsay, *English Urban Renaissance*, p. 302.

33. Buckley, *18th-Century Cricket*, p. 19. WSRO, Goodwood MS 23 (Accounts, 1694–1704), fol. 51. Lord Harris (ed.), *History of Kent County Cricket* (London: Eyre and Spottiswoode, 1907), pp. 1, 11, 34. George B. Buckley, *Fresh Light on Pre-Victorian Cricket: A Collection of New Cricket Notices from 1709 to 1837* (Birmingham: Cotterell, [1937]), p. 1.

34. BL, Egerton MS 2609 (Diary of Thomas Minter), fol. 108b. CKS, U442/ 045 (notebook of Paul d'Aranda), 30.9.1708; I am indebted to Norma Landau for this reference.

35. Marchant, MS Diary, *passim*. Many years later, between 1790 and 1815, a 'Marchant of Hurst' was a leading player for a team at nearby Oakenden Green, and a player of the same name regularly turned out for both Brighton and Sussex. This could very well have been Will's grandson: *S&B*, I, 130, 137, 139–41, 273; Buckley, *18th-Century Cricket*, pp. 148–51, 156.

36. Marchant, MS Diary, *passim*; also *VCH, Sussex*, VII (1940), 172–6, and *SAC*, XI (1859), 75–6.

37. Marchant, MS Diary, 12.6.1717; 14.5.1722.

38. David Vaisey's estimate is 350: *Diary of Thomas Turner*, pp. xxviii–xxix, while Dean K. Worcester, Jr, *The Life and Times of Thomas Turner of East Hoathly* (New Haven: Yale University Press, 1948), p. 2, suggests 400.

39. Vaisey, *Diary of Thomas Turner*, pp. 9, 40, 64, 102, 159, 205–6, 209, 274–5, 322.

40. Ibid., pp. 61–3, 208. For the 'best ball in the game' see above, p. xx.

41. Blencowe, 'Journal of Walter Gale', pp. 198–202.

42. Buckley, *18th-Century Cricket*, p. 3.

43. *Sussex N&Q*, XI (1946–7), 133. WSRO, Goodwood MS 136 (Steward's papers), R. Buckner to Duke, 5 June 1744. John Marshall, *The Duke Who Was Cricket* (London: F. Muller, 1961), p. 139. BL, Add. MS 28230 (Caryll MSS), fol. 402, T. Hunt to Caryll, 6 June 1747. Waghorn, *Dawn*, p. 29. Buckley, *Pre-Victorian Cricket*, pp. 2–3. *Sussex Weekly Advertiser*, 29.5.1749; 12.6.1749; 10.7.1749.

44. Vaisey, *Diary of Thomas Turner*, pp. 63–4.

45. Ibid., pp. 292–4, 326–39.

46. Ibid., pp. 102, 274–5.

47. W. S. Norton, 'Kent Cricket, 1705–50', in Harris, *Kent County Cricket*, pp. 12–13, 17, 22–3, 34. Marshall, *Duke Who Was Cricket*, pp. 115, 139, 157. Buckley, *18th-Century Cricket*, p. 23.

48. Buckley, *18th-Century Cricket*, p. 3; *Pre-Victorian Cricket*, p. 1. Historical Manuscripts Commission, *Portland MSS*, VI, 76. The estimate of the population of Dartford dates from 1676: K. M. Roome, 'Dartford 1660 to c.1720', *Arch. Cant.*, CXI (1993), 113. [John Goulstone], *The History of Cricket in Dartford* [1978], p. 7.

49. Buckley, *Pre-Victorian Cricket*, pp. 2–3. Norton, 'Kent Cricket, 1705–50', pp. 21–38. Henry T. Waghorn, *Cricket Scores, Notes, etc. from 1730–1773* (Edinburgh and London: Blackwood, 1899), pp. 45, 52–3. Waghorn, *Dawn*, p. 28. Ronald D. Knight (ed.), *Hambledon's Cricket Glory* (Weymouth, 1975–), vol. II, pp. 33–4; vol. VII, p. 17.

50. Buckley, *18th-Century Cricket*, p. 48. Goulstone, 'Some Cricket Grounds', 37–8; *Cricket in Dartford*, pp. 17–25. Hampden, *Eighteenth-Century Journal*, p. 16.

51. Buckley, *18th-Century Cricket*, p. 17; *Pre-Victorian Cricket*, p. 3. H. F. and A. P. Squire, *Henfield Cricket and its Sussex Cradle* (Hove: Cambridge's, 1949), p. 38. Waghorn, *Dawn*, pp. 29–30; *Cricket Scores*, pp. 26–7. *DA*, 30.7.1743. Norton, 'Kent Cricket, 1705–50', pp. 21–2. *Sussex Weekly Advertiser*, 29.5.1749.

52. E. P. Thompson, *Whigs and Hunters: The Origin of the Black Act* (New York: Pantheon Books, 1975), p. 92. Waghorn, *Cricket Scores*, p. 54 and n. F. S. Ashley-Cooper, 'Register of Kent County Cricketers, 1729–1906', in Harris, *Kent County Cricket*, p. 259.

3   Peers, Patrons and Professionals

1. John Brewer, *The Pleasures of the Imagination: English Culture in the Eighteenth Century* (London: HarperCollins, 1997). The following pages owe much to this fine book.

2. BL, Add. MS 28229, fol. 426: J. Magill to Caryll, 11.12.1739. Henry Raynor, *A Social History of Music* (New York: Schocken Books, 1972), pp. 261–2, 320. 'Ancient' was defined as having been composed at least twenty years earlier!

3. James Rosenheim, *The Emergence of a Ruling Order: English Landed Society 1650–1750* (London: Longman, 1998), p. 98. Lybbe Powys is a good example: see Climenson, *Powys Diaries*.

4. L. P. Curtis, *Chichester Towers* (New Haven: Yale University Press, 1966), pp. 47–8.

5. Marchant, MS Diary, p. 187. Paul Monod, 'Dangerous Merchandise: Smugg-

ling, Jacobitism, and Commercial Culture in Southeast England, 1690–1760',
Journal of British Studies, vol. 30 (1991), 159–60. *SJ*, 18.9.1739. The warmth
of the reception is confirmed by a letter in the Caryll MSS: BL, Add. MS 28229,
fol. 400. The Carylls seem to have been an exception to the growing aristocratic
withdrawal from local society described in Rosenheim, *Emergence of a Ruling
Order*, esp. p. 96.

6. BL, Add. MS 28229 (Caryll MSS), fol. 187: Lady Mary Caryll to John
Caryll, 18.1.1737/38. For Caryll, see Monod, *Jacobitism and the English People*,
pp. 83, 137; and 'Dangerous Merchandise', 179.

7. BL, Add. MS 28231, fols 195, 201v. *SJ*, 21.4.1766.

8. *SJ*, 18.8.1760; 29.10.1764; 15.4.1765; 24.8.1767.

9. Vaisey, *Diary of Thomas Turner*, pp. 11–12, 107, 161, 188.

10. G. W. Eustace (ed.), 'The Tomkins Diary', *SAC*, LXXI (1930), 19–20. *SJ*,
8.10.1750. CKS: U269/A232 (Sackville MSS). On the decline of aristocratic
charity, see Rosenheim, *Emergence of a Ruling Order*, p. 183. Thompson,
Customs in Common, pp. 45–8, describes other ways in which elite authority
was projected.

11. Roger Longrigg, *The English Squire and His Sport* (London: Michael Joseph,
1977), pp. 114–36, 222. For Ridge, see below, p. 132.

12. Torr, 'Tour through Kent', 277. Borsay, *English Urban Renaissance*,
pp. 187, 189. Vamplew, *The Turf*, pp. 26, 78–9. *SJ*, 11.9.1738; 22.4.1751.

13. Ibid., 9.9.1740; 28.5.1750. Borsay, *English Urban Renaissance*, p. 279.

14. Ibid., pp. 173–5. *DA*, 30.8.1756. *SJ*, 27.4.1767.

15. Ibid., 4.12.1739. *DA*, 17.5.1742; 20.7.1743. Dennis Brailsford, *Bareknuckles: A Social History of Prize-Fighting* (Cambridge: Lutterworth Press,
1988), pp. 7, 9–14.

16. Longrigg, *History of Horse-Racing*, pp. 46–7. WSRO, Goodwood MS 23
(Accounts, 1694–1704), fol. 51. Whether the Duke consumed the brandy
himself, or shared it with his team, is not known.

17. This account of Richmond is based on Timothy J. McCann (ed.), *The
Correspondence of the Dukes of Richmond and Newcastle 1724–1750* (Lewes:
Sussex Record Society, 1984) (hereafter, *Richmond–Newcastle Correspondence*), Introduction, and Curtis, *Chichester Towers*, pp. 35–9. Several payments for cricket matches are recorded in the Duchess's 'Household Book' for
1731–43: WSRO, Goodwood MS 127.

18. Ibid. 108, fol. 815; 120, fol. 96.

19. Curtis, *Chichester Towers*, pp. 36–7. Langford, *Public Life*, p. 120.
McCann, *Richmond–Newcastle Correspondence*, pp. xxxiv, 25–6. BL, Add.
MS 28230 (Caryll MSS), fol. 7: Richmond to Caryll, 3.3.1740. In the previous
October Richmond had angrily reproved Caryll for not declaring his neutrality,
and thus allowing the Whigs to canvass his tenants, as other Catholic landowners
had done. But in the subsequent by-election Caryll was indeed neutral, and sent
Richmond a gift of venison: ibid., fols 78–9, 145–7, 179.

20. WSRO, Goodwood MSS 117, p. 76; 120, fols 150–57, 167, 173. March, *A Duke and His Friends*, vol. I, pp. 148–51. Marshall, *Duke Who Was Cricket*, pp. 45–6.

21. Buckley, *18th-Century Cricket*, p. 4; *Pre-Victorian Cricket*, p. 1. Marshall, *Duke Who Was Cricket*, pp. 61, 66, 69. Lord Harris and F. S. Ashley-Cooper, *Kent Cricket Matches 1719–1880* (Canterbury: Gibbs, 1929), p. 6. Squire and Squire, *Henfield Cricket*, p. 37.

22. WSRO, Goodwood MS 108, fol. 819. Marshall, *Duke Who Was Cricket*, p. 72. Waghorn, *Cricket Scores*, p. 4.

23. Edmund Esdaile, 'Their Chivalry Was Cricket,' *JCS*, vol. 4 (1969–70), 25–49. Neil Caplan, 'The Sussex Catholics c. 1600–1800,' *SAC*, CXVI (1978), 21–8; and see also note in ibid., XLV (1902), 213. McCann, *Richmond–Newcastle Correspondence*, pp. xxxv, 38, 93.

24. Ibid., pp. 62–3, 67, 73. Timothy J. McCann, 'The Duke of Richmond, Slindon, and the 1741 Cricket Season in Sussex', *JCS*, vol. 11, no. 1 (autumn 1982), 29–30. Marshall, *Duke Who Was Cricket*, pp. 112–13, 119–24.

25. *DA*, 6–13.9.1744. Marshall, *Duke Who Was Cricket*, pp. 139, 156. Norton, 'Kent Cricket 1705–50', p. 22. Waghorn, *Dawn*, p. 29. Esdaile, 'Their Chivalry Was Cricket', 48. W. A. Walton, 'The Slindon Cricket Grounds and Teams', *West Sussex History*, no. 31 (1985), 27–8; I am indebted to Tim McCann for this reference.

26. In that year a Sussex player listed as 'Nyland' appeared for 'England' against Dartford; it is also possible that this was Richard Nyren, who had not yet moved to Hambledon and thus would still have been a Sussex player. For all this, see Esdaile, 'Their Chivalry Was Cricket', 25–9, 45–9 (the list of Slindon players in the second part of the article is questionable). W. D. Cooper, 'Royalist Compositions in Sussex during the Commonwealth', *SAC*, XIX (1867), 116–19. Edwin H. W. Dunkin (ed.), *Calendar of Sussex Marriage Licences ... for the Archdeaconry of Chichester, June 1575, to December 1730* (Sussex Record Society, 1909), p. 153. Norton, 'Kent Cricket, 1705–50', p. 38.

27. Timothy J. McCann, 'Edward Aburrow, Cricketer and Smuggler', *JCS*, vol. 10, no. 2 (spring 1981), 17–19. Waghorn, *Dawn*, p. 26; *Cricket Scores*, pp. 47–9. Thompson, *Whigs and Hunters*, pp. 229–30. ESRO, QI/EW9 (Indictment Book, 1732–49), fol. 55v; QZ/EW4 (Recognizance Book, 1738–52). For the treatment of informers by smugglers, see Cal Winslow, 'Sussex Smugglers', in Douglas Hay et al., *Albion's Fatal Tree: Crime and Society in Eighteenth-Century England* (New York: Pantheon Books, 1975), pp. 145–6.

28. March, *A Duke and His Friends*, vol. I, p. 260. McCann, *Richmond–Newcastle Correspondence*, pp. 4, 7.

29. *SJ*, 31.7.1739; 28.8.1739; 26.8.1740. McCann, *Richmond–Newcastle Correspondence*, pp. 35–8. For the general election campaign, see Curtis, *Chichester Towers*, pp. 43–6.

30. BL, Add. MS 32697 (Newcastle MSS), fols 295, 405: Gage to Newcastle,

9.7.1741, and Jewkes to Newcastle, 9.8.1741. WSRO, Goodwood MS 127 ('Household book' 1731–43), 1.4.1741.

31. Lewis et al., *Walpole Correspondence*, vol. XL, p. 6. Waghorn, *Cricket Scores*, pp. 12–13. Norman Sykes, *Church and State in the XVIIIth Century* (Cambridge: Cambridge University Press, 1934), p. 82. McCann, *Richmond–Newcastle Correspondence*, pp. 62–3. For Richmond's use of cricket in elections, see also McCann, 'Cricket and the Sussex County By-Election of 1741', 121–5.

32. McCann, *Richmond–Newcastle Correspondence*, pp. 40, 62, 69. Curtis, *Chichester Towers*, pp. 43, 58. BL, Add. MS 32697 (Newcastle Papers), fols 388–9: Gage to Newcastle, 5.8.1741. See also McCann, 'Cricket and the Sussex County By-Election of 1741'; 'The Duke of Richmond, Slindon, and the 1741 Cricket Season in Sussex', 29–31.

33. McCann, *Richmond–Newcastle Correspondence*, pp. 67, 73. Curtis, *Chichester Towers*, p. 84. CKS, U269/C150 (Sackville corr.): Richmond to Duke of Dorset, [10.6.]1741. BL, Add. MS 32698 (Newcastle Papers), fol. 229: Board to Newcastle, 29.10.1741.

34. McCann, *Richmond–Newcastle Correspondence*, p. 23.

35. Waghorn, *Cricket Scores*, p. 13. Marshall, *Duke Who Was Cricket*, pp. 90–91. Buckley, *18th-Century Cricket*, p. 25. The standard biography of the Prince is Sir George Young, *Poor Fred: The People's Prince* (London and New York: Oxford University Press, 1937), which, however, ignores his cricketing interests.

36. Waghorn, *Cricket Scores*, p. 6; *Dawn*, p. 10. Norton, 'Kent Cricket, 1705–50', p. 16. Harris and Ashley-Cooper, *Kent Cricket Matches*, p. 9. W. V. Crake, 'Correspondence of John Collier', *SAC*, XLV (1902), 67–8. Waghorn's collections contain numerous other reports of the Prince's presence at matches: e.g., *Cricket Scores*, pp. 13, 22. For Stead, see Marshall, *Duke Who Was Cricket*, pp. 39–40.

37. *DA*, 7.9.1743. Waghorn, *Cricket Scores*, pp. 34–5.

38. Waghorn, *Cricket Scores*, p. 40.

39. CKS, U269/A301/1 (Gardener's accounts, 1735, 1738). *Lloyd's Evening Post*, 5–7.10.1757. *DNB*: Sackville, Lionel, first Duke of Dorset (1688–1765). Piers Mackesy, in his *The Coward of Minden: The Affair of Lord George Sackville* (London: Allen Lane, 1979), does the best he can in Lord George's defence.

40. *DNB*: Sackville, Charles, second Duke of Dorset (1711–1769). Harris and Ashley-Cooper, *Kent Cricket Matches*, p. 9. CKS, U269/A237 (Sackville MSS). Lewis et al., *Walpole Correspondence*, vol. XL, p. 6. BL, Add. MS 5957 (Whaley's travel journal), fols 11–12.

41. Lewis et al., *Walpole Correspondence*, vol. XXXVII, p. 270. Waghorn, *Cricket Scores*, pp. 7–8. Harris and Ashley-Cooper, *Kent Cricket Matches*, pp. 11–12. Marshall, *Duke Who Was Cricket*, pp. 119–24. Buckley, *18th-Century Cricket*, pp. 15–16.

42. 'The British Champion', in *Gentleman's Magazine*, vol. 13 (1743), 486. March, *A Duke and His Friends*, vol. II, p. 597.

43. Lewis *et al.*, *Walpole Correspondence*, vol. XX, pp. 74, 235. N. A. M. Rodger, *The Insatiable Earl: A Life of John Montagu, Fourth Earl of Sandwich* (London: HarperCollins, 1993), pp. 78, 86. Farmington, Conn.: Lewis Walpole Library, 1757, 3581 BMC. Waghorn, *Cricket Scores*, pp. 27–8, 31; *Dawn*, p. 13. *DA*, 3.8.1743; 17.7.1744.

44. Waghorn, *Cricket Scores*, pp. 18, 49–52; *Dawn*, pp. 26–9. *SJ*, 13.5.1751; 10.6.1751; 8.7.1751. Buckley, *18th-Century Cricket*, p. 25.

45. Alfred Spenser (ed.), *Memoirs of William Hickey* (London: Hurst and Blackett, 1913–25), vol. I, pp. 68, 99–106. Hickey says the match was arranged by Dorset, who in 1768 would have been the second Duke. But the third Duke is more likely, being much closer in age to Hickey, and he succeeded to the title only a year later, which would account for Hickey's error.

46. Marshall, *Duke Who Was Cricket*, p. 52. WSRO, Goodwood MSS 123, p. 69; 126, p. 45.

47. Marshall, *Duke Who Was Cricket*, pp. 66, 69, 118–19, 122–3, 158, 182. Waghorn, *Cricket Scores*, pp. 37, 41, 43. 'H. P.-T.', *Cricket's Prime* (Nottingham: Richards, 1925), pp. 15–16. *Sussex Weekly Advertiser*, 4.9.1749.

48. Marshall, *Duke Who Was Cricket*, pp. 123, 154. Waghorn, *Cricket Scores*, pp. 34–5. CKS, U269/A12 (Sackville MSS), 7.1.1768.

49. Huntington Library, Stowe MS 164 (Account Book, 1732–79), 1741 account. I am grateful to Leland Bellot for this reference.

50. CKS, U269/A232 (Sackville MSS): 'Expences of the Three Cricket Matches, 1745'.

51. March, *A Duke and His Friends*, vol. II, pp. 604–5. Henfield was one of the great centres of Sussex cricket: see Squire and Squire, *Henfield Cricket*.

52. WSRO, Goodwood MS 120, fol. 41. March, *A Duke and His Friends*, vol. I, pp. 191–2. Waghorn, *Dawn*, p. 11. *DA*, 27.8.1743. ESRO, SHR 1373 (Bridger accounts, 1751–90); 1374 (Accounts, 1760–5). Bridger also records winning 7s.6d. at a game called 'laugh and lay down'.

4 Cricket in Metropolitan Culture

1. Peter Earle, *The Making of the English Middle Class: Business, Society and Family Life in London, 1660–1730* (London: Methuen, 1989), pp. 17, 80. Brewer, *Pleasures of the Imagination*, p. 28.

2. Ibid., p. 3.

3. Warwick Wroth, *The London Pleasure Gardens of the Eighteenth Century* (London: Macmillan, 1896), pp. 286–305.

4. Ibid., pp. 199–212. These figures dwarf those for London theatres. The 'little theatre in the Haymarket' was built in the 1720s for as little as £1,500, and in

1731 a subscription of only £6,000 was required to launch the Theatre Royal, Covent Garden; see John Baker, *History of the London Stage* (London, 1904), pp. 113, 211.

5. Wroth, *London Pleasure Gardens*, pp. 93–109. Brewer, *Pleasures of the Imagination*, p. 379. Yorke, *Diary of John Baker*, p. 197 and n.

6. *DA*, 24.8.1744. *SJ*, 4.6.1750. Wroth, *London Pleasure Gardens*, pp. 247–54.

7. Ibid., pp. 33–6, 43–50, 77–8, 131–3. Arthur H. Scouten (ed.), *The London Stage 1660–1800*, pt III: *1727–47* (Carbondale, Ill.: University of Illinois Press, 1961), p. xxxix. *DA*, 9.6.1742; 27.8.1743; 31.8.1743; 8.9.1743; 25.8.1744.

8. Ned Ward, *The London Spy*, ed. Arthur L. Hayward (London: Cassell, 1927). *DA*, 11.5.44. Wroth, *London Pleasure Gardens*, pp. 9–10, 36.

9. Wroth, *London Pleasure Gardens*, pp. 40–9. James P. Malcolm, *Anecdotes of the Manners and Customs of London* (London: Longmans, 1810), vol. II, p. 150.

10. *DA*, 13.7.1742; 1.9.1742; 8.6.1744; 9.6.1744; 11.7.1744. Malcolm, *Anecdotes*, vol. II, pp. 149–50.

11. *DA*, 10.5.1742. Malcolm, *Anecdotes*, pp. 117, 125, 143, 147. Hampden, *Eighteenth-Century Journal*, p. 321.

12. Brailsford, *British Sport*, pp. 45, 52; *Bareknuckles*, pp. 3–14. Malcolm, *Anecdotes*, vol. II, pp. 135–6, 164–77. Earle, *Making of the Middle Class*, p. 58. *Sporting Magazine*, October 1792, p. 17. *DA*, 4.6.1743. *SJ*, 3.4.1738; 12.2.1739; 16.4.1750; 9.6.1760.

13. V. A. C. Gatrell, *The Hanging Tree: Execution and the English People 1770–1868* (Oxford: Oxford University Press, 1996), chaps 2–3. Peter Linebaugh, 'The Tyburn Riot against the Surgeons', in Hay *et al.*, *Albion's Fatal Tree*, pp. 66–7.

14. *SJ*, 13.5.1740; 20.5.1740.

15. Malcolm, *Anecdotes*, pp. 155, 170–1. Brailsford, *Sport, Time, and Society*, p. 134. *SJ*, 30.9.1765.

16. *DA*, 13.9.1742; 13.6.1743; 24.6.1743; 28.8.1743; 7.9.1743; 29.6.1744; 4.7.1744. *Lloyd's Evening Post*, 19.6.1764; 3.10.1764.

17. *SJ*, 27.7.1737; 8.1.1740; 22.1.1740; 22.7.1751. Hickey, *Memoirs*, vol. I, pp. 95–7. By 1773, Hickey says, rowing had ceased to be fashionable and the elite had taken up sailing: ibid., pp. 297–9.

18. Wynne-Thomas, *History of Cricket*, p. 9.

19. Malcolm, *Anecdotes*, vol. II, p. 126.

20. Buckley, *18th-Century Cricket*, pp. 1–2. Harris and Ashley-Cooper, *Kent Cricket Matches*, p. 5. Norton, 'Kent Cricket, 1705–50', p. 12.

21. A. S. Turberville (ed.), *Johnson's England: An Account of the Life and Manners of his Age* (Oxford: Clarendon Press, 1933), vol. I, p. 193. Buckley, *Pre-Victorian Cricket*, p. 4. Harris and Ashley-Cooper, *Kent Cricket Matches*, p. 10. *SJ*, 2.4.1755.

22. Marshall, *Duke Who Was Cricket*, p. 91. Waghorn, *Dawn*, p. 9. Harris and Ashley-Cooper, *Kent Cricket Matches*, p. 11. Waghorn, *Cricket Scores*, p. 55. Buckley, *Pre-Victorian Cricket*, pp. 8–9.

23. Buckley, *18th-Century Cricket*, pp. 8, 15. Waghorn, *Cricket Scores*, p. 58.

24. Ibid., p. 56. Buckley, *18th-Century Cricket*, p. 18.

25. Marshall, *Duke Who Was Cricket*, pp. 147–8, 156–7. Waghorn, *Cricket Scores*, pp. 59, 65; *Dawn*, pp. 91, 123. Hampden, *Eighteenth-Century Journal*, p. 198.

26. Buckley, *18th-Century Cricket*, pp. 11, 16, 30, 40. Waghorn, *Dawn*, pp. 7, 23, 28–30. *DA*, 4.6.1743; 11.7.1743; 3.8.1743; 19.8.1756.

27. Yorke, *Diary of John Baker*, p. 128.

28. George G. Walker, *The Honourable Artillery Company 1537–1926* (London: John Lane, 1926), pp. 85–6, 109–10, 116–17, 135–6, 146. Ward, *London Spy*, p. 45. James Love, 'Cricket: An Heroic Poem' (1744). HAC MSS, Minute Book D (1714–42), pp. 77, 148; Cash Book, 1703–30. 'HAC Cricket', in *Honourable Artillery Company Journal*, vol. 57 (1980), 69 (I am indebted to Sally Hofmann for this reference).

29. Walker, *Artillery Company*, pp. 146–7. Buckley, *18th-Century Cricket*, p. 35; *Pre-Victorian Cricket*, p. 1. *SJ*, 4.6.1750; 23.7.1750; 20.8.1750. *Lloyd's Evening Post*, 7.9.1757; 31.7.1765. Anthony Highmore, *History of the Honourable Artillery Company* (London, 1804), p. 233. *Sporting Magazine*, vol. 12 (1798), 199.

30. Waghorn, *Cricket Scores*, pp. 40–41. Brewer, *Pleasures of the Imagination*, p. 74. Smith's engraving of Hayman's painting was by 'Mr Grignion'. An earlier (1743) engraving is reproduced in Neville Cardus and John Arlott, *The Noblest Game: A Book of Fine Cricket Prints* (London: Harrap, 1969), plate 4.

31. 'The British Champion', in *Gentleman's Magazine*, vol. 13 (1743), 486. One of the admission tickets is reproduced in John Ford, *Cricket: A Social History 1700–1835* (Newton Abbot: David and Charles, 1972), p. 118; the 2s.6d. price is evidently a dealer's later addition. I am grateful to Stephen Green for this point.

32. *DA*, 12.6.1742; 29.6.1744; 4.7.1744. Waghorn, *Cricket Scores*, p. 38. Harris and Ashley-Cooper, *Kent Cricket Matches*, p. 7. HAC MSS, Minute Book E (1742–58), p. 26.

33. *DA*, 29.6.1744. Waghorn, *Cricket Scores*, pp. 33–4, 38–9; *Dawn*, p. 20. Buckley, *18th-Century Cricket*, pp. 19, 21, 27, 40. Smith was turned down several times before the Company at last admitted him: HAC MSS, Minute Book D, p. 355; E, pp. 84, 95–6, 165, 208.

34. *Gentleman's Magazine*, vol. 13, 486. *DA*, 13.8.1742; 6.9.1743.

35. *DA*, 12.7.1744. Buckley, *18th-Century Cricket*, pp. 28, 30.

36. Waghorn, *Cricket Scores*, p. 9. The passage from Dance's poem is quoted in Wynne-Thomas, *History of Cricket*, p. 15.

37. Waghorn, *Cricket Scores*, pp. 18–19, 65.

38. *DA*, 1.9.1743; 7.9.1743; 5.7.1744; 7.7.1744; 18.9.1744; 26.9.1744.

39. Waghorn, *Cricket Scores*, p. 41.

40. Yorke, *Diary of John Baker*, p. 111. Waghorn, *Dawn*, p. 10; *Cricket Scores*, pp. 8, 13–14. Buckley, *18th-Century Cricket*, p. 11.

41. Waghorn, *Cricket Scores*, pp. 30, 34, 47–9, 59. The early professionals are discussed in Brookes, *English Cricket*, pp. 60–63.

42. *Sporting Magazine*, vol. 11 (1797–8), 26–7. [Goulstone], *Cricket in Dartford*, p. 19.

43. John Goulstone, ' "Long Robin" and the Cricketing Colchins', *Genealogists Magazine*, vol. 24, no. 9 (1994), 389–93. I am indebted to Sally Hofmann for this reference.

5 Hambledon: the Players and the Community

1. Green, 'Some Cricket Records', 191. I am grateful to Mr Green for reminding me of this passage.

2. Ashley Mote, *The Glory Days of Cricket: The Extraordinary Story of Broadhalfpenny Down* (London: Robson Books, 1997), p. 21. For Hambledon's earlier history I have relied heavily on John Goldsmith, *Hambledon: The Biography of a Hampshire Village*, rev. edn (Chichester: Phillimore, 1994). See pp. 65–9 for the 1726 fire.

3. *VCH, Hampshire*, III, 237–44; V, 440. W. R. Ward (ed.), *Parson and Parish in Eighteenth-Century Hampshire: Replies to Bishops' Visitations* (Winchester: Hampshire County Council, 1995), p. 65.

4. Goldsmith, *Hambledon*, pp. 50–51. HRO, 46M69/PO2 (1716 Poor Rate). Thompson, *Whigs and Hunters*, p. 122.

5. G. N. Godwin, *The Civil War in Hampshire (1642–45)* (Southampton, 1904), pp. 128, 183. The story of Charles II's flight has been often told: his own account of the Hambledon episode is printed in William Matthews (ed.), *Charles II's Escape from Worcester* (Berkeley and Los Angeles: University of California Press, 1966), pp. 66–71.

6. Arthur J. Willis (ed.), *A Hampshire Miscellany* (Folkestone, 1963–7), pp. 116–17. Ward, *Parson and Parish*, p. 65. Goldsmith, *Hambledon*, p. 65.

7. Thompson, *Whigs and Hunters*, pp. 165–6. HRO, 21M65/CP/53, 1723 (Winchester Consistory Court papers).

8. White, *Selborne*, pp. 32–3.

9. Robert Mudie, *Hampshire: Its Past and Present Condition, and Future Prospects* (Winchester, [1838]), vol. II, p. 160.

10. For the earlier conflicts, see Buchanan Sharp, *In Contempt of All Authority: Rural Artisans and Riot in the West of England, 1586–1660* (Berkeley and Los Angeles: University of California Press, 1980); for the ones after 1700, see Thompson, *Whigs and Hunters*, pt II.

11. Willis, *Hampshire Miscellany*, p. 280. Thompson, *Whigs and Hunters*, p. 122n. White, *Selborne*, p. 30.

12. Thompson, *Whigs and Hunters*, p. 136.

13. White, *Selborne*, pp. 30–32. Thompson, *Whigs and Hunters*, pp. 144n., 161–2.

14. *London Gazette* 29.1.1725/6–1.2.1725/6. Thompson, *Whigs and Hunters*, pp. 166, 228.

15. *SJ*, 28.6.1737; 9.4.1750. BL, Add. MS 32696 (Newcastle papers), fol. 267. McCann, *Richmond–Newcastle Correspondence*, pp. 58–9. Thompson, *Whigs and Hunters*, pp. 228–32.

16. Mote, *Glory Days*, pp. 39–40. *DA*, 28.8.1756. A few days later the same paper confusingly stated that Dartford had won all three games in the series: ibid., 3.9.1756.

17. Mote, *Glory Days*, pp. 18–19. Borsay, *English Urban Renaissance*, p. 359. *SJ*, 28.8.1739.

18. Buckley, *18th-Century Cricket*, p. 18. *SJ*, 19.8.1771. BL, Add. MS 28230 (Caryll MSS), fol. 369.

19. Waghorn, *Dawn*, pp. 24–5; *Cricket Scores*, pp. 59, 65.

20. Paul Langford, *A Polite and Commercial People: England 1727–1783* (Oxford: Oxford University Press, 1989), p. 150, surveys the prevailing opinion.

21. Knight, *Hambledon's Cricket Glory*, vol. XXVI, pp. 9, 37.

22. Esdaile, 'Their Chivalry was Cricket', 25–9, 45–9. Dunkin, *Sussex Marriage Licences 1575–1730*, p. 80.

23. Waghorn, *Cricket Scores*, pp. 56–7. *Lloyd's Evening Post*, 14–17.9.1764; 19–21.9.1764. The Lands were moving up in the world during the century: in the 1790s a third 'Squire Land', of Park House, was Master of the Hambledon Hunt: F. S. Ashley-Cooper, *The Hambledon Cricket Chronicle 1772–1796* (London: Herbert Jenkins, 1924), p. 19 and n.

24. *SJ*, 18.6.1764; 2.6.1766. Waghorn, *Cricket Scores*, p. 60. Knight, *Hambledon's Cricket Glory*, vol. III, p. 117; vol. IV, p. 17.

25. Mote, *Glory Days*, pp. 165–8. Buckley, *18th-Century Cricket*, pp. 50–51.

26. Yorke, *Diary of John Baker*, p. 205.

27. Blunt, 'Baker's Horsham Diary', 47–8.

28. Ibid., 55–6.

29. Waghorn, *Cricket Scores*, pp. 64–5. Ashley-Cooper, *Chronicle*, p. 102.

30. For this and the following paragraph: Mote, *Glory Days*, pp. 87–8, 169–91.

31. Yorke, *Diary of John Baker*, p. 315.

32. Walker, *Honourable Artillery Company*, p. 147. Mote, *Glory Days*, pp. 172, 180, 189, 197. Goulstone, ' "Long Robin" ', 393.

33. Besides Nyren, I have relied for biographical information on Ashley-Cooper, *Chronicle*; Mote, *Glory Days*; Knight, *Hambledon's Cricket Glory*; and E. V. Lucas (ed.), *The Hambledon Men* (London: Henry Frowde, 1907).

34. *HC*, 26.7.1773; 16.8.1773; 30.8.1773. Knight, *Hambledon's Cricket Glory*, vol. X, pp. 52–3. HRO, 65M82/2: Diary of John Thorp, 30.5.1778.

35. Ward, *Parson and Parish*, pp. 33, 171.

36. Nyren, ed. Ashley-Cooper, p. 88.

37. Ibid., p. 77; Nyren's italics.

38. Ibid., pp. 73–4.

39. Nyren, ed. Mote, pp. 75–6.

40. Mote, *Glory Days*, pp. 73–4.

41. Ibid., p. 214. *HC*, 12.7.1783.

42. Nyren, ed. Ashley-Cooper, pp. 75–6, 99–100.

43. Knight, *Hambledon's Cricket Glory*, vol. XI, p. 56; vol. XIII, pp. 14, 59, 69. Nyren, ed. Mote, p. 84.

44. Pycroft, *Cricket Field*, p. 97. Knight, *Hambledon's Cricket Glory*, vol. X, p. 35.

45. Ashley-Cooper, *Chronicle*, pp. 49–50, 66, 117–39. Goldsmith, *Hambledon*, pp. 84–5. For the post-1808 evidence, see below, chapter 8.

46. W. A. Armstrong, 'Rural Population Growth, Systems of Employment and Incomes', in G. E. Mingay (ed.), *Agrarian History of England and Wales*, vol. VI: *1750–1850* (Cambridge: Cambridge University Press, 1989), p. 697. Nyren, ed. Mote, pp. 66–7. Buckley, *Pre-Victorian Cricket*, p. 34.

47. Lucas, *Hambledon Men*, p. 138.

48. HRO, 46M69/PO3; 46M69/PW14. Knight, *Hambledon's Cricket Glory*, vol. X, pp. 47, 57.

49. *SJ*, 31.5.1756; 11.5.1767; 27.7.1767; 3.8.1767; 24.4.1769. Nyren, ed. Mote, pp. 60–61. Knight, *Hambledon's Cricket Glory*, vol. XII, pp. 48–9.

50. Nyren, ed. Ashley-Cooper, p. 103.

51. Francis W. Steer (ed.), *Memoirs of James Spershott* (Chichester: Chichester City Council, 1962), pp. 13–14. *SJ*, 2.6.1766. Knight, *Hambledon's Cricket Glory*, vol. XII, p. 23. Newspaper advertising of cocking mains was so common in this period that it seems superfluous to give specific references.

52. Buckley, *18th-Century Cricket*, p. 41. The half-notch was presumably derived from the practice in single-wicket matches, in which a complete run was scored only if the batsman ran to the bowler's end and back, hitting what would normally be scored as a two. It is not clear whether these local matches in Kent were played entirely under single-wicket rules. For another example, see Waghorn, *Cricket Scores*, pp. 72–3.

53. *HC*, 29.7.1782; 12.7.1783; 26.7.1783.

54. *SJ*, 30.5.1768. *HC*, 7.9.1772; 28.5.1781; 16.7.1781; 6.8.1781; 10.9.1781. HRO, 65M82/2, pp. 138, 140.

6 Hambledon: the Club and the Patrons

1. Often reprinted; e.g., in Mote, *Glory Days*, pp. 403–5.

2. Marchant, MS Diary, for example 22.10.1719; 28.3.1727; 12.12.1727. For clubs in general, see Langford, *Polite and Commercial People*, pp. 99–100, and Borsay, *English Urban Renaissance*, pp. 124, 135–6, 145, 268.

3. W. S. Norton, 'Kent Cricket, 1751–1848', in Harris, *Kent County Cricket*, pp. 28–9. Waghorn, *Dawn*, pp. 90, 100. Goulstone, 'Some Cricket Grounds', 38–9.

4. Goulstone, 'Some Cricket Grounds', 34–5, 37. Waghorn, *Dawn*, p. 82. *SJ*, 15.9.1788 (I owe this reference to Christine Ferdinand). Buckley, *Pre-Victorian Cricket*, p. 5.

5. Pycroft, *Cricket Field*, p. 47. Ashley-Cooper, *Chronicle*, p. 155. Lewis Walpole Library, Clement Correspondence: Powlett to William Sloper, 2.8.1760. For the 1768 women's match, see above pp. 111–12.

6. *SJ*, 28.10.1771. Knight, *Hambledon's Cricket Glory*, vol. XXVII, p. 77. There is a list of Hambledon members in the period 1771–96 in Ashley-Cooper, *Chronicle*, pp. 143–61.

7. These and other subsequent references to the minutes are from Ashley-Cooper, *Chronicle*, pp. 41–97, *passim*.

8. Knight, *Hambledon's Cricket Glory*, vol. XII, pp. 12–14; vol. XXVII, p. 79.

9. CKS, U269/F14 (Sackville MSS). Buckley, *Pre-Victorian Cricket*, p. 6.

10. Nyren, ed. Mote, pp. 62, 72.

11. Claire Tomalin, *Jane Austen: A Life* (New York: Viking, 1997), p. 85.

12. Hickey, *Memoirs*, vol. II, pp. 307–9.

13. For the members I again rely mainly on Ashley-Cooper's *Chronicle*, with some further information from Knight's *Hambledon's Cricket Glory*, and Goldsmith's *Hambledon*.

14. Blunt, 'Baker's Horsham Diary', 48.

15. Roger Ingpen, *Shelley in England* (Boston and New York: Houghton Mifflin, 1917), pp. 4–15. Buckley, *Pre-Victorian Cricket*, p. 6. Knight, *Hambledon's Cricket Glory*, vol. VII, pp. 36, 42; vol. X, p. 44; vol. XII, p. 15.

16. See ibid., vol. VI, pp. 6–12; Ward, *Parson and Parish*, p. 235.

17. G. E. C. [G. E. Cokayne], *Complete Peerage*, vol. II, pp. 212–14.

18. Knight, *Hambledon's Cricket Glory*, *passim*. B. B. Woodward *et al.*, *A General History of Hampshire* (London: Virtue, 1861–9), vol. II, p. 55. Ashley-Cooper, *Chronicle*, pp. 21, 155. *SJ*, 29.8.1757; 22.4.1771. Ward, *Parson and Parish*, pp. 76, 196. HRO, Q27/3/24; also Quarter Sessions, Calendar of Prisoners 1743–87, Mich. 1777.

19. *Complete Peerage*, vol. II, pp. 214–15.

20. *SJ*, 22.5.1769; 5.6.1769. *Kentish Weekly Post*, 5–12.6.1769.

21. *Complete Peerage*, vol. III, pp. 131–3. Joan Johnson, *Princely Chandos: James Brydges 1674–1744* (Gloucester: Alan Sutton, 1984), pp. 158–61. *Hampshire N&Q*, V (1890), 142. *SJ*, 19.8.1751.

22. Sir Lewis Namier and John Brooke, *The House of Commons 1754–1790* (London: HMSO, 1964), vol. I, p. 302. HC, 15.1.1780. The continuing Bolton influence is apparent from *SJ*, 23.6.1766; 20.7.1767; 19.9.1768.

23. Ibid., 19.6.1769; 21.8.1769; 18.9.1769; 2.10.1769; 9.10.1769; 13.11.1769; 27.11.1769.

24. Ibid., 14.5.1770. Knight, *Hambledon's Cricket Glory*, vol. IX, pp. 31–4. *HC*, 29.7.1782.

25. *SJ*, 9.7.1770; 15.7.1771; 20.7.1772. *HC*, 5.7.1773; 20.12.1773.

26. Namier and Brooke, *House of Commons 1754–1790*, vol. I, p. 293.

27. *A Collection of All the Handbills, Squibs, Songs, Essays, etc. Published during the Late Contested Election for the County of Hampshire* (Winchester, 1780), esp. pp. 107, 116–27. See also Langford, *Public Life*, pp. 94, 531; and Knight, *Hambledon's Cricket Glory*, vol. XI, pp. 38–45.

28. *HC*, 8.1.1780; 15.1.1780; 22.1.1780.

29. On the origins of the Association movement, see Ian R. Christie, *Wilkes, Wyvill and Reform: The Parliamentary Reform Movement in British Politics 1760–1785* (London: Macmillan, 1962), pp. 70–77, 89–95, 129, 169n.; and Eugene C. Black, *The Association: British Extraparliamentary Political Organization 1779–1793* (Cambridge, Mass: Harvard University Press, 1963), pp. 42, 188.

30. *HC*, 13.5.1782. Christie, *Wilkes, Wyvill and Reform*, p. 171.

31. Knight, *Hambledon's Cricket Glory*, vol. XI, p. 45.

32. Ibid., vol. IX, pp. 31–40; vol. XI, pp. 38–45; vol. XII, pp. 11–12; vol. XIII, pp. 8–9; vol. XIV, pp. 10–11. *Collection of All the Handbills*, pp. 61–2, 118, 126.

33. *SJ*, 18.8.1760; 29.7.1760; 9.9.1765; 18.9.1769. *HC*, 7.9.1772; 16.8.1773; 13.9.1773.

34. *SJ*, 14.5.1750; 29.7.1765; 4.8.1766; 3.8.1772. Yorke, *Diary of John Baker*, pp. 160–2, 323–6. *HC*, 26.7.1773. For the Southampton social scene, see also Robert Douch (ed.), *Southampton 1540–1956: Visitors' Descriptions* (Southampton: Southampton Corporation, 1961), pp. 16–18; and Phyllis Hembry, *The English Spa 1560–1815: A Social History* (London: Athlone Press, 1990), pp. 242–3.

35. *HC*, 9.8.1773; 16.8.1773; 23.8.1773; 6.9.1773; 13.9.1773. Mote, *Glory Days*, p. 175.

36. *HC*, 23.8.1773; 30.8.1773; 13.9.1773; 20.9.1773.

37. Marchant, MS Diary, 19.5.1727. BL, Add. MS 5957 (Whaley's travel journal), fols 14–15. *HC*, 29.7.1782. *SJ*, 8.7.1751; 19.5.1755; 13.8.1764.

38. Ibid., 21.5.1764; 22.9.1766; 1.6.1767; 8.6.1767; 5.8.1767; 5.9.1768; 19.6.1769; 17.7.1769. Raynor, *Social History of Music*, p. 263.

39. Borsay, *English Urban Renaissance*, pp. 139–42. Climenson, *Powys Diaries*, pp. 134, 178–91, 237, 240.

40. *SJ*, 31.8.1772.

41. Ralph Arnold, *A Yeoman of Kent: An Account of Richard Hayes, 1725–1790, and of the Village of Cobham* (London: Constable, 1949), p. 195. 'The Jovial Cricketers' (1776), in Waghorn, *Dawn*, p. 44. Yorke, *Diary of John Baker*, pp. 181, 235, 243. Blunt, 'Baker's Horsham Diary', 46, 55.

42. Pycroft, *Cricket Field*, p. 82. Waghorn, *Dawn*, p. 51.

43. Lucas, *Hambledon Men*, p. 226. Pycroft, *Cricket Field*, p. 49. Knight, *Hambledon's Cricket Glory*, vol. XIII, p. 64.

44. *Complete Peerage*, vol. XII, pt i, pp. 634–5. Lucas, *Hambledon Men*, pp. 122, 199–200. Ashley-Cooper, *Chronicle*, p. 173. Buckley, *Pre-Victorian Cricket*, p. 215. Knight, *Hambledon's Cricket Glory*, vol. VII, p. 34; vol. X, pp. 25, 41; vol. XII, p. 32.

45. Goulstone, 'Some Cricket Grounds', 35, 38. Waghorn, *Cricket Scores*, pp. 71–3, 78, 84–8, 101, 111–13. Namier and Brooke, *House of Commons 1754–90*, vol. III, p. 100. Lewis *et al.*, *Walpole Correspondence*, vol. XXI, p. 129.

46. Goulstone, 'Some Cricket Grounds', 34–5. [J. Duncombe], 'Surry Triumphant: Or the Kentish-Men's Defeat' (1773), in *S&B*, I, 9–11. The poem is a parody of the well-known ballad, 'Chevy Chase'.

47. Nyren, ed. Mote, pp. 84–5. Knight, *Hambledon's Cricket Glory*, vol. X, p. 59; vol. XIV, p. 54. Pycroft, *Cricket Field*, p. 50. Mote, *Glory Days*, pp. 218–19.

48. Lewis *et al.*, *Walpole Correspondence*, vol. XXII, p. 563; vol. XXIII, p. 495; vol. XXV, p. 312n. Knight, *Hambledon's Cricket Glory*, vol. XII, p. 65; vol. XIV, pp. 54–5.

49. This account of Dorset is based mainly on V. Sackville-West, *Knole and the Sackvilles* (London: Heinemann, 1923), pp. 176–200; supplemented by *Complete Peerage*, vol. IV, pp. 428–9, and Buckley, *Pre-Victorian Cricket*, p. 11.

50. Lewis *et al.*, *Walpole Correspondence*, vol. XXIV, p. 435 and n.; vol. XXXII, p. 145. Langford, *Polite and Commercial People*, p. 576. John Goulstone and Michael Swanton, 'Carry on Cricket: the Duke of Dorset's 1789 tour', *History Today*, vol. 39 (August 1989), 19.

51. Buckley, *Pre-Victorian Cricket*, pp. 10–11. Climenson, *Powys Diaries*, pp. 148–50. Langford, *Polite and Commercial People*, p. 120. Brewer, *Pleasures of the Imagination*, pp. 255, 309. Lewis *et al.*, *Walpole Correspondence*, vol. XXXIII, p. 224. CKS, U269/C197: Dorset to George III, 26.8.1785.

52. Langford, *Polite and Commercial People*, p. 576. CKS, U269/A12 (Expenses, 1766–9); U269/A240/2 (Bills, 1769); U269/A47/2 (Accounts, 1777–88). *HC*, 11.1.1773.

53. Nyren, ed. Ashley-Cooper, pp. 98–9. Payments to Minshull and other cricketers on the Knole staff are repeatedly recorded in CKS, U269/E301/1 (Gardeners' vouchers, 1718–39); U269/A28 (Accounts, 1769–79); U269/A47/2 (Accounts, 1777–88); and U269/31 (Wage book, 1769–84).

54. Goulstone and Swanton, 'Carry on Cricket', 19.

55. CKS, U269/F14 (cricket papers). Scores in the 1777 Guildford match are given in Mote, *Glory Days*, pp. 195–6.

56. Knight, *Hambledon's Cricket Glory*, vol. VI, pp. 13–14. Another poem celebrating a Kent victory (over Surrey in 1773) devotes some space to the

achievements of the lower-class players, but still gives greater prominence to Dorset, Mann and the other gentlemen: John Burnby, *The Kentish Cricketers* (Canterbury, 1773). 'Surry Triumphant' (see above, n. 46) also emphasizes the roles of the nobility and gentry.

57. Quoted in Knight, *Hambledon's Cricket Glory*, vol. XII, p. 55. For the macaroni, see Langford, *Polite and Commercial People*, pp. 576–7.

58. Burnby, *The Kentish Cricketers*, pp. 4–6, 12.

7 The MCC and the Decline of Hambledon

1. Nyren, ed. Mote, p. 79. Ashley-Cooper, *Chronicle*, pp. 63, 67–8, 117.

2. Knight, *Hambledon's Cricket Glory*, vol. XIV, pp. 39–40. *Complete Peerage*, vol. IV, p. 428n. Goulstone and Swanton, 'Carry on Cricket', pp. 20–3. Rumours of Dorset's 'too great an intimacy' with Marie Antoinette were already circulating in 1784: A. Aspinall (ed.), *Later Correspondence of George III*, vol. I (Cambridge, 1962), p. 9, n.

3. CKS, U269/A13 (Sackville accounts, 1780–82). The earliest Hambledon match recorded in 1780 began on 30 August (Mote, *Glory Days*, p. 205), but it seems unlikely that none was played before then. Dorset's movements suggest that there was cricket at Broadhalfpenny sometime between 28 July and 4 August, and again between 12 and 17 August.

4. *Complete Peerage*, vol. XII, pt ii, p. 787. Langford, *Public Life*, p. 561. E. E. Snow (ed.), 'Extracts, Related to Cricket, from the Private Accounts of the 9th Earl of Winchilsea, 1788–99', *JCS*, vol. 8, no. 1 (1976–7), 26–7.

5. Snow, 'Cricket Accounts', 29–31, 35–6. Ashley-Cooper, *Chronicle*, pp. 160–61. Harris and Ashley-Cooper, *Kent Cricket Matches*, pp. 59–63.

6. Wynne-Thomas, *History of Cricket*, pp. 24–5. Mote, *Glory Days*, p. 220.

7. Nyren, ed. Mote, pp. 93–8. Mote, *Glory Days*, pp. 109–13. Pycroft, *Cricket Field*, p. 72. Lucas, *Hambledon Men*, p. 154.

8. Mote, *Glory Days*, pp. 123–7. Nyren, ed. Mote, pp. 85–7. Shepheard's sketches (which also included the other Hambledon players, Harris and Beldham) have been often reproduced, for example in Cardus and Arlott, *The Noblest Game*, plate 2.

9. Ashley-Cooper, *Chronicle*, pp. 74, 176. Pycroft, *Cricket Field*, p. 46. Knight, *Hambledon's Cricket Glory*, vol. XIV, p. 42. Mote, *Glory Days*, pp. 113–21.

10. Pycroft, *Cricket Field*, p. 96. Knight, *Hambledon's Cricket Glory*, vol. XII, pp. 72–3, 80. If Beldham was right about the date being 1784, the match cannot have been on Broadhalfpenny, as Hambledon had by then already moved to Windmill Down.

11. Knight, *Hambledon's Cricket Glory*, vol. X, p. 62; vol. XIV, pp. 14–15.

Wynne-Thomas, *History of Cricket*, pp. 34–6, shows the continuity between the Star and Garter, White Conduit and Marylebone Clubs.

12. Knight, *Hambledon's Cricket Glory*, vol. XII, p. 53; vol. XIII, pp. 59–61; vol. XIV, pp. 17–21.

13. Ibid., vol. XIV, pp. 44–8, 54–6. Mote, *Glory Days*, p. 220.

14. Wynne-Thomas, *History of Cricket*, pp. 31–3.

15. *S&B*, I, 70–71, 74–5. Ashley-Cooper, *Chronicle*, pp. 78 and n., 101, 113. One of Winchilsea's kinsmen, Charles Finch, had been married at Assheton Smith's house: *SJ*, 2.1.1779.

16. Pycroft, *Cricket Field*, p. 64. Ashley-Cooper, *Chronicle*, pp. 36, 81. Harris and Ashley-Cooper, *Kent Cricket Matches*, pp. 65, 69. *S&B*, I, 110.

17. Ashley-Cooper, *Chronicle*, pp. 32, 87–8, 170. For other 1790–91 examples, see *S&B*, I, 103–8, 113–22.

18. Ibid., 137, 154, 156. The preference for Stoke Down after 1795 is clear in ibid., 201–2, 224, 240, 331–2.

19. Pycroft, *Cricket Field*, p. 82. *S&B*, I, 165–77.

20. Pycroft, *Cricket Field*, pp. 80, 97.

21. Ibid., pp. 49, 93–4.

22. Ibid., pp. 95–100.

23. Ford, *Cricket: A Social History*, pp. 101–2. Wynne-Thomas, *History of Cricket*, p. 56.

24. Frederick Gale, *The Game of Cricket*, 2nd edn (London: Swan Sonneschein, 1888), pp. 19, 22, 127.

25. For a survey of these matters, see Douglas Hay and Nicholas Rogers, *Eighteenth-Century English Society: Shuttles and Swords* (Oxford: Oxford University Press, 1997), esp. chap. 7.

26. Crabbe, 'The Village'. I have quoted both Goldsmith and Crabbe from M. H. Abrams *et al.* (eds.), *The Norton Anthology of English Literature*, 3rd edn (New York: Norton, 1974), vol. I, pp. 2405–22.

27. *SJ*, 30.3.1772. *HC*, 14.12.1772. White, *Selborne*, p. 28.

28. CKS, U269/A47/3 (Knole accounts, 1788–90). HRO, 44M69/F10/13/25 (Jervoise MSS). Ashley-Cooper, *Chronicle*, p. 95. The entry shows that Nyren did not leave Hambledon in 1791, as often supposed.

29. Tomalin, *Jane Austen*, pp. 104, 151–2. Langford, *Public Life*, p. 455. BL, Add. MS 33106 (Pelham MSS), fols 408, 417–20.

30. Waghorn, *Dawn*, pp. 59, 86. L. J. Maguire (ed.), *Journal and Correspondence of John Burgess from 1785 to 1819* (Ditchling: privately printed, 1982), pp. 59–61. Sawyer, 'Extracts from the Journal of John Burgess', 156.

31. Waghorn, *Dawn*, p. 125. Ernest Cox, 'An Old Sussex Household Diary', *SAC*, LXVII (1926), 198. *Cantium*, vol. 6, no. 3 (autumn 1974), 54. *Sporting Magazine*, vol. 12 (1798), 178, 270, 309. John Mockett, *Mockett's Journal* (Canterbury, 1836), p. 35. A. L. Macfie, 'The Pattenden Diaries 1797–1819', *Arch. Cant.*, XCIV (1978), 146.

32. Waghorn, *Dawn*, p. 118. *VCH, Berks.*, II, 318. Lucas, *Hambledon Men*, p. 138.

33. Pycroft, *Cricket Field*, p. 62. William Gilpin, *Observations on the Western Parts of England* (1798, repr. Richmond: Richmond Publishing, 1973), p. 39.

34. Ashley-Cooper, *Chronicle*, pp. 86–95, 114–38.

35. Ibid., pp. 95n., 114–42.

36. Ibid., pp. 114–42.

37. *S&B*, I, 126, 137. Ashley-Cooper, *Chronicle*, pp. 101, 113. *Sporting Magazine*, May 1793, 122. *Gentleman's Magazine*, vol. 61 (1791), 232. *Hampshire Repository* (Winchester, 1799–1801), II, 197.

38. Ashley-Cooper, *Chronicle*, pp. 93–6.

39. Ibid., pp. 97, 101n. Buckley, *18th-Century Cricket*, p. 179.

40. For the political background in general, see E. P. Thompson, *The Making of the English Working Class* (New York: Vintage Books, 1966), chap. 5.

41. PRO, ASSI 23/8 (Western Circuit Gaol Book), p. 474. Black, *The Association*, pp. 258–9.

42. John Keane, *Tom Paine: A Political Life* (London: Bloomsbury, 1995), pp. 430, 605. See also Jack Fruchtman, Jr, *Thomas Paine: Apostle of Freedom* (New York: Four Walls Eight Windows, 1994), p. 350.

43. Keane, *Tom Paine*, pp. 62, 71. [Rowland Bowen], 'Citizen Tom Paine "Author of the Rights of Man"', *Cricket Quarterly*, vol. 7, no. 2 (spring 1970), 93–4.

44. Ashley-Cooper, *Chronicle*, pp. 97, 114–42. Mote, *Glory Days*, pp. 236–7. For the Club's history after 1796, see the next chapter.

8 The Hambledon Club's Last Years

1. *Hampshire N&Q*, I (1883), 3–5. I have used the 1982 Oxford University Press edition of Mitford's *Our Village*. See pp. 96–105 for the cricket match.

2. Ibid., pp. 167–8.

3. Charles Vancouver, *General View of the Agriculture of Hampshire* (London: Board of Agriculture, 1813), pp. 384–5.

4. *HC*, 11.6.1814–25.7.1814. Mitford, *Our Village*, p. 163.

5. *HC*, 8.5.1815; 12.6.1815; 26.6.1815; 3.7.1815. Linda Colley, *Britons: Forging the Nation 1707–1837* (New Haven and London: Yale University Press, 1992), pp. 222–6, 237.

6. E. J. Hobsbawm and George Rudé, *Captain Swing* (New York: Pantheon, 1968), p. 15.

7. *HC*, 26.6.1826. Yale University, Beinecke Library, General Collections, 20 (Diaries of Peter Hawker, 1795–1853), XIII, 10.7.1827; 10.7.1828.

8. *HC*, 31.5.1820; 3.6.1822; 30.5.1825.

9. Brailsford, *Sport, Time, and Society*, p. 71. *HC*, 6.6.1814; 3.7.1815. *Sporting Magazine*, vol. 52 (1818), 24, 147; vol. 64 (1824), 60.

10. Mockett, *Journal*, pp. 106–7, 170. *Arch. Cant.*, XXVII, 208. F. S. Andrus, 'Extracts from the Miscellany and Farm Accounts of Francis Andrus of Seadbury in the Parish of Southfleet', *Arch. Cant.*, C (1985), 375–6. Richard Hayes watched cricket at Meopham Fair in 1778: Arnold, *Yeoman of Kent*, p. 195.

11. *Sussex N&Q*, XV (1958–62), 331; XVI (1963–7), 247. *HC*, 21.9.1822; 4.8.1823; 13.6.1825. Wynne-Thomas, *History of Cricket*, pp. 48–9.

12. *HC*, 11.5.1807; 10.8.1807; 11.5.1812; 19.6.1815–1.8.1815; 30.6.1828. Brailsford, *Sport, Time, and Society*, p. 73.

13. *S&B*, I, 307, 310, 325–6, 331–2, 335, 388, 390, 432, 443, 527. *Sporting Magazine*, vol. 62 (1823), 226. *HC*, 28.9.1822; 9.8.1824; 20–27.6.1825.

14. Mitford, *Our Village*, p. 96. Pycroft, *Cricket Field*, pp. 80, 90. Wynne-Thomas, *History of Cricket*, pp. 52–3.

15. Ibid., pp. 53, 55–6.

16. Ashley-Cooper, 'Register of Kent County Cricketers, 1729–1806', p. 312. Nyren, ed. Mote, pp. 101–3.

17. Buckley, *Pre-Victorian Cricket*, pp. 37, 40, 48. Mote, *Glory Days*, p. 240. The 1808–25 account book is in HRO, 76M92/1. References to Hambledon members, matches, and players in the following pages are derived from this manuscript, unless noted otherwise. At this time anniversaries were not necessarily on a fixed date; between 1804 and 1821 Hambledon's took place on dates ranging between 1 May and 27 September. However, they still commemorated the founding of the club.

18. HRO, 76M92/1. Buckley, *Pre-Victorian Cricket*, p. 40.

19. Ibid., pp. 72–4, 106. Buckley, unpublished MS notes, Lord's, MCC Library, p. 102. *HC*, 13.8.1821; 8.7.1822; 21.7.1823; 28.7.1823; 11.8.1823; 16.8.1824; 30.8.1824.

20. Buckley, *Pre-Victorian Cricket*, pp. 72–3.

21. The accounts for 1791–6 are in Ashley-Cooper, *Chronicle*, pp. 114–41.

22. Buckley, MS Notes, p. 87.

23. *HC*, 21.8.1820. For Beagley, see *S&B*, I, 114, 388–549 *passim*; and Lucas, *Hambledon Men*, pp. 129, 132.

24. *S&B*, I, 114.

25. Ibid., 115.

26. *Hampshire Repository*, II, 196. Ashley-Cooper, *Chronicle*, p. 150. Knight, *Hambledon's Cricket Glory*, vol. XIII, pp. 60–61. HRO, 46M69/PO3, 5 (Poor Rate assessments, 1799, 1819).

27. *HC*, 27.4.1812; 18.5.1812. Ashley-Cooper, *Chronicle*, p. 153. Goldsmith, *Hambledon*, pp. 6, 17–18, 101. *VCH, Hants*, V, 524–5, 543. *Sporting Magazine*, vol. 52 (1818), 43–4. Gale, *The Game of Cricket*, pp. 36, 249.

28. Buckley, *Pre-Victorian Cricket*, p. 95. Information on the local players is

taken mainly from HRO, 46M69/PO5 (1819 rate); 46M69/PR6, 8, 10 (parish registers); and 'Inscriptions in St Peter's, Hambledon' (folder in HRO).

29. For wages, see Mingay, *Agrarian History*, vol. VI, p. 1082; and Hobsbawm and Rudé, *Captain Swing*, pp. 174, 243.

30. *HC*, 18.8.1823; 30.8.1824.

31. Ibid., 20.6.1825.

32. *S&B*, II, 78–9, 83. Buckley, MS notes, p. 259. *Hampshire Advertiser and Salisbury Guardian*, 29.6.1833.

33. William Cobbett, *Rural Rides*, ed. George Woodcock (Harmondsworth: Penguin, 1983).

34. Ibid., pp. 76–9. Ashley-Cooper, *Chronicle*, p. 166. Goldsmith, *Hambledon*, p. 106.

35. Cobbett, *Rural Rides*, pp. 477–8. Goldsmith, *Hambledon*, pp. 101–3.

36. Hobsbawm and Rudé, *Captain Swing*, pp. 38–47.

37. For a balanced discussion of 'Speenhamland', see J. P. Huzel, 'The Labourer and the Poor Law, 1750–1850', in Mingay, *Agrarian History*, vol. VI, at pp. 773–90.

38. Hawker Diaries, vol. VIII, 24.10.1820 and 27.12.1820; vol. X, 28.12.1821; vol. XII, 16.1.1826. On the decay of paternalism, see W. A. Armstrong, 'The Position of the Labourer in Rural Society', in Mingay, *Agrarian History*, vol. VI, pp. 821–4.

39. Hawker Diaries, vol. VIII, 1.9.1819; vol. IX, 27.1.1821; vol. XIII, 1–6.9.1827.

40. Ibid., vol. XII, 28–29.12.1821; vol. XIV, 5.11.1828.

41. For this and the following paragraphs: *VCH, Hants*, V, 440; HRO, 46M69/PO5 (Rate book, 1811–21); 46M69/PO9 (Poor Law accounts, 1805–34); Hobsbawm and Rudé, *Captain Swing*, p. 76.

42. Nationally poor relief expenditure appears to have reached its peak in 1818: Huzel, 'The Labourer and the Poor Law', at pp. 761–2.

43. Hobsbawm and Rudé, *Captain Swing*, pp. 50–51. Parliamentary Papers, 1822, V: *Report from the Select Committee on Poor Rate Returns*; 1830–31, IX: *Account of the Money Expended for the Maintenance and Relief of the Poor, 1825–1829*.

44. HRO, 46M69/PV1 (Vestry minutes, 1824–66).

45. HRO, 46M69/PO9 (Poor Law accounts, 1805–34); 46M69/PV1 (Vestry minutes, 1824–66).

46. Mingay, *Agrarian History*, vol. VI, p. 977. *HC*, 8.11.1830. HRO, 46M69/PV1.

47. The best account of the Hampshire riots is in Hobsbawm and Rudé, *Captain Swing*, chap. 6. There is a very full collection of documents in Jill Chambers, *Hampshire Machine Breakers: The Story of the 1830 Riots*, 2nd edn (Letchworth: J. Chambers, 1996).

48. Bushaway, *By Rite*, pp. 70–71. Hobsbawm and Rudé, *Captain Swing*,

pp. 116–18. Chambers, *Hampshire Machine Breakers*, pp. 21–2, 26. *HC*, 22.11.1830.

49. Hawker Diaries, vol. XVI, 20.10.1830–4.12.1830. PRO, ASSI 21/57 (W. Circuit Minute Book, 1828–33), Lent Assizes, Winchester, 1831: ASSI 25/22/5 (Indictments, Lent Assizes, 1831).

50. Hobsbawm and Rudé, *Captain Swing*, pp. 118–20. PRO, ASSI 25/22/5 (Indictments, Lent Assizes, 1831). Chambers, *Hampshire Machine Breakers*, pp. 29, 32–4, 38–41, 101.

51. PRO, ASSI 25/22/5 (Indictments, Lent Assizes 1831); HO 40/27, fol. 557 (Home Office papers). HRO, 46M69/PV1 (Vestry minutes, 1824–66).

52. Goldsmith, *Hambledon*, pp. 107, 116. HRO, 46M69/PV1 (Vestry minutes, 1824–66). *HC*, 19.11.1830.

53. Hobsbawm and Rudé, *Captain Swing*, pp. 258–61. Chambers, *Hampshire Machine Breakers*, pp. 55, 121–30, 202.

54. Chambers, *Hampshire Machine Breakers*, pp. 87, 99–100. *Middle Temple Admissions Register*, II, 437. *Pigot's Commercial Directory, 1832–4*, col. 1090. Ashley-Cooper, *Chronicle*, p. 155. HRO, 76M92/1.

55. *HC*, 20.12.1830. HRO, 46M69/PO9 (Poor Law accounts, 1805–34).

56. Thompson, *The Making of the English Working Class*, p. 267.

57. HRO, 46M69/PO5 (Poor Rate Book, 1811–21). HRO, 46M69/PV1 (Vestry minutes, 1824–66). *HC*, 12.7.30.

Epilogue: Beyond Hambledon

1. Paul Weaver, 'Slaves to the Corporate Rhythm', the *Guardian*, 27.7.1999.
2. *Manchester Guardian Weekly*, 17.1.1999.
3. The *Guardian*, 30.6.1999.
4. Stephen Chalke, *Runs in the Memory: County Cricket in the 1950s* (Bath: Fairfield Books, 1997), pp. 195–6.

Note on Sources

Research on early cricket history necessarily begins with Frederick Lillywhite's classic *Cricket Scores and Biographies of Celebrated Cricketers*, vol. I, 1744–1826 (London: Lillywhite, 1862), which contains notices of eighteenth-century matches. Many additional ones were printed from the newspapers in two collections by Henry T. Waghorn: *Cricket Scores, Notes, etc. from 1730–1773* (Edinburgh and London: Blackwood, 1899); and *The Dawn of Cricket* (London: MCC, 1906); and two by George B. Buckley: *Fresh Light on 18th-Century Cricket: A Collection of 1000 New Cricket Notices from 1697 to 1800 A.D.* (Birmingham: Cotterell, [1935]); and *Fresh Light on Pre-Victorian Cricket: A Collection of New Cricket Notices from 1709 to 1837* (Birmingham: Cotterell, [1937]). Buckley assembled a further collection covering matches between 1744 and 1845, which remains unpublished; I have used the typescript in the MCC Library at Lord's.

Our knowledge of cricket at Hambledon begins, of course, with John Nyren's 'The Cricketers of My Time', printed in F. S. Ashley-Cooper's edition of *The Young Cricketer's Tutor* (London: Gay and Bird, 1902). There is a splendid recent edition, from a slightly different text, by Ashley Mote: *John Nyren's The Cricketers of My Time: The Original Version* (London: Robson Books, 1998). E. V. Lucas (ed.), *The Hambledon Men* (London: Frowde, 1907) also reprints Nyren, with supplementary material that includes the Revd John Mitford's review in *The Gentleman's Magazine*, 1833. The surviving records of the Hambledon Club down to 1796 are printed in F. S. Ashley-Cooper's *The Hambledon Cricket Chronicle 1772–1796: Including the Reproduction of the Minute and Account Books of the Club* (London: Herbert Jenkins, 1924); the work also contains lists of matches and members. Ronald D. Knight has published a still incomplete and undigested collection of historical materials pertaining to Hambledon and the Club in *Hambledon's Cricket Glory* (15 vols to date: Weymouth, 1975–94). The original manuscripts of the Club's minute and account books, printed by Ashley-Cooper, are in the Hampshire Record Office (HRO, 4M85/1–3); the Record Office also contains the hitherto neglected account book for the years 1808–25 (HRO, 76M92/1).

The historian of Hambledon village is descended from a family whose name will be already recognizable to readers of this book: John Goldsmith, *Hamble-don: The Biography of a Hampshire Village* (Chichester: Phillimore, 1994) – this, the second edition, has a foreword by the former England captain David Gower, also a descendant of a Hambledon Club member. In addition to Knight's collections, I have also used manuscripts pertaining to the village (including the Vestry minutes) in the Hampshire Record Office; all are in the category 46M69. Also of great value has been Ashley Mote's *The Glory Days of Cricket: The Extraordinary Story of Broadhalfpenny Down* (London: Robson Books, 1997), which contains notices of the leading players, and accounts of the Club's matches down to 1794.

Much of the information about cricket in the works already listed comes originally from local newspapers. I have found both the *Salisbury Journal* and, from 1772, the *Hampshire Chronicle* to be goldmines of information about the social, cultural and political life of Hampshire and the neighbouring counties, as well as the cricket. But I have also made occasional use of other Kent, Sussex and London newspapers, to which references will be found in the end notes. Of the London papers, the *Daily Advertiser* proved to be the most useful in its reporting of cricket news. For London cricket before 1760 I have also benefited from having had access to the archives of the Honourable Artillery Company. The Waghorn and Buckley collections miss a number of post-1815 matches which are reported in the local newspapers. From 1792 the *Sporting Magazine* is a valuable source of information about cricket and many other sports. William Beldham's vivid recollections of professional cricket in the period 1780–1820 are in James Pycroft, *The Cricket Field: Or, the History and the Science of Cricket* (London: Longmans Green, 1851); I have used a later American edition (Boston, Mass.: Mayhew and Baker, 1859).

Several diaries illuminate both the cricket and other aspects of life in the rural southeast. Almost all the important ones are from Sussex. The earliest is by Thomas Marchant of Hurstpierpoint, largely a record of his farming activities between 1714 and 1728, but also including material about other local matters, including cricket. There are extracts in *SAC*, XXV (1873), but I was able to use a microfilm of the complete diary in the Sterling Memorial Library at Yale University. A diary with even more plentiful information about village cricket in Sussex is the one kept by the East Hoathly shopkeeper Thomas Turner: David Vaisey (ed.), *The Diary of Thomas Turner 1754–1765* (Oxford: Oxford University Press, 1984). From further up the social scale is the diary of the lawyer John Baker, who frequently attended cricket matches, including several involving Hambledon. Two different selections have been printed, with some overlap, but each containing material that is not in the other: one is in *SAC*, LII (1909); the other is P. C. Yorke (ed.), *The Diary of John Baker* (London: Hutchinson, 1931). References to a few other diaries will be found in the end notes.

The papers of two of the great aristocratic families who supported eighteenth-century cricket have been immensely useful. For Sussex, both the political and the cricketing interests of the second Duke of Richmond are illuminated by Timothy J. McCann's superb edition of *The Correspondence of the Dukes of Richmond and Newcastle 1724–1750* (Lewes: Sussex Record Society, LXXIII, 1984). I also used the Goodwood MSS in the West Sussex Record Office; there are some extracts in the Earl of March, *A Duke and His Friends: The Life and Letters of the Second Duke of Richmond* (London: Hutchinson, 1911). There is much less printed source material available for Kent's great patron of cricket: the Duke of Dorset and his family at Knole. But the Sackville MSS in the Centre for Kentish Studies are, like the Goodwood archives, extremely valuable both for the family's cricket and for other historical information. Of the local gentry families, the Carylls of Ladyholt have left the most extensive correspondence; I found the volumes in BL, Add. MSS 28229–28231 to be the most relevant.

For the many other primary sources which I used less frequently, the reader is referred to the end notes. So too with the large number of secondary works on general history which make the task of any historian exploring the eighteenth century so much easier. Cultural history, however, deserves special mention, and in this field two recent books stand out: Peter Borsay, *The English Urban Renaissance: Culture and Society in the Provincial Town, 1660–1770* (Oxford: Clarendon Press, 1989); and John Brewer, *The Pleasures of the Imagination: English Culture in the Eighteenth Century* (London: HarperCollins, 1997). In several important books Dennis Brailsford has done much to clarify sport's historical significance: *Sport and Society: Elizabeth to Anne* (London: Routledge, 1969); *Sport, Time, and Society: The British at Play* (London: Routledge, 1991); and *British Sport: A Social History*, rev. edn (Cambridge: Lutterworth Press, 1997). Brailsford's history of boxing, *Bareknuckles: A Social History of Prize-Fighting* (Cambridge: Lutterworth Press, 1988), is valuable for its discussion of professional–amateur relations in another, more brutal, sport. Another important work on eighteenth-century sport, though disappointing on cricket, is Robert W. Malcolmson, *Popular Recreations in English Society 1700–1850* (Cambridge: Cambridge University Press, 1973).

General histories of cricket are legion, beginning with H. S. Altham, *A History of Cricket* (London: Allen and Unwin, 1926). More recent ones include Rowland Bowen's quirky but stimulating *Cricket: A History of its Growth and Development throughout the World* (London: Eyre and Spottiswoode, 1970); Christopher Brookes, *English Cricket: The Game and its Players through the Ages* (London: Weidenfeld and Nicolson, 1978); and Peter Wynne-Thomas, *The History of Cricket: From the Weald to the World* (London: HMSO, 1997). The literature in books and journal articles on specific aspects of cricket is even more voluminous; as the end notes will show, I have used many articles from the *Cricket Quarterly* and the *Journal of the Cricket Society*. There are accounts of early Sussex cricket in two books by John Marshall: *Sussex Cricket: A History*

(London: Heinemann, 1959); and *The Duke Who Was Cricket* (London: Muller, 1961). For Kent, the most useful of the older works are Lord Harris (ed.), *History of Kent County Cricket* (London: Eyre and Spottiswoode, 1907), especially the article by W. S. Norton; and Lord Harris and F. S. Ashley-Cooper, *Kent Cricket Matches 1719–1880* (Canterbury: Gibbs, 1929). Several more recent articles by John Goulstone are also valuable for Kent cricket; references can be found in the end notes.

No one can seriously explore all the vast and complicated literature of cricket history without recourse to the MCC Library at Lord's, so expertly cared for by Stephen Green, and I am no exception. Apart from the newspapers, almost all the printed materials on cricket that have been used in this book can be found there. All serious cricket historians will sooner or later find their way to Lord's, and will find there far more information than can possibly be described in this brief note.

Index